Supportive Parenting

of related interest

Speaking Up
A Plain Text Guide to Advocacy (4-volume set)
John Tufail and Kate Lyon
ISBN 978 1 84310 474 2

Building a Joyful Life with your Child who has Special Needs
Nancy J. Whiteman and Linda Roan-Yager
ISBN 978 1 84310 841 2

The Complete Guide to Asperger's Syndrome
Tony Attwood
ISBN 978 1 84310 495 7

Mothering Special Needs
A Different Maternal Journey
Anna Karin Kingston
ISBN 978 1 84310 543 5

Parenting Across the Autism Spectrum
Unexpected Lessons We Have Learned
Maureen F. Morrell and Ann Palmer
ISBN 978 1 84310 807 8

Parenting the ADD Child
Can't Do? Won't Do? Practical Strategies for Managing
Behaviour Problems in Children with ADD and ADHD
David Pentecost
ISBN 978 1 85302 811 3

Parenting a Child with Asperger Syndrome
200 Tips and Strategies
Brenda Boyd
ISBN 978 1 84310 137 6

How to Live with Autism and Asperger Syndrome
Practical Strategies for Parents and Professionals
Chris Williams and Barry Wright
Illustrated by Olive Young
ISBN 978 1 84310 184 0

Asperger Syndrome and Bullying
Strategies and Solutions
Nick Dubin
Foreword by Michael John Carley
ISBN 978 1 84310 846 7

Supportive Parenting

Becoming an Advocate
for Your Child with Special Needs

Jan Starr Campito

Jessica Kingsley Publishers
London and Philadelphia

First published in 2007
by Jessica Kingsley Publishers
116 Pentonville Road
London N1 9JB, UK
and
400 Market Street, Suite 400
Philadelphia, PA 19106, USA

www.jkp.com

Copyright © Jan Starr Campito 2007

Library of Congress Cataloging in Publication Data
A CIP catalog record for this book is available from the Library of Congress

British Library Cataloguing in Publication Data
A CIP catalogue record for this book is available from the British Library

ISBN 978 1 84310 851 1

Printed and bound in the United States by Thomson-Shore, Inc.

To Marcus and Michael
I'm so happy and proud to be your mom

Contents

Boxes

Preface

This book was ten years in the living, and over four in the writing. During that time, my life was enriched by discussions with many people, from many different perspectives and on many different issues. I've found that you can't spend very much time talking to advocates without talking about the language we use when we talk about people with disabilities. For example, the term, "disability," implies that something is making one less able. Many individuals find that offensive, feeling (rightly so!) that they may do some things differently from normal, or have some limitations on what they can do, but they are not "dis-abled," and I certainly agree.

When I polled a number of advocates on my language concerns, I received almost as many suggested substitutes as I found people to poll. For example, some prefer "individuals with learning differences," "children with health issues," or "children with disABILITIES." After a great deal of thought, I've chosen to keep the term "children with special needs" as most appropriate for this book. To me, of all the options offered, "special needs" is the most encompassing and the one easiest to understand. As much as I appreciate the intent behind the other suggestions, I don't want vulnerable parents having to wonder whether children with learning disabilities or cerebral palsy or autism spectrum disorders (for example) are covered under my title, and so hesitate to pick up my book. Yes, I agree that we are still just talking about people, period, and it is more than ironic that some needs are considered normal, and that other needs are considered special—but my children's needs *are* sometimes special in the sense that the usual treatment of children will not meet those needs. In fact, federal and state laws have been enacted to recognize my children's differences from the norm, and, specifically, to protect their rights to have their needs met.

Throughout this book, I try to avoid any labels of our children. I work to always put the child as an individual first, with the disability as only a secondary characteristic. But in the interest of clarity, I also often talk about special needs. If this language puts any reader off, I apologize. Please choose another term to substitute. Sharing my thoughts with you and engaging you in dialogue is far more important to me than any particular word choice I have made. As I ask your tolerance, please keep in mind that I am also writing this as a mother of two children with "special needs," very much aware that my children often stop to look over my shoulder at what I am writing. Odds are that Marcus and Michael will some day pick up this volume, seeking to understand how their mother viewed them. The answer is: with love, respect, and appreciation for *all* of their qualities. I do therapy with them to help with areas that challenge them. I never hesitate to go to bat for them, or whisper guidance to them to better enable them to tackle things on their own. I always try to help make their dreams happen. This is the only type of parenting I know how to do, for any child. So, if my terminology is getting in your way, just read this book as *Supportive Parenting: Becoming an Advocate for Your Child*. I certainly wrote it about becoming an advocate for my own.

Jan Starr Campito

Acknowledgements

There are many people I want to thank for their various forms of encouragement, inspiration, and support as I worked on this project for, what feels like, all my life. I know math doesn't work that way, but to each of you I owe 100 percent gratitude!

To Bill Kessen and Bob Sternberg—two former professors who had a tremendous impact on developing my abilities as a writer and as a thinker. Your influence extends beyond academia.

To Anna Bray, who asked a very simple question one day that has been a continuing touchstone for me as I wrote this book: "How do I do it?" This book describes what's working, so far, for me.

To Janet McLeod, for her willingness to let parents into the special ed process and for her dedication to finding ways to help parents and children in her care. Janet, you may have to deal with more vocal parents as a result of my book, but I hope they won't be as quick to yell!

To Gary Griffieth, pediatrician extraordinaire, for his expertise and his willingness to learn yet more, and for the unstinting gift of his time and attention. And to his office staff, for their long hours due to the resulting backlog in his waiting room. I wish every child with special needs could be so fortunate as to be under the care of your practice.

To Theresa Bancheri, Dave De Bonis, Lisa Braun, Alison Curley, Jeff Daly, Robert Fox, Kerry Frank, Heather Daniels, Shauna Evans, Priscilla Griffin, Mary Marro-Gireau, Tracey Maynard, Myra Nathan, Dawn Osuch, Barb Phelps, Debbie Shea, Jeanne Shub, Karen Sroczynski, Kathaleen Stewart, Carolyn Turner, and Donna Ware—my children's therapists and members of our team over the past ten years. Thank you for all the help you've given Michael and Marcus, and for taking the time to teach me. I have learned so much from you, and I don't *just* mean professional techniques. Also to Kim Salmon, Barbara Collins, Pat Schuler, Sandy Hutchison, and Debbie May, each of whom offered information and guidance when it was most needed.

To Kim Kelly, Becky Dustin, Dan Dunford, and Kristen Frank. As aides you've been much-appreciated supports to my children's developing abilities. Thank you for being my eyes and hands, thanks for your insights, and thanks for your patience in deciphering my scrawls in our communiqué books. I also thank all of my children's teachers at Loudonville Elementary School, but my experiences with four in particular have been exceptional. Jean Van der Carr's calm, pragmatic approach eased me through my panic when my oldest child first started floundering. Sue Breslin's warmth and hugs were most appreciated by Marcus and by me, at a particularly emotional time in our lives. Donna Chittenden and Shanon Newcomb, I love the way you naturally adjust your teaching style to meet the individual needs of your students. If there were more teachers like you, there would be less need for "special" education. Loudonville Elementary is a very warm educational community, and that sense of family extends from classroom, to lunchroom, to staff offices, to custodial services. Thank you all for the role you play in making my sons' world a good place to be.

To all those people I've chatted with on playgrounds and airplanes, at ski lodges, walking the dogs, or long-distance through e-mails and over the phone. To the members of the Asperger's Syndrome Advocacy Support Group of Schenectady, for the insights provided by your e-mail postings. And especially to my richly diverse Partners in Policy-Making group—I am honored to be included among you. You have definitely had a tremendous impact on how I view my sons and my goals as their parent. Thank you for your fellowship and for that education. I highly recommend the Partners experience to anyone who wants to learn to see the world in a different way.

Writing is a lonely business, made even lonelier when much of one's "free time" is spent trudging along unmarked pathways for one's kids. Thank you to all my friends who helped me feel less alone. Thanks also to the hallway parents at school, and to the regulars in Randi's yoga group. Your support mattered, especially when other things seemed to keep pulling me down. A special thanks to Mary Chew and Karen Hertel for keeping my body going when challenged by serious injury.

Thanks also to Helen Ibbotson and the staff at Jessica Kingsley Publishers, for your patient support and for making this book possible. Thanks to Phyllis Ferguson Bottomer, who provided such good company as we explored this publishing process together. And thanks to all those who read earlier drafts of my manuscript, and tried to help me iron out some of my book's kinks: Kathy Berggen, Karen Boliver, Lynn Goliber, Chad Hotaling, Tracey Maynard, Janet McLeod, Myra Nathan, Steve Oill, Barb Phelps, Betsy Schilling, Debbie Shea, Deborah Whitfield, Kim Willman—and especially Kitty Fitzgerald. I learn best when I can see from the perspective of others, and your generous gift of time and feedback has helped me tremendously.

To my parents, Ruby and Jan Hooft for believing in me. Knowing I could always count on you has helped more than you can know. My parents always modeled giving of themselves to others. I hope with this book, I've carried on that legacy in a way that makes them proud. To my deceased father, Ken Starr, who showed me that love comes in many forms. And to all my brothers, sisters, in-laws, nieces, and nephews. Growing up in a large family instilled in me a deep sense of the benefits of flexibility, cooperation, and communication. I care deeply about each of your lives. My sister, Kim, has been particularly helpful, and I thank her for her many e-mails. Piet, Chris, Nannie, John, Ka, and the rest, thanks for adding some down-home experiences to my boys' summers. Special thanks for my New York family, the Campito clan. I know that you are private people and I appreciate your acceptance of my need to share our lives. Speaking of sharing lives, Mom and Laurie, it's always been so great to have you around for that steady cycle of baseball, soccer, science fairs, and concerts. Peter and Mary Beth, your willingness to carry on for us if we were no longer around makes such a difference to our peace of mind.

Finally, and most of all, to my husband, Mark, and my sons, Marcus and Michael—so full of laughter, surprises, and adventures. What a gift God gave me, when He brought each of you into my life. I love ya'll. Period, exclamation point!

1
Why This Book?

Welcome. If you have picked up this book, you are probably wrestling with some serious issues concerning your child. Perhaps you are scared and worried, beginning to realize that you need to explore the warning signs you are getting about your child's development. Perhaps you are grieving and scared because your child, who you love so much, has recently been identified as having some sort of special needs. Perhaps you are angry and frustrated because your child's school isn't meeting his or her needs. You've tried asking for more help, but nothing seems to work, and you don't know what to do. Perhaps you are just feeling overwhelmed and tired of fighting for your children.

You are not alone. You are in the company of many, many people who are trying everything they know (and then some) to make the world the best possible place it can be for their kids. We're normal, loving parents; it's just that parenting is a little more involved for us than "normal." We're parents of kids who have special needs.

My husband, Mark, and I have two sons: Marcus, age 13, and Michael, age 11. At two-and-a-half, Marcus's speech was very difficult to understand, and his coordination and physical skills were different enough from his peers that we sought formal evaluation. We knew from our pediatrician that Marcus had low muscle tone, poor coordination, and speech articulation difficulties. We were totally unprepared, however, for the diagnosis we received from the developmental specialist: Asperger's Syndrome. Asperger's is a type of high-functioning autism. It is a pervasive condition, affecting language, social relationships, and those cognitive abilities that are called "executive processing skills." This diagnosis meant more than just a description of our child's difficulties. It was an entry into a new way of being for all of us. A few months after leaving the specialist's office, we entered the world of Early Intervention to begin the process that would obtain for us the support services that we so needed in our lives.

In comparison, Michael's development seemed to be progressing much more smoothly than his older brother's. Past experience, however, taught us to recognize subtle warning signs with speech articulation and hand coordination in him as well. Just to be "safe," we began investigating Michael's development at age two, and found that he also was showing some significant, although "spotty," developmental delays requiring therapeutic intervention. Later, at age six, Michael was diagnosed with Attention Deficit Disorder (ADD)/Inattentive Type, and a mild Central Auditory Processing Disorder. Still later, neuropsychological evaluations confirmed that although my son is gifted intellectually, he also has significant executive processing difficulties, and many autism spectrum characteristics. After Michael recently experienced a bout of clinical depression at age ten, I realized that we still do not have a total understanding of the complexities underlying Michael's abilities and disabilities. But that's true of all children: as they develop, new characteristics sometimes unfold.

In the ten years since I officially entered the world of parenting children with special needs, one or both of my boys have received speech therapy, physical therapy, occupational therapy, auditory integration training, vision therapy, play therapy, and most recently, social skills training. At the height of our intensive early intervention, we had 17 therapies going on *every week*. The boys have made incredible progress and have graduated, at least for the moment, from the need for most of their therapies, although I am always vigilant for signs that may need renewed attention. My home interventions with my children, however, remain extensive. Ours is a success story. My kids are usually happy, and function quite well given the proper support. It's the "given the proper support" part of the statement that this book is about. How do we, as parents, identify and acquire the supports needed to help our children blossom? How do we advocate for our children to make sure they receive the help they need? My goal in this book is to help you answer these questions for your own child and family.

Despite the marketing claims of some experts, there is no official owner's manual for how to parent children, even when our kids are "normal." A peek at any playground or classroom confirms the obvious:

there's a tremendous range of individual differences among children, even those of the same age or those raised in the same family. But the differences are not just between *children*. A look at parents also reveals a tremendous range of parenting styles. Parents differ in their backgrounds, goals, and preferences, and these characteristics affect child-rearing decisions. Are some parents getting it right and the rest of us, who differ from these "ideal parents," not? I doubt it. Although some parenting practices are clearly better than others, a lot of what is "good" needs to be looked at closely to see if it is good for *your* child. I would argue that "the" proper path for a child, and "the" parenting or teaching style, that would hold true across all children, probably doesn't even exist. One model of car certainly isn't best for all family incomes and needs. In the same way, what parenting choices are best really depends a lot upon your family's situation and values, as well as your child's abilities, personality, and interests.

Parenting is a difficult job to do well. Parenting a child who has special needs adds another layer of complexity to parenting decisions. Our kids don't come with God-given labels identifying each of their disabilities, explaining what the disability is, and detailing how it will manifest itself in our particular child. Nor, unfortunately, do our children come with instructions on how best to support their healthy development. Seldom in the past ten years, has it been *obvious* what I should do with my kids, or when I should do it. When it comes to parenting my children, I live in a world of gray areas. Asperger's Syndrome, for example, has only become widely recognized as a disorder in the past 20 years or so. Researchers and clinicians are still working to understand it. The educational system is even further behind in this process. This is often true with disabilities—not because schools are incompetent, but because the medical aspects of dis-abilities are usually explored before the intervention aspects. We don't always know enough about intervention alternatives to make informed choices. Even if I wanted to try all the therapies possible to see for myself how much they could help my children, my own time and financial resources—not to mention my children's time, energy, and tolerance—are limited. We can't do it all. We have to make choices, and the choices and their consequences are seldom laid out for us in black and white.

In fact, the world of special needs is gray from the beginning. Your pediatrician will look for developmental checkpoints to see if your child is developing within the normal range. But what if your child is hitting some checkpoints on time, and not others? This certainly was the case with my boys. And what if the delays are not forming a consistent pattern over time? A lot of disabilities are not obvious, especially in the early stages, and pediatricians are understandably reluctant to alarm parents, or to advise intrusive testing or consultations with experts until they are fairly sure the child has a developmental problem. Right from the beginning, you may find yourself bogged down in a morass of questions, looking for answers that are difficult to come by, and less straightforward than you crave.

When my husband and I initially realized that our first-born son was not following a typical developmental pattern, we were devastated (as I imagine most parents are when they discover problems are in store for their loved ones). It took time to recognize that actually, in some respects, we were fortunate. I taught full-time at an excellent local college. My graduate training, at Yale University, was in cognitive developmental psychology and I had eight years' experience teaching child development, adolescent development, and educational psychology courses to undergraduate and graduate students. Although not specifically in the area of special needs, my field of training provided relevant background knowledge, and people tended to listen to me with respect. I had colleagues who taught special education courses in graduate programs, and I could call upon them for advice and help with networking with other professionals. Mark and I met and married when we were older and more secure in our finances. He has his own successful, international business. We could more easily afford a wide range of intervention options, including my staying home for a while, when we decided that would best help our children.

Despite all of these advantages, entering the world of special needs threw us for a total loop. I am normally a competent and outspoken woman, but suddenly I found myself depending totally upon the knowledge of others, and passively accepting their advice. My normal approach to almost anything in life is to ask questions, seek explanations and elaborations, and actively pursue knowledge, but now I found myself just listening, trusting, and obeying. I was in a foreign land, these were the experts, and I would do what they said to help my sons. Does this sound familiar to you? I've heard similar attitudes expressed by others who've had to start this process. We feel lost, without the knowledge we need to help our children. Even for those of us with relevant professional knowledge, the world looks different when the problems are *your* child's, and *you* are the one consulting the experts.

It took a while for me to realize that trusting and following the experts' advice was not the way to go! Exactly because I wanted to do the best possible for my sons, I could not continue in this passive, accepting attitude. Although, admittedly, the subject matter was new, I had to do what I had always done. I had to go back to using my own intelligence and following my own instincts. I had to research, question, gather my resources, and pull everything together in a way that made sense to me. If a therapeutic approach didn't make sense to me, how could I entrust my children to it? How could any parent? And if I could so completely lose my voice in a situation with such high stakes, what about the parent without my advantages? I can't tell you the number of impromptu conversations I've had with worried parents who would spontaneously share with me, simply because I was a willing and sympathetic listener, that their son or daughter had recently been identified as having special needs, and they were wrestling to get the help they wanted for their children. It was in those conversations that I realized how much of a leg up my developmental training had provided me, and how much I have learned over the past ten years of living with my children and their needs. I listened to parents who were hurting and lost—hungry for guidance on what to do or how to do it, or just wanting reassurance that they were not the only ones struggling. We'd talk while our kids played, and they'd sometimes follow up with phone calls to my home. I realized that in living and breathing in my children's world, I *had* gained a lot of experience, the hard way, and that sharing my training and experience seemed to help other parents. So I decided to write this book. I almost entitled it *Things I Wish Someone Had Told Me*, because that's what it is. I hope it can help you feel less lost and more in control of the decisions you will have to make about how best to deal with your child's needs.

Throughout this book, I invite you to filter my words through the knowledge and wisdom you have gained from dealing with your own children. Our situations may vary in severity or type of disability, but I believe that the desire to speak up for our children is something we share in common. I will not presume to tell you what you should do. Even for my own children, although I can anticipate some of their future needs, I do not know what challenges will arise next month, or even next week. But I have developed a set of strategies and a proactive mindset for dealing with whatever those problems may be. It is "advocacy as a way of life," that I will describe to you in the pages that follow. I invite you to create your own version, molding it to fit your particular family values and vision. As you'll see in the following chapters, autism spectrum disorders require a particularly intense type of parent involvement. Other disabilities will vary as to what they involve. The one advantage in having dealt with such a wide variety of issues for my children, is that I can offer lots of examples of different types for you to think about for your own.

My sister-in-law called some time ago, to ask my opinion about her own son who had a developmental disability. He was transitioning from having therapies provided by individually contracted providers, to having them provided by the publicly funded school system. As I spoke with her, I realized that as important as this transition was for my nephew, an even more important transition had already happened, *within her*. Like me, she had made the journey from being a parent who looked to be told what to do, to being a parent who asks questions and vigorously advocates for her child. We still consult the professionals, but we don't give up our parenting responsibilities, and we don't take lightly our own unique knowledge of our children. We are experts in our own right, and we seek to apply that expertise to this new territory that our children's lives now include. Our children's welfare matters to us. We seek not just to respond to situations as they arise; but also to anticipate them. We research and we plan. We run obsessive double-checks on those things that could have been misunderstood, overlooked, or neglected. We ask others for advice, but we do so ready to decide for ourselves how this advice meshes with our own views of our children and their needs. It is this immersion of oneself in the process that I mean when I encourage advocacy as a way of life. I offer this book to you in the hope that it will help you also, to make that transition from passive acceptance, to active—and even proactive—involvement.

How to use this book

I have organized this book into 11 chapters, discussing the sorts of issues my husband and I addressed as we began to recognize and deal with our sons' needs. Feel free to turn ahead to those chapters that correspond to where you currently are in this whole process, but at least skim all the chapters. You very well may find, as I have, that just when you think you have things settled with your child, you have to backtrack and re-diagnose, or add new dimensions or therapies to your current repertoire. Similarly, although the book is laid out in a linear fashion, as is necessary when dealing with printed text, the issues addressed in various chapters overlap. I offer a wide variety of examples from my experience, to encourage you to look with fresh eyes at your own children, perhaps to gain ideas for approaching current difficulties, or even to re-examine old problems that may have been only temporarily settled for you.

The next chapter, Chapter 2, is on pre-diagnosis, the time when you first start to suspect that the difficulties you are experiencing with your child may be outside the realm of typical parenting concerns. You want to do what is best for your child, but I understand your hesitation to open the scary door that leads out of the familiar. In this chapter, I help you face your worries and explore the questions you are likely to be raising. Chapter 3 then walks you through the process of obtaining an evaluation and an official, clinical name for those difficulties your child and family are experiencing. A formal diagnosis can be very liberating. It helps you make sense of what is happening with your child, and it is the doorway into help. However, the process of seeking a diagnosis is a very difficult and emotional one for parents. Therefore, I also include in this chapter an extensive discussion of feelings—both the complexities of your own, and the emotional reactions you are likely to encounter from people around you.

Chapter 4 begins to discuss what to do with your child's diagnosis. It addresses finding out what those formal-sounding words really mean, how the condition is manifesting in your particular child, and what treatment options are available. Learning is hard work, all the more so when it is learning about something so important for your child's well-being. In recognition of this, I also offer emotional strategies for supporting yourself as you work to learn more about your child's diagnosis. This chapter also discusses talking to your child about his or her disability.

Chapter 5 discusses beginning therapeutic interventions with your child. It discusses how to select and schedule therapists, and your role in the therapeutic intervention process. I am a strong proponent of parental involvement, and have found that the more knowledgeable I am about what is going on in my children's therapies, the better advocate I can be for my children. Because therapies are not the only types of supports your child may need, this chapter also includes a discussion of other types of resources and funding sources you may wish to explore.

In Chapter 6, I use the last ten years with my son, Marcus, to show how the manifestation of a child's disability can change over time, and how our supportive parenting efforts need to change in response. You may feel overwhelmed by the advocacy task ahead of you, and so this chapter illustrates the concept of prioritizing, or identifying and focusing one's parenting energies on those issues that are most important at any given time. This chapter also demonstrates an important thing to keep in mind: kids change; skills can improve; abilities develop. Each year brings new struggles, but every year I also have the thrill of seeing how far my children have come. Mapping Marcus's change over ten years had another, unexpected effect as well. As I proofread this chapter discussing the patterns we saw in Marcus, I realized that those same patterns apply to my second son, Michael, as well. I am now convinced that Michael's developmental path also falls on the autism spectrum, although I believe his unique strengths and the supportive parenting in our household often keeps his diagnosis skimming just under the surface, often unrecognizable except in times of stress.

Chapters 7 and 8 discuss the implications of your child's diagnosis for parenting your child. I firmly believe that one reason my boys have blossomed is the work I have done to ensure they are supported in all areas of their lives. Basically, this has involved a push on two fronts: home and school. I have teamed closely with a variety of teachers and therapists to provide strong educational supports. But I also take full responsibility for creating a welcoming and supportive home life for my children. The remaining chapters of this book discuss this two-pronged approach to supporting your children in *both* home and school. Not only do I try to extend the knowledge and approaches I learn from therapists into our home, but I am also constantly watching and experimenting on my own, to learn from my children what works to meet their needs. My expertise on my children has strong, deep roots in this way of life at our home.

Chapter 7 looks at how to structure your home for your child's success, and it helps you understand and manage problem behaviors. Actually, this chapter could equally apply to parenting *any child* supportively, whether or not they have a diagnosis. In it, I include specific examples to help you understand your child's perspective. Our children are often dealing with many other issues that typically developing children never have to face. Understanding their needs is key to creating home and learning environments that are part of the solution, instead of part of the problems facing our children.

Chapter 8 looks at working to support and to build your child's strengths. It introduces the concept of scaffolding, which involves working to support your child's functioning at his or her highest level. Several teaching strategies are also discussed. One of these is task analysis, by which one can break any task down into its component parts, and then identify and train those parts causing difficulty. Providing supportive assistance, or scaffolding, is also discussed as a teaching tool, as well as the effective use of modeling and practice to help a child learn. Homework and other examples are used to illustrate these concepts.

Chapter 9 is designed to help you navigate the special education labyrinth and work with the schools to create a welcoming and supportive learning environment for your child (for readers elsewhere, please note that I use the US model and terminology as an example here, and the special needs education system will work differently in other countries). Yes, the process is complex, and quite daunting, but armed with your newly heightened awareness of the things you can do to advocate for your child, you will be more likely to hold your own as you work with your special education team to develop an Individualized Education Plan (called "IEP" for short, and sometimes termed Individualized Education Program) to help meet your child's needs. This chapter describes the parts of the IEP, and the collaborative process by which the IEP is created. It also discusses what you should look for in the resulting product, and how you can work to make the special education process best work for your child.

Chapter 10 is where I spend most of my advocacy life nowadays—monitoring and following up on the provisions set in place in my sons' IEPs, and working to adjust those plans as new complexities arise. Your child's special needs are not static. They will change as she or he grows, and they will change as the demands of his or her environment changes. Monitoring these changes and ensuring that appropriate supports are always in place for your child is a continuous and vitally important task. Chapter 10 also includes a section on conflict and how to deal with it. Interestingly enough, although I am often quite assertive and vocal in requesting change to meet my sons' needs, I actually seldom see myself as being in conflict with others. Rather, my view of advocacy is that I'm providing information and a perspective that the professionals who teach and work with my children, need to know. I'm providing a service, not only for my children, but also to those who have as their jobs the responsibilities of helping meet my sons' needs. My attitude is that we are partners working together, and the professionals need my input as much as I need theirs.

Chapter 11, the final chapter of this book, revisits the notion of what advocating for your child means. Advocating means more than doing things for our children. It also means helping them become more competent, independent, and able to do things for themselves. This chapter includes a discussion of helping our children prepare for adulthood and become strong advocates for themselves. This chapter describes some of the cultural and political issues likely to shape our children's world. Finally, I discuss the many faces of advocacy and explore some of the other things you may do if you wish to take a larger, societal advocacy role, such as forming a parent advocacy or support group (or writing a book or article on your own experiences!).

Before we move to the next chapter, I'd like to add a personal note. I was nervous when I broached to my husband my desire to write this book. After all, as I share with you the knowledge that I've gained over the past ten years of my life—it's not only *my* life I'm describing, it is his and those of our children. My husband is a very private person, and I appreciate his willingness to let me share with you some of what goes on inside our home. I wish you could meet our boys; they are great kids. I'm sure I'd enjoy meeting yours, too. As you read some of the details of what we have done to try to help our children, I invite you to keep your own children firmly pictured in your mind. They are the ones for whom we do all this. And they are worth it.

2

Pre-diagnosis: Is it Normal for Everything to be so Hard?

It's difficult for me to remember back before we received our children's diagnoses, or to reconstruct what warning signals made us even question whether their development was proceeding as it should. Of course, if enough time has gone by, it's hard for any of us to look back and recall elaborate details from a particular period of our lives, even precious images that we thought we could never, ever forget. Luckily, the seemingly unending nature of the paperwork involved in the special needs process (three, 4-inch binders' worth, and counting) makes reconstruction of that time period more possible. I will use those records to share some of our experience with you now.

It's a scary thing to turn an objective lens on your child and on your family's functioning. We all want to be "normal," or even "above normal." We take seriously the privilege and responsibility of parenting, and secretly worry whether we're doing a good enough job. Recognizing that not only are things hard for you and your child, but they even may be "abnormal," takes a lot of courage. Acknowledging that you may need help is a giant first step in becoming an advocate for your child's special needs. In this chapter, I'll discuss daring to take that first step of voicing your concern. It's hard, I know. My husband and I have been there too.

For us, recognition that our oldest son, Marcus, was different from other children came in two phases. The first phase, resulting in an initial diagnosis, came after a long, frustrated period spent grappling with an increasing collection of disquieting evidence, embedded in a life that was otherwise "new parent normal." This was a time of trying to learn how to parent, becoming familiar with our son, and worrying a lot about whether we were doing it right. As first-time parents, we had no standards with which to compare our experience, and it was a long time before we even thought to question its normality. The second phase of our recognition of the extent of our differences from the norm resembled more a "crash-and-burn" family scenario, when all of our carefully constructed supports collapsed. My husband and I were left bewildered, trying to comprehend what had happened, and overwhelmed as to what to do next. Desperation led to our acknowledgement that even our therapy-supported routines had become too difficult, and we needed further diagnosis and intervention. I'll share each of these accounts with you here, because something in them may resonate with you and help you on your road to diagnosis.

Our long journey to initial diagnosis

Twelve years ago, my husband and I were thrilled by the long-awaited birth of our first child, a gorgeous (to us at least!) 9 lb. 1 oz. boy we named, "Marcus." As with most new parents, we had no idea how he would change our lives. Well, maybe it is truer to say "little idea" because actually some change had already begun as soon as we knew he was conceived. Ours was a high-risk pregnancy. My age (then 38), the presence of fibroid uterine tumors, and faulty coordination between the various natural hormones governing pregnancy were all problematic. In fact, I had a miscarriage the year before I became pregnant with Marcus. My obstetrician/gynecologist came up with a plan to make it more likely that I would be able to maintain this pregnancy, and I religiously did what she advised. So began the frequent doctor visits required of a high-risk pregnancy, the weekly shots of progesterone and occasional injections of hCG (human chorionic gonadotropin), the frequent fetal heartbeat checks, and the restricted diet because of gestational diabetes. Like the destruction of innocence occasioned by my earlier miscarriage, this difficult prenatal process left its own, slightly sour legacy: I became resigned to the idea that nothing is ever as easy as we've been led to believe it would be. My conversations with others reinforced my sense that for many, many people, complications are the norm and nothing should be taken for granted. This realization led to one of the founding principles of my later advocacy work: *ignorance is for the lucky. Staying informed and on top of things is essential for the rest of us.*

Although I was physically fit, the pregnancy was hard on my 38-year-old body. I was working full-time at a local college, and I have many memories of interrupting afternoon and evening lectures to run down the hall and take care of "morning sickness" before returning to resume my class. My patient educational psychology students saw the latest installments of my ultrasounds. They heard almost weekly updates on what parts of my unborn child were developing at any given time. Occasionally, we would have brief discussions of later educational and other difficulties that could be related to things going wrong at any prenatal point.

Then, when my pregnancy was 27 weeks along, I tripped on a Venetian-blind cord. A trivial little stumble—I didn't even fall—but a stumble that set contractions into motion. Three days later, I left the hospital, confined to bed rest and mild barbiturates for the next seven weeks. This was another indication that parenting would require the development of totally foreign characteristics and skills. As active as I had been before, suddenly, just lying there and staying calm was the best thing that I could do for my unborn child. My previously homemaking-illiterate, executive husband had a sudden crash course in running a house with a bedridden wife.

Again, the outcome was eventually a positive one. After sweating through a full-term pregnancy, our obstetrician and my husband chanted, "Come on Marcus!" for what felt like hours in the delivery room, and our gorgeous baby was born. He was bruised and cone-headed from coming out elbow first, facing backwards, with his umbilical cord wrapped around his neck and elbow, but he was indescribably beautiful to us. We felt blessed and awed and deliriously happy—and totally overwhelmed. In other words, we were typical, new parents. Our lives were difficult, but no more so than we expected. Life was busy, but good.

As time passed, we started getting messages from others that we were *not* typical new parents. Or rather, that the child we adored, was not typical. In hindsight, I can see these messages as early warning signs. At the time, we saw them as critical comments on our child and our parenting abilities. Marcus was, what my mother called, "colicky." He needed to be held—a lot! I nursed him, and he thrived. But forget about sleeping through the night! For the first five months of his life, he woke up every two hours for nightly feedings, never missing a one. He was a happy baby, as long as he was held, but seemed to be easily over-stimulated. He'd be fine, and then suddenly break down. The least bit of moisture in his diaper would set off wails and squirming—or at least that's the only explanation we could come up with for these mysterious meltdowns. He was most readily comforted by being held up against my shoulder with *hard*, rhythmic pats on his back. I still remember the strange looks I'd get from relatives when the sounds of those thumps would resound across the room.

When Marcus was a little over three months old, I resumed my teaching responsibilities at the college. I engaged a neighbor with three children of her own, to watch Marcus in her home. The situation seemed ideal. One of her sons was only two months older than Marcus, and we were able to pay her well enough that she did not need to take in any more children. Marcus seemed to be thriving, although he was still prone to intense emotional meltdowns that were difficult to calm. Whereas many children use pacifiers for comforting, Marcus would go to sleep with literally six or eight "binkies" scattered inside his crib, to help him self-soothe. He'd often doze off with one in his mouth, and another clenched in each fist. I remember, on more than one occasion, leaving the house to teach my evening seminars, and coming home three hours later to a dazed, shell-shocked husband who reported that our infant refused his bottle and screamed inconsolably the entire time I was gone.

The months went on, and our sitter started telling us that she did not think things were quite right with Marcus. She noted how hard it was to interact with him and how easily he got upset. She commented repeatedly on his physical awkwardness, and she made a big deal out of the way he would sit on the floor, with his bottom directly on the floor, his knees pointing forward, and his legs splayed backwards, so that his legs formed a "W." Our response was to get defensive, and we tended to discount Meg's concerns. We knew Marcus could be hard to read, but her sons were all small, slight children, with quiet, easy-going personalities. We thought she just didn't understand his personality type; or, since Marcus was actually taller than her son, I thought that perhaps Meg expected Marcus to act older than he was. I did not recognize the sensory implications of Marcus's intense cravings for swaddling and the reassurance provided by weight and pressure against his body.

By the time Marcus was ten months old, we started getting "spotty" developmental feedback from our pediatrician, meaning that although most things were developing right on schedule, there were some areas of concern. For example, Marcus was a little slower to sit up than expected, and rolling rather than crawling seemed to be his preferred method of locomotion. Yet each time we would start to worry, Marcus would have a developmental spurt, suddenly acquiring the overdue ability. The developmental delays were not across the board, but rather in seemingly unconnected spots. Our pediatrician noted that Marcus had low muscle tone, meaning that the resting state of his muscles was looser than normal, as though he were a marionette whose strings were loosened instead of pulled taut and ready for movement. The pediatrician also told us that it looked as though Marcus just had his own developmental timetable, and we would watch and learn that timetable from him.

When Marcus was 18 months old, the disquieting feedback got noisier and noisier—and he got quieter! From steadily gaining new words every month, beginning with his first word at ten months, his language suddenly went underground. There were no obvious new vocabulary additions, and he stopped using some of the vocabulary he'd already acquired. This is when I started becoming alarmed. I kept detailed records of every new word, and in his baby calendar I noted my confusion about their sudden absence. Although Marcus seemed to understand us, and loved being read and sung to, he didn't initiate social interactions as I'd noticed other infants doing. He would avoid eye contact when I looked in his face as I rocked him to sleep. He didn't point to communicate. Nor did he ask the interminable "What's that?" or "Why" questions the toddler literature led me to expect. Again, the warning signs seem so clear when pulled out of context like this, but they weren't when viewed as just *some* of *many* behaviors exhibited by a bright, healthy, happy—and adored—child.

Around this time, I became pregnant with our second son. Mark and I were incredibly busy, with both of us continuing full-time work, and trying to keep up with an active toddler. Fortunately, this pregnancy went easier, but I still was in a medically high-risk category, and so continued with frequent prenatal visits and first-trimester progesterone shots. My record-keeping, which continued to be almost obsessively archival for

Marcus, was almost non-existent for the second pregnancy (a not un-common phenomenon for later-born children). Eventually, our beloved Michael, again a whopping 9 lb. 1 oz., healthy baby, was born. For this birth, we reluctantly agreed to the planned cesarean section recommended to us by our obstetrician when, a month before our son was due, he turned in the uterus so that he was no longer presenting in the preferred, head-down, birth-ready position. The cesarean section proceeded un-eventfully, although we did discover that Michael's umbilical cord also was wrapped around his neck, and so it was fortunate for us that my obstetri-cian hadn't tried to turn him to proceed with the vaginal birth. Even as a newborn, Michael was an incredibly easy baby. But then, anything would seem easy in comparison, when my yardstick was Marcus! It took a while for me to realize that Michael could, indeed, be hitting the developmental checkpoints infinitely easier than Marcus, but still have significant devel-opmental issues of his own.

By the time Michael was seven months old (and three months before Marcus turned three), after yet another anxious discussion with our pediatrician, we jointly decided to "play it safe" and have Marcus formally evaluated for special needs. I'll talk about the process of obtaining a diag-nosis in the next chapter. For now, let me just say that like innumerable other parents, we had no idea how to begin, and no idea what to do with the information we started collecting along the way. We were totally over-whelmed, emotionally and cognitively, with what we were finding out. Frustration, anxiety, loneliness, and fear—yes, those were pretty common emotions to me in this pre-diagnosis time. Sound familiar to you?

Why wasn't it obvious that we had a problem?

We, laypeople, tend to think of the medical field as relatively straightfor-ward and objective. In reality, medical decisions also draw on a doctor's judgment, with experience and intuition shaping the judgment as much as objective "facts." Our pediatrician is very aware of the burden that facing the possibility of their child's developmental abnormalities places on parents, and he does not rush to raise that specter. What I describe above was a sustained period of small concerns with Marcus's development: there were no loud, impossible-to-ignore signals that Marcus's development was not proceeding according to a normal timetable. In retrospect, I think such ambiguity is probably normal. I believe there are four main reasons for this, which I'll lay out for you now. They may help as you muddle through your own ambiguities.

First, the normal path of child development is not a single, narrow path. Rather, the "normal" covers a wide range, and the timing of the acquisition of particular abilities can vary from child to child. Pediatricians use statistical curves to decide whether or not a child is far enough at either end of that range of normal to cause concern. (Let's face it, we're really only talking about the bottom end of the developmental range—I doubt any of us would look panic-stricken to be told our child is significantly *above* normal, at least on most dimensions!) The pace of development will vary from child to child. As we saw with Marcus, the developmental curve may even be marked by developmental plateaus before new abilities emerge. Child development just does not proceed on an even, invariable timetable, and with this in mind, a pediatrician is not likely to label a child's development as "abnormal" based on a single check-up. It often takes time for suspicious patterns to emerge.

Second, child development is a complicated process, involving many different dimensions. More than mere physical growth, it includes fine and gross motor development, language development, the development of thinking and problem-solving skills, and social and emotional develop-ment. Yet your pediatrician can only observe a few of those dimensions easily in his or her office. In order to screen for abnormalities in areas other than the physical dimension, the pediatrician needs to interact with your child, either directly or indirectly. Your pediatrician needs to be able to watch your child think, follow directions, carry on a conversation, and interact socially with other people. She or he needs to get a sense of your child as a *person*—as more than just a physical machine—and then look for warning signs of potential problems. Even the most charming, engaging, and enterprising pediatrician is limited in this screening by the constraints of a brief office visit. Marcus's low muscle tone was relatively easy to observe in a doctor's office, and was one of the first abnormalities we flagged. Other difficulties were less likely to be displayed in the doctor's office. Marcus's inability to engage in pretend play and his limitations in pragmatic language, are two such examples. I did not realize these were areas of development I should question. Since our pediatrician does not regularly screen for these characteristics in his normal developmental evaluations, even he was somewhat surprised when a developmental specialist later diagnosed our son with an autism spectrum disorder.

This brings us to the third reason it is so difficult for a pediatrician to identify abnormal development in our children: the expert, our pediatrician, is limited not only by the range of things he can directly observe, but also by the quality of the information we provide about those things she or he cannot observe. We are flawed reporters. We go to these check-ups frazzled from trying to keep our children entertained and relatively well behaved. We don't know what questions the pediatrician is going to ask, and we may not think to bring our baby calendars along so we can accurately report dates of significant developmental accomplishments—assuming we even recorded them. Under pressure, it is difficult to focus on our pediatrician's questions and to think whether we truly have noticed our child exhibiting a particular skill, or to report with accuracy the relative frequency of that behavior.

Sometimes, the developmental indicator of an abnormality is obvious if you know what you are looking for, but technical and specific enough that the parent, as a layperson, has trouble recognizing its significance. I mentioned earlier Marcus's lack of pretend play, and his limited use of pragmatic language to get his needs met as a few examples of significant signs that passed us by, but in our case there were many more. Michael was skilled enough at manipulating his physical environment that I never thought (or knew) to check whether he was picking up small objects by using his thumb and forefinger, instead of his fingers and palm. Marcus's "W-sitting" (the technical term for the splayed-leg way he would sit on the floor, with his bottom between his knees) is a common indicator of low muscle tone and possible gross motor difficulties. Both of these were physical deviations from the norm that my own experience and knowledge did not allow me to recognize. We need our pediatricians to help us know what to look for in our children, and our pediatricians need *us* to help them picture our children's typical functioning outside of the pediatrician's office. Some pediatricians further this parent partnership, by offering short seminars on various developmental topics as a way of educating parents and raising awareness of developmental concerns.

Fourth, and finally, is the fact that even though we are talking medicine and "hard science," sometimes "we just don't know." Pediatricians' offices are full of children who may seem a little quirky or odd, but we aren't sure that we would call it a *developmental abnormality* or *disability*. Sometimes, it may take years for developmental patterns to become clear. This is why we need to be always ready to ask, and ask again if things don't feel right. Sometimes, we may never know for sure.

Your child's pediatrician will weigh a number of factors as they perform your child's developmental check-ups, and because some of these factors involve a physician's own experience and belief systems, two different physicians may take two different approaches to the same child. Some physicians are quick to send patients off for further tests to rule out possibilities. Other physicians prefer to wait before raising the fear that something might be wrong. The indicators for further testing are not always as clear-cut as parents sometimes believe.

How good parenting can actually mask developmental abnormality

Unless the child is born with an obvious physical condition, or experiences a serious disease or accident, special needs do not suddenly and dramatically appear. Rather, just as the abilities of normally developing children emerge over time, so do the abilities—and the special needs—of children with disabilities. The many small adjustments that we, as parents, make to accommodate those special needs happen so gradually, and are often such a collection of small things, that it may be hard for us, or for others, to discern the pattern that is emerging.

From before they are born, we arrange our children's environments to keep them safe and to allow our children to have what they need or want. We adjust our behaviors too, to meet their physical, emotional, and social needs. In fact, we learn to read our children so well that we can often anticipate their needs before those needs are even expressed. We also protect our children in the social world. We know when they want to be held, when they're open to interaction with others, and when they want just to observe from a safe distance. We learn to read their emotional signs to see when they are being over-stimulated or over-tired, and to anticipate what's likely to set off a meltdown, so we can intervene before it happens. When our children's needs change, our behaviors as caregivers change as well, and we adjust to newly developed competencies or to new challenges posed by our children's engagement in new developmental tasks or unfamiliar environments.

As you work to meet your children's needs, you may not think to question whether you are expending a "normal" amount of effort doing so, or whether the range of adjustments and interventions you have to provide is "normal." Monitoring and unobtrusively slipping in support often becomes automatic, so that you're not even aware of what you're doing. Because you're anticipating your child's needs and filling them before they become obvious, the snags and the difficulties may never become apparent.

For example, I developed a series of what I can see, in retrospect, were fairly elaborate accommodations to help Marcus dress himself in the mornings when he was five years old, and seeking to be more independent. In those days, I found I had to supervise closely both of my children's dressing—so closely, in fact, that it would have been much easier for me to actually dress them myself! But my children needed to feel competent and independent, and so my job as their parent was to let them learn to dress themselves. Every morning was a major hurdle for us. Michael, the three-and-a-half-year-old, needed what I thought of as the usual prompting for a preschooler to stay on task, as well as my help with buttons or getting into turtlenecks. My kindergartener, Marcus, on the other hand, required very much more, and so that was what I provided. First, I minimized distractions, making sure his brother was in another room, the TV was off, and the targeted clothes were placed in a pile in front of him. Marcus would occasionally stare off into space or get distracted, but more often, the problems arose when he actually appeared to be on task. Clothing reversals were common, but there were more serious difficulties as well.

His dressing difficulties are a classic example of motor planning difficulties. Motor planning is the ability of the brain to conceive, organize, and carry out a sequence of physical activities. Motor planning affects a great number of one's physical skills, including gross motor activities (crawling, walking, climbing stairs, skipping), fine motor activities (feeding oneself, blowing bubbles), and speech. When we first learn a new skill, we may have to consciously rehearse the motor planning (as when we learn to tie our shoelaces into a bow), but then it becomes automatic. For a child with motor difficulties, it may take much longer for motor planning to become automatic, and motor skills may have to be separately mastered before they can be combined into a smooth sequence.

I have seen Marcus take off his pajamas and then start to put them back on again. I have seen him put a sock on one foot, and then put the second sock on the same foot. I have seen him put his pajama shirt back on, layering it on top of his clothing, with no awareness of what he had just done. He would forget underwear. Often I intervened with a reminder, because usually he would not catch these problems himself. At age five, checking how everything looked or felt was not a natural behavior for him. In fact, Marcus did not show much body awareness, in general. Yet, the physical organization difficulties were alleviated if I presented a challenge for him. For example, I would set a timer, allowing one minute for each item of clothing that needed to be put on, and then I would challenge him to beat the timer. This worked well because it redirected the emotional component of the challenge towards an outside entity, the timer, instead of towards me. Beating the timer was fun; being nagged by Mom was not. Or I would sit in the room with his pile of clothes beside me, and I would toss Marcus one item of clothing at a time to put on. My goal was to keep his energy and attention heightened, and to simplify and structure the dressing task so he was more likely to be successful in the task. This, I felt, was much better for his developing independence than my constantly commenting on his performance and verbally cuing the next step every morning. Yet even with these dressing games in place, every morning was a major hurdle for us. When we were finally ready to go out the door to the car, I'd ask him to think what else he needed to put on. I would see him literally stop and think before he could say, "Shoes, Mom." If I asked a second time, he'd do the same full-body stop, pause, and then say, "A coat Mom." *Nothing* physical was automatic for him, and the amount of energy and attention that attending to these daily tasks required from both of us was exhausting.

Transitions were difficult for Marcus as well, and I spent much time rehearsing with both boys what our schedule would look like for a given day. Therapists call this behavior, in which you rehearse what to expect, "pre-setting"—much in the same way that TV or movie theatres provide previews of upcoming shows. I didn't only rehearse schedules, or review behavioral rules and expectations. Detailed *social* pre-setting was also a normal part of our day. For instance, if Marcus was invited to a birthday party, I went through an elaborate ritual preparing him for the party. I'd talk to him about where the party was going to be, and what the entertainment and food were likely to be. Marcus has strong taste and texture aversions to certain foods, therefore I would need to reassure him that it was ok not to eat the ice cream. We would rehearse how to say "Happy Birthday" to the birthday child, and "Thank you for inviting me" to the parent. I'd tell him that not every child opens their birthday presents at their party; some families like to wait until later. Without this rehearsal, Marcus would be very upset and melt down at the party's end if he did not get to watch the child open his gift. We would rehearse specific situations as well: what if someone else gives the birthday child the same present that you brought? Well that just means you made a great selection that kids like. What if the child says they already have this one? Again, that just means you guessed correctly that this gift would be something that child would like! It's ok, we'll include the gift receipts so that the child can exchange your gift for something else good. Who do you think you might want to look for, to play with at the party? What will you do if you realize you need to go to the bathroom? Mind you, this pre-setting was never in response to my children's questions. My boys tend to be very quiet and passive in unfamiliar situations. The burden was always on me to anticipate ahead of time what might happen, and what might solve the potential problem for my children. Most of these were preparations we learned to do the hard way, following a previous meltdown. I learned to expect a need for quiet after each of these social outings because of the tremendous excitement and sensory overload of a loud party.

The upshot of all this pre-setting, rehearsal, and attention to transitions, is that most people had no idea of the extent or difficulty of the challenges facing Marcus. They thought he was just a shy child. The pre-setting helped demystify life for him, and the verbal rehearsals prepared him to cope more smoothly with situations that arose. My parenting efforts helped him function more easily, and because these accommodations were hidden, it was much less evident to anyone that Marcus was developmentally different, or that we were having a problem.

Parental monitoring and intervention are a part of good parenting of any child. What seems to be different for the parent of a child with special needs, however, is the *extent* of the parental interventions that need to occur, and the fact that it doesn't let up as quickly with age. Interestingly, I was going to suggest an age at which one can typically expect increased independence and decreased parental supervision. But at least with my children, no such age comes readily to mind. Yes, my children's competencies have grown tremendously. I am so thankful that our mornings are no longer the tremendous ordeal that they were for Marcus when he was five. In fact, by second grade, these particular challenges were pretty much mastered by both my children. Other challenges, however, quickly replaced them.

The biggest clue for me that perhaps I had passed beyond normal parenting accommodations was my emotions. Now, when I find myself increasingly feeling exhausted, impatient, or irritated because it feels like the demands on my attention are unending, I have finally learned to step back and question what I am doing, and why. It is very easy for me, as a child-centered, involved parent, to keep piling on accommodations, each of which alone may seem minimal. Added together, however, they become overwhelming, so that I feel myself starting to collapse under the load. It's hard to recognize that your child has special needs because each individual accommodation may come about naturally and seem normal. You do it unquestioningly because it is necessary, and you seldom have the time or the perspective to ask, "Is it normal to have to do this much?"

I realize that in many ways, my parenting style with my elementary school children more resembles that of a parent of a preschool child. Are you horrified at these descriptions of how much structure is necessary in our lives? Or are you nodding your head in recognition that this is your world as well? The sort of mothering I do to keep my sons safe and to help them be successful in the tasks they set themselves, would perhaps be "smothering" if my children were typically developing. Yet it is based on my perception of my children's current needs. Intervening the way I do is, paradoxically, what fosters my children's *independence* instead of their *dependence*. My own goal is to provide the supports for my children, to enable them to keep up with their peers and not be restricted in the activity choices they make. In fact, I often use that goal of developing increased competence and independence as my guide when I decide when and how to intervene with my children.

It is when your parenting efforts break down that you realize that you have a problem. Your routine adjustments no longer seem sufficient. You realize that your child is struggling, and your efforts aren't enough. Or perhaps, as is natural as children grow older, your child moves outside the protective and supportive environment you've been able to provide for them, and she or he starts to crash. Starting school can be one such traumatic eye-opener for the parent of an atypical child. It certainly was for us. Yes, there is the usual panic that most parents of kindergarteners feel when you don't have your little one with you any more. But even more significantly, your child is away from the protective and supportive cushion you provide around him or her. Starting school, your child is faced with a new, exciting (and stressful) environment, posing new academic, physical, and social challenges, without one of their major coping tools—you! Because we are often unaware of the extent of the support we provide, both our children and ourselves may be devastated by the extent of the crash when they try flying solo.

Many children with special needs are not identified until they are placed in an environment where the difference between their performance and that of their peers is obvious. One such environment is a same-age daycare or preschool grouping. Yet the developmental range appearing in the preschool years is so broad, it is hard for the untrained eye to know which differences are significant and which are not. Also, preschool environments tend to allow children many choices, seldom forcing an activity on a child. This makes it difficult to discern whether a child's avoidance of certain tasks is due to the child's preferences, or to the child's lack of ability.

As a preschooler, Marcus never engaged in pretend play. He would play, using physical objects in a physical way, but never in a symbolic way. He would never *pretend*. "So what?" other parents, particularly of boys, would say to me. "My son doesn't like to do that pretend stuff either." The difference was that Marcus couldn't. It was not a matter of preference for him. He didn't know how. He might like to put on a fireman costume, but the concept of pretending to be a fireman putting out a pretend fire didn't exist for him. He might push a fire truck, recognizing that it was a toy fire truck, but he never drove the truck to a pretend fire, or made engine or siren noises while he pushed it. Since I never saw Marcus even try to engage in pretend play, I didn't know he couldn't. You have to see someone try repeatedly and fail before you know they can't.

By the time of entry into kindergarten, with particular activities *required* of the child, peer-group comparisons are easier to make and deficiencies or differences are more obvious. In this setting, the child is thrown into a sort of line-up, where his or her competencies and behaviors are compared with other children their age—their new peer group. Perhaps your child's friends are talking about successfully taking the training wheels off their two-wheeler bicycles, and you realize that your child seldom even rides a trike. You may have been using a sippy cup to prevent your child's frequent spills at home, but now he or she's having snack time with his or her peers and no one uses a sippy cup. Now, with the child's emergence into a new social world, the "normality" of the accommodations you as a parent have made for your child, comes under the spotlight. The careful rehearsals and pre-settings you do with your child to help with the day's schedule and to ease him through transitions, don't happen. You will have to see whether your child can adjust. Perhaps those supports you've been providing were superfluous, or perhaps not. Marcus's entry into kindergarten was certainly such an eye-opener for us. I thought that I had arranged adequate supports for his transition into his kindergarten classroom. I certainly did not expect how easily the whole façade would crash when given the increased demands of his school situation.

An overload to our family's functioning

I remember the August Marcus turned five and began kindergarten. In retrospect, I should have considered delaying his kindergarten entry for a year, but Marcus was a bright boy, and his birth date was well before our school's cut-off date of December 1. I didn't realize then that most people in our particular community hold their fall-born children back, and what a disadvantage being so much younger would be for a physically and socially challenged child. (However, as I found later with Michael, receiving services for special needs when the child is school-aged, but voluntarily withheld from the publicly funded school system, poses its own set of problems.)

Marcus was enrolled in kindergarten, with a slightly extended day twice a week to accommodate his physical therapy and speech therapy. Everything seemed to be going ok at school, although our home life continued to be intensely challenging, due to Marcus's difficulties with motor planning and self-care activities. Then a series of events happened that put our accommodating system over the edge. I call this our "crash-and-burn scenario."

First, in November, I had to have a hysterectomy to deal with my uterine fibroids. The surgery itself was not as invasive to our home life as the lifestyle accommodations that preceded it, when back pain seriously restricted my usual parenting style. The week of the surgery finally came. My parents, who live out of state, graciously agreed to come spend two weeks helping until I could get on my feet again. This was wonderful for me, but a *major* stressor to Marcus, who did not deal well with transitions! Not only was I less available to help him emotionally or physically, but Marcus also had to deal with people who were pretty much strangers from his perspective, since he only saw them twice a year. To make matters worse, the week following my surgery, Marcus's kindergarten teacher, who had planned to start her pregnancy leave of absence during the Christmas break, experienced pregnancy complications and had to take her leave early, giving only three days' warning to the children.

My husband and I despaired when we saw how all of these changes were totally overwhelming Marcus. My memory glides over much of that time; it is so painful to remember. My son had a tendency to turn inward and shut down when he felt stressed. You could watch him fall apart. His body movements became less coordinated. His clothing was less likely to be put on correctly. He had more frequent toileting accidents. He would get halfway through a task and then stop, not realizing he wasn't finished. It would be obvious that he was trying hard, but it was totally beyond his ability to cope.

At school, he was having a rough time unpacking his backpack and hanging up his winter clothing in the morning. Snack times were physically challenging for Marcus, not just opening the juice boxes and snack packaging, but also coordinating clean up. His lunch box would come home a mess, because when it was time to clean up after snack time, he could not distinguish between garbage and items to be saved. Consequently, half-empty juice boxes would be thrown in with soggy pretzels or cheese sticks.

In kindergarten, much instructional time is spent in a circle on the floor. Due to Marcus's low muscle tone, sitting on the floor was very tiring for him. He would slump or lie down instead, because he didn't have the torso strength to sit erect without support for long periods of time. His Asperger's Syndrome meant he had little awareness of the body language and eye contact desired by teachers to indicate attention. Because Marcus was a sweet, non-aggressive child, he was slower to rush to the rug to sit for circle time. As a result, he would usually end up in the back rows, where attending to instruction was even harder for him to manage. Marcus was always losing his belongings, and asking him to prepare his table space for work was like asking me to do an advanced calculus problem. Marcus was constantly dropping, picking up, or looking for items while the teacher was giving class instructions. His new teacher was struggling with routines and transitions herself. Not only could she not help him, but also the changes in her style from that of his previous teacher confused Marcus even in those few expectations and routines he had been able to internalize.

If I hadn't been recovering from surgery and forced to take more of a backseat and observer role to all of Marcus's struggles, would I have been able to acknowledge that, in accommodating our son's needs, we had moved far beyond the range of "normal" family functioning? It may not be until your family's coping mechanisms overload and fail, that you can see the size of the elephant that your family is carrying around every day. I watched my son crash. I was doing everything I knew to do, and yet it was obvious that he needed more. I realized my love and willingness to work hard to support my child were not enough. Our family system was breaking down. We needed help. It couldn't possibly be normal for things to be this hard. As difficult as it was to live through, that collapse—that crash-and-burn scenario—was one of the most constructive things that could have happened to our family. I didn't know how or where to start to get the help we needed, but I had to find out. My kids needed me to do this. We had to seek further diagnosis. We had to find the door that would open toward help.

My advice to you?

What have I learned from facing this process of identifying developmental abnormalities in my own two children? As I found out, the divide between normal and abnormal isn't as great as I would have thought. Special needs may first manifest in a collection of nagging, small things rather than in an obvious revelation. Obviously, you can't respond to every comment made to you about your children's development. But if you start hearing concerns raised across different contexts or by different people, it is probably worth bringing these to the attention of your pediatrician or other health care professionals.

Watch your children with others in their same age group. Talk to people you trust and listen as they share their experiences. I'm not talking about those general comments that people make, complaining about how hard it is to get their kids out the door on time, or how messy their kids are. I'm talking about the more detailed descriptions of their children's accomplishments and difficulties. Do they seem to be similar to your concerns or different? How so?

Take charge of finding out more about child development. Parenting magazines or the family and child section of your local bookstore are two sources of information, as are television and radio programs. Many of you are familiar with the books, *What to Expect When You Are Expecting* (Murkoff, Eisenberg and Hathaway 2002), or *What to Expect in the First Year of Life* (Murkoff, Eisenberg and Hathaway 2003). The Gessell Institute publishes an old, but still wonderful series of similar books for each year of life until adulthood (Bates Ames and Chase Haber 1985, 1989, 1990; Bates Ames, Ilg and Chase Haber 1988). The American Academy of Pediatrics has a similar, more modern series (Shelov and Hannemann 2004; Schor 1999). Dr. Berry Brazelton has a wonderful, parent-friendly television series on child development issues (called *What Every Baby Knows*) that can help you put your experience in context. You'll find that every stage of development presents some natural problems and challenges for the child and for the family. But each stage of development is also marked by an array of developmental abnormalities that may begin to appear. Is your challenge one that you would normally expect to arise at your child's age? Does the extent or severity of the difficulty seem normal? Is your family able to cope with the problem? Do you need to consult with an expert for advice?

Similarly, if you, or your spouse, have a nagging sense that something isn't right with your child, flag that concern and investigate it. Raise it on your next visit to your pediatrician. If your pediatrician isn't concerned, ask him or her to explain to you the difference between what you are afraid you are seeing, and what your pediatrician thinks it is. Think about what your pediatrician says. Then revisit your concern at another time and see if it is still there. If so, then raise it with your pediatrician again. As we have seen, sometimes it takes time to recognize that an abnormal pattern is emerging. Your pediatrician is an important source of information for you. However, she or he does not see your child in the different settings you do, and pediatricians are not infallible. If something still doesn't feel right to you, seek another opinion.

Why not just wait until it is *obvious* that there is a problem? For one thing, some disabilities may always appear gray to a layperson, but clear to an appropriate expert. By waiting to seek help until your child is clearly drowning, your child has struggled much more and much longer than is necessary. Diagnosis and intervention can open up a whole new world of possibility for your child. You don't want to deny your child the experience of that full life. Also, there are other advantages to seeking help early. Younger children have become less entrenched in bad habits and potentially limiting compensatory behaviors. Younger children are less likely to feel a stigma of "difference." Younger children have fewer school responsibilities and commitments to interfere with scheduling therapies. Although "better late than never" certainly applies to meeting your child's special needs, my own personal view is that "earlier is even better."

Sometimes, we are almost superstitiously afraid of even asking whether our child is normal, as though voicing a fear that she or he is not, will conjure up a demon and make the fear come true. Trust me, developmental abnormalities don't work that way. If they exist, they will be true whether we name them or not. Finding out more about them, however, is the ticket to getting those special needs met. Worried? Check it out. Still worried? Check some more. Don't give up until those worries are satisfied. I can reassure you from the other side of this process, that the gains possible from early intervention are more than worth it.

3

Obtaining a
Formal Evaluation

Starting the diagnostic process is not as hard as you would expect. In fact, you've already done the hardest part of it, which is confronting your fears and deciding to go for help. The next step is like entering one of those whirlpool rides in a water park. Once you step out into the current, the process itself will sweep you along. You're sure to start some movement right away. Perhaps not the most efficient movement, but that's okay. As for learning how to control the whirlpool to arrive at a complete and accurate diagnosis of your child—that part may be more difficult, but just step in and you'll start encountering people who can help you.

If you've already obtained a diagnosis for your child that seems to account satisfactorily for the nature and extent of your child's difficulties, feel free to skip this chapter and move on to the next ones on dealing with the diagnosis. But, if your child's diagnosis doesn't feel right to you, or your child doesn't seem to be making the progress expected, you may want to reopen the diagnostic question. Many children actually have a constellation of disabling conditions. Identifying and putting the ones that apply to your child into perspective may take time and multiple trips through the diagnostic process, as it did for us. As for you first-timers, I hope sharing with you what I've learned about obtaining a diagnosis gives you some guidance and reassurance.

Referring your child for
evaluation: an overview of the process

In 1975, the United States federal legislature passed the Education for All Handicapped Children Act (PL 94-142). This law states in no uncertain terms that a free, appropriate public education must be provided for our children, regardless of disabling conditions that might exist. Since then, the law has undergone several revisions and reauthorizations. Its most recent incarnation is the Individuals with Disabilities Education Improvement Act of 2004, known as IDEA 2004. Because of the protections provided by this series of federal laws, determining that your child has special educational needs does not exclude your child from publicly funded schools, nor does it necessarily exclude your child from inclusion in regular classrooms. Those of us who remember what education for differently-abled children looked like in the 1950s and 1960s understand what a huge commitment the United States government made to American children by enacting this law. The passage of these federal acts marked society's acceptance of its responsibility to provide an appropriate education for *all* children, regardless of possible disabling condition. Furthermore, IDEA details possible avenues for identifying children with disabilities or with special educational needs through evaluations funded at public, not private expense. All children, from newborn to age 21, have access to this process. The federal legislation includes a Child Find provision, in which the schools have an obligation to seek out families and children who may be in need of special education or related services. But under IDEA, anyone can refer a child for evaluation: you, your pediatrician, a child's teacher, a friend… The parent or guardian of the child will then be asked to give consent for the evaluation to occur.

Requesting and receiving an evaluation is fairly simple. No rigid burden of proof is placed on the parent to show that an evaluation is needed. The special needs identification system is not like Medicaid, where you must fit in a particular lower income bracket to be eligible for services. Again, these battles have been fought for you. Although you always have the option of paying privately for evaluations, most evaluative needs can be met by going through public sources. This is a very good thing too, because even if financially secure, you'd be amazed at how quickly the evaluation and therapy bills can accumulate. So my first advice to you, regardless of your income, is to *try going through the appropriate county or public school services for evaluation and treatment first*. Save your own funds for use if your needs are not met through normal channels, or to supplement your child's program with additional services and therapies.

What are the "normal channels" for obtaining an evaluation to determine whether your child has special needs? In the United States, the process is, in large part, determined by what state you live in, and the age of your child. The federal laws governing services for children with special needs apply to every state. The system through which those services are administered, however, varies across states. There are different supervising entities, different public funding sources, and different procedures applicable to children in different age groups. You are eligible for one set of services from birth to age three, another from three to five years old, and yet another for school-aged children and adolescents. You are *always* eligible to request a publicly funded evaluation for your child, but which particular fund will pay for it varies with your child's age. So, starting the formal evaluation process first involves connecting with the appropriate supervising entity and getting its approval for the publicly funded evaluations you are requesting. Within the United States, you would contact your state's Department of Education, Department of Social Services, or Department of Health and Human Services to find out how the process works in your state. Every state also has a Parent Training and Information Center (PTI for short), which can be accessed for a wide variety of information. To me, the clearest outline of the process for each state was available through the National Dissemination Center for Children with Disabilities (NICHCY). NICHCY has been established as the national clearing house for information related to children with disabilities. It publishes resource sheets for each state, and a "cheat sheet" guide for how to use these sheets. NICHCY also publishes a very clear, informational brief for parents on PTIs. (See Useful resources for contact details of NICHCY and other resources at the end of the chapter.) There's an incredible network out there to help you. Be sure to take a look.

When you make your initial phone call, don't worry about whether you've got the right terminology, or even the appropriate initial phone number. I've been told that for elementary school-aged children and younger, by far the majority of evaluation requests are initiated by parents, not professionals. The special needs system actually expects to walk you through the process. Just briefly explain to the person on the other end of the phone line that you want to request a formal assessment to determine whether your child has special needs. If that particular person is not the appropriate contact, odds are that she or he can give you the number of the person who is.

Once you have made your initial inquiry, you will then be provided with the first round of paperwork. One of the most important documents is a "Consent to Evaluate" form. Signing this document not only authorizes the evaluation of your child, it also sets in motion an official, 60-day time clock regulating the evaluation process. Other paperwork included will ask for background information on your family and your child's developmental history. These questionnaires will ask very specific questions about your child's development in a number of areas, including his or her cognitive or intellectual development, social development, emotional development, language development, and physical development. They will ask you to report, if known, the dates of your child's major developmental milestones, the history of your concerns, and your perception of your child's current level of functioning. The information you provide is important for helping the professionals put into context the behaviors and abilities they will later observe in their evaluations. Knowledge of the approximate age of onset of certain behaviors (or the lack of certain behaviors at various ages) may be important cues for helping your evaluators determine the likelihood of various possible diagnoses. This background information will also help the evaluating agency decide which specialists to include on your child's evaluation team. Work carefully through these forms, and fill them out as accurately and completely as possible, for these will become your child's official personal history for the professionals you are bringing on board. I usually go over the questionnaires several times, marking those items that I am not sure about and returning to them again on later days to see if I have had any further thoughts. After you have compiled this information once, any subsequent questionnaires will be easier in that you will often be able to use these first records for reference. You will also be asked to authorize the release of your child's medical records to assist in the evaluation.

Along with this initial round of paperwork, you should receive literature outlining your child's basic educational rights, and how the educational process works for individuals with special educational needs. Sometimes the literature they'll send is physically illegible, in legalese, or difficult to understand, so feel free to call back and ask questions. Again, within the United States, your state's PTI can also help. As always, other parents can be a wonderful source of information. If you wish for more detail on the general process, two parent-friendly publications are:

Anderson, Chitwood and Hayden's *Negotiating the Special Education Maze* (1997) and *The Complete IEP Guide* (2001), by attorney Lawrence M. Siegel. A little more intimidating because of their thoroughness, but clearly the king of navigating the system and translating special educational law into parents' and children's rights, are the Wrightslaw books and web resources, provided by Pam and Pete Wright. Two in particular are *From Emotions to Advocacy* (2nd edn, 2006) and also their detailed guide and discussion, *Special Education Law* (2nd edn, 2007). I strongly encourage you to acquire a copy of both volumes to guide you in the specifics of the process.

The following pages discuss some of the specifics of the evaluation process in the United States for each of the major age groupings. Although the details will vary from state to state, this description will give you an idea of what to expect.

The evaluation process for children from birth to age three

In the United States, a child eligible for special services can begin to get help long before she or he enters the publicly funded school system. Here, public law and public policy wonderfully match the science of what we know about children and the importance of early experiences. In my opinion, the hardest part of applying for Early Intervention services is finding out who administers the programs! In New York, it is through the State Department of Health's Bureau of Early Intervention. In other states it may be through the State Department of Health and Welfare, State Education, or other departments. To my dismay, the phonebook does not provide listings simply under "Early Intervention." The easiest way to find out who administers Early Intervention programs in your state is to first contact the National Dissemination Center for Children with Disabilities, as listed in Useful resources at the end of the chapter. If you prefer, a quick call to your school district or to your pediatrician's office may provide the contact information you want.

When you call, you will be assigned a caseworker, whose responsibilities include walking you through the steps to obtain Early Intervention (often called EI) services. The EI caseworker will attend your meetings and represent you when the evaluation report is submitted and services are requested. Your caseworker should also guide you to other resources for which you are eligible, including income supplements, respite care, social security benefits, and the like. Our EI caseworker also attended my son's evaluations. When your child becomes three years old and ages out of Early Intervention, your caseworker's job is to help you navigate the transition to the preschool services administered through the school district.

Early Intervention is designed to be extremely family-friendly. The meetings usually take place in your own home, making them more convenient and less intimidating. The evaluations also often take place in your own home or your child's daycare; occasionally a particular evaluation requires a more specialized setting. Once you have submitted your initial application, you will receive packets of information, including a list of agencies or individuals approved by your county for evaluating the major areas of child development. These areas include speech therapy, physical therapy, occupational therapy, or special education. The county will also ask if you wish to access your health insurance to help pay for the evaluation. Free Early Intervention evaluations are available to everyone, regardless of whether they have insurance. Allowing the county to bill your insurance company simply allows them to stretch their funding further, and the law requires that this be at no financial disadvantage to you. You may go outside the approved list for your child's evaluation, but then you may need to pay through your family's medical insurance or out of your own pocket. Because Early Intervention referrals are a major source of their clientele, most, if not all of the major evaluation providers in your area are likely to be on the county's lists.

An alternative route to contacting the appropriate state agency directly, is to access Early Intervention services through your child's physician. Parents of premature and other at-risk newborns are often automatically referred to the Early Intervention programs through the hospital where their children are born. Do not assume, however, that any applicable Early Intervention programs for which your child may be eligible will contact you automatically. A friend of mine had a child born with some very obvious developmental abnormalities. Because her baby stayed in intensive care for some time at a well-regarded local hospital, my friend assumed that she was being guided to all the Early Intervention services that were applicable. She discovered four months later, that Early Intervention offered a wonderful support for families of newborn to three-month-olds, but by then, her infant was already too old to be eligible. (The county helped connect her to another program later.) My point is that automatic referral channels take time. With them, as with everything in the special needs system, you are safest never relying on the automaticity of the process. That's another part of the mindset that I recommend in advocating for your child with special needs: *never assume or take anything for granted. Always check for yourself.*

The evaluation process for preschool children

In the United States, once a child attains three years of age, she or he is still eligible for intervention, but the supervisory and approval responsibility is now shared between your local school district and the state agency responsible for preschool intervention services. Your contact is usually through your local school district offices. In New York, for example, you would call your school district and ask for the chair of the Committee on Preschool Special Education (also known as the CPSE). Don't be thrown off by the name "special education." All special education means is that the children have special needs that may not be met by the "regular" education process. The chair of the CPSE will send you a Consent to Evaluate form and information on the special needs identification process.

What happens next may vary from state to state. The parent and the other members of the CPSE together decide what types of evaluations to perform. In some states, your child's local school personnel conduct the evaluations. In other states, such as New York, the school district will provide a list of independent providers contracted by the school district to perform evaluations for preschool children. This list may be different from that provided for the younger age group. When you call the agency you have selected, summarize your concerns for them, and they will help you put together an evaluation team. The CPSE chair may also be able to help you with this, based on his or her experience. My experience with both Early Intervention and the CPSE is that they are truly there to help families. Although I would not count on them as the *only* source of expertise, their guidance is valuable because of their knowledge of the special education process and their familiarity with local schools and professionals.

The evaluation process for a school-aged child

In the United States, once a child is either "kindergarten-eligible" or officially enrolled in a public or private kindergarten-to-twelfth-grade-program, then you must proceed through your local publicly funded school to request an evaluation for special needs. In our school district, kindergarten-eligible means that the child would turn five years old before December 1 of that year. The cut-off age may be different in your school district, and the committee names may vary depending on where you live. In New York, you go to the Committee on Preschool Special Education (the CPSE) for preschool children, and the Committee on Special Education (the CSE) for school-aged children. Even though we elected to delay our second son's entrance into kindergarten to give him an extra developmental year, we still had to switch to using the CSE for formulating and providing his special needs services.

You may start the CSE process in several ways. You may contact the psychologist, special education teacher, or social worker at the institution your child currently attends (if any). You may call your local publicly funded school and ask to be put in touch with a special needs specialist on its staff. Or you may once again call the offices of your local school district and ask to speak to the CSE chair. They will send you information outlining the process, and a form requesting your consent to evaluate your child. They will also ask you to sign a release for your child's medical records. Again, put your request for an initial evaluation in writing, and describe your areas of concern and the reasons why you are requesting an evaluation. Putting your request in writing officially starts the 60 days that the law allows for your school district to follow through on your request.

In the case of a school-aged child, the relevant specialists in your child's local school district usually perform the evaluations. In some states, this is also the case for a preschool-aged child. You always have the option to employ private practitioners instead, or to supplement the process with outside evaluators and request that the school district pay for these. The district is more likely to do this if your school's specialists have already done an initial, base evaluation looking for the most common areas of concern. Having the school district perform at least some of the evaluation is likely to benefit you by minimizing your cost. One thing to keep in mind, however, is that if the district pays for the evaluation, they are also entitled to see the results. Sometimes parents prefer to review the evaluation results before deciding whether or not to share them with the district. The Wrightslaw resources mentioned earlier offer excellent discussions of these issues.

The CSE chair or your local school psychologist can be sources for guidance and referral for outside evaluators. Your pediatrician is another. If you have access to them, other parents with experience can be very helpful in directing you to appropriate individuals, and walking you through this evaluation process. In some school districts, you may feel like you are encountering resistance to your efforts to have your child's needs identified. If so, any of the resources referenced earlier can help you to navigate obstacles thrown your way.

Can starting the evaluation process hurt my child?

What I've just given you is the "official" answer to the question of how you start the formal evaluation process for a school-aged child. There's another answer, though, because there's another question. When a friend of mine called to ask me how to start the process for her second grader, what she really wanted to know was, "What do you tell the school, and when?" What we're talking about here is the power and the risk of knowledge, especially when it is knowledge of a vulnerability your child has, or the perception of a difficulty your child may pose to others. This fear is founded in some social realities. I felt it when I was interviewing preschools for my sons, and one well-respected private school acted as though I'd passed gas when I asked the question, "How does your school work with kids with special needs?" The issues are sharper and of even greater consequence when the child is school-aged and a formal school record begins tracking your child's school career. Telling the school that we are concerned that our children may have special needs certainly does not feel like a risk-free venture for us as parents. I can understand my friend's temptation to wait until an outside evaluator confirmed the extent of her son's challenges.

My advice to you, however, is the same advice I gave my friend. Yes, it may feel risky, but tell your school as soon as possible. Your child's teacher probably already suspects there's some sort of problem, even if she or he doesn't know exactly what it is. Telling the school that you want to pursue an evaluation for special needs alerts the school to your level of concern and your commitment to helping your child. The school district has tremendous resources in place. Use those channels and those resources. The risk is not anywhere near as great as you think it is. Teachers and other school personnel are professionals whose responsibility is to educate your child. If your child has special educational needs, they are the people who most need to work with you to get them identified. On a purely practical level, you must tell the school eventually, in order to receive special education services through them, so I recommend including the school early in the process.

My friend was worried that if she started with the school professionals and they told her they saw no evidence of special needs in her son, she then would be bound by their decision and stymied in her attempts to get help. This is not the case. In the United States and in many other countries, there are legal safeguards in place protecting the rights of parents and allowing you to contest the school district's decision. For instance, IDEA states that if you disagree with an evaluation, you have the right to request another one from an outside, independent evaluator at public expense. Other people may worry that the special education process will take on a life of its own, and you will lose the right to make choices for your child. This fear is also unfounded. The special educational system is in place to *assist* families. You do not abandon your parenting rights by entering the special needs network.

Finally, the same system of federal laws and regulations establishing the special needs system also addresses the confidentiality of your child's records. The Family Educational Rights and Privacy Act (FERPA) is a federal statute protecting parent and child privacy by limiting who has access to your child's educational records. It also allows you the right to inspect and review their contents. Any evaluations performed by the school, and any evaluations or medical information released to the school, will become a part of those records and protected by these privacy laws. Your CPSE or CSE chair can provide you with information regarding how your particular school district addresses student privacy. If you have confidentiality concerns, I refer you to one of the legal advocacy resources described at the end of the chapter.

How do you bring the school into the process?

When you are ready to talk to your school, a good place to start is by conferencing with your child's teacher. He or she has knowledge of your child in the classroom context—an experience different from your own. Your child's teacher is familiar with the range of characteristics and behaviors often encountered at your child's age level. Listen carefully to the teacher's descriptions of the strengths and weaknesses she or he sees in your child. Ask for specific examples of things you do not understand. Come to the conference prepared with a list of your concerns, and specifically ask the teacher what she or he thinks about those concerns. Sharing perspectives through this give-and-take dialogue can be very useful to both parent and teacher, and can foster a sense of teamwork, with your child as the beneficiary. You are not bound by the judgment and advice of your child's teacher, but I do believe in asking their professional opinion. Again on a practical level, the evaluators are going to do so anyway, and it will help you to know the teacher's overall impression ahead of time! If you disagree with the teacher's opinions, you can specifically address the areas of disagreement with the evaluators.

If your school uses parent volunteers in the classroom, try to volunteer, even if only occasionally. Not only will your child's classroom benefit from the extra pair of hands, there is nothing like this opportunity for you to see first-hand the extent to which your child is having problems, and how your child compares with his or her same-aged peers. This is also a good way to get a sense of how well your child fits into the particular educational setting in which she or he is placed.

After you have a sense of your child's performance in the classroom, I would recommend scheduling an appointment with the school psychologist, or with the school's CSE team. Bring a list of your concerns with you and discuss them at this meeting. This may help you gain additional perspective on your child's difficulties, and what assistance the school can provide, even without a formal evaluation. If needed, the school psychologist can then guide you through the appropriate steps for evaluation within your school. If you are considering bringing in an outside evaluator, talk to the team about that as well. Although the choice is yours, the team may have helpful suggestions or advice. Whenever you meet with the school team, let them know what you've done thus far and what your future plans are. No one likes to be blindsided by unexpected information, and sharing your plans helps give school personnel time to adjust.

Selecting evaluators for your child

If your local school is not going to perform your child's evaluations, you will have to choose someone to do it for you. The first, and obvious step is to check that the person has appropriate credentials for your child's type of problem(s). The second is to check that the proper assessment tools are used. You may wish to see the Wrightslaw or the NICHCY resources for more on this. IDEA provides for the use of multiple assessment measures. These include standardized tests and "functional assessments" of your child's abilities, which provide additional descriptions of your child's abilities within the context of his or her daily activities.

For the initial evaluation, at least a two-person team will evaluate your child. One individual will be someone trained in overall child development. She or he will provide a comprehensive developmental screening, more thorough than that provided by your pediatrician, and designed to help determine whether additional areas should be looked at more intensely. A second evaluator will be a specialist in the area of your particular concerns. If you have multiple areas of concerns, you should request a specialist to represent each area.

Our county sent out quite a daunting list of evaluators from which I was supposed to make my selection, but a closer look at the list helped me to see that they didn't all apply to me. The list should be categorized in multiple ways. For example, evaluators will be classified by the types of evaluations they provide. Although you may not be proficient in the technical jargon various specialists use, you probably know at least the basic areas of your concern. Coordination, muscular, and other physical movement concerns will probably involve the services of an occupational therapist (OT) and/or a physical therapist (PT). Speech and language concerns merit the attention of a speech and language pathologist (SLP). I use the terms speech therapist, speech pathologist, and speech and language pathologist interchangeably to mean a professional who provides support for children with articulation, language, and communication issues. Behavioral and cognitive concerns will involve a psychologist and/or a special educator. Most evaluating agencies employ a variety of specialists and can put together an appropriate team for your child's evaluation based on their initial conversations with you about the nature of your child's difficulties.

Evaluators differ in their skills and in their approaches. You may need to do some sleuthing to find out which ones are most likely to provide a good fit for your child and your concerns. Other parents are often the best source of recommendations, so it is worth contacting a parent advocacy group in your area, such as Parent to Parent, or ask around among your friends. Your pediatrician may be able to make a recommendation. Local treatment centers are another information source. Because agencies are vying with one another for the opportunity to provide evaluations and receive payment for these services, your caseworker or CPSE or CSE chair is not *supposed* to select an evaluator for you. Doing so is feared to show favoritism or undue influence on the parent's right to choose. However, you can always ask for guidance as to which individuals or agencies may be the best place to start, and you may very well get off-the-record advice. Even if the caseworker or CPSE or CSE chair does not feel comfortable recommending one agency over another, they will be able to answer specific questions. Perhaps, they can also steer you towards some individuals or away from others, based on the particular concerns you raise. Local sources have usually been able to help me with most general evaluations, but for other, more specialized evaluations, I have been willing to look further afield. National advocacy groups focused on your child's suspected disorder may have lists of specialists on file. I have even e-mailed authors of books I've encountered, asking for referrals in my geographical area. Wrightslaw publishes a website, www.yellowpagesforkids.com, which provides a state-by-state listing of a wide variety of additional resources. These include the names and contact information of Parent Training and Information Centers and Community Parent Resource Centers in each state. Its entries are updated frequently, and grouped both by type of resource and by state. The website includes grassroots organizations, national, and even some international resources. It is an excellent place to start your search. Many of these resources are referenced in Useful resources at the end of the chapter.

If you are feeling overwhelmed by the responsibility of making a selection, take a deep breath and remind yourself that attention to this detail is important. A sense of trust in your evaluator is very helpful for getting you through all the unknowns that will follow. There may not be an obvious, perfect choice of evaluators for your child, but do look for one or more individuals with good reputations, who are likely to provide a good, solid first pass evaluation. Note that I wrote, "first pass evaluation." If later experience shows that the evaluation was insufficient to diagnose your child's difficulties, then you can always request another one, fine-tuning your request based on the results of your first evaluation experiences. For example, my son Michael's initial evaluation was performed by an occupational therapist and a special educator. I did not agree with their findings that his delays were only slight and not needing intervention. I had Michael re-evaluated a few months later by a different agency. I specifically requested that a physical therapist and a speech and language pathologist be included on this new evaluation team, to target the areas that I felt had not been adequately addressed before.

We have used our local school for some evaluations and therapies, and employed outside specialists in autism spectrum disorders for others. It is also important for you to know that the school district is not *obligated* to approve treatment plans recommended by outside evaluators. These recommendations must be argued for and approved by your school district CSE or CPSE meetings. Whether you go through your home school or through an outside practitioner, it is important to keep your home school CSE team aware of what you are doing and the results of any relevant outside evaluations you have performed. This communication helps avoid redundant testing of your child, and enables better planning and coordination of any services offered.

You will also discover that, in the world of schools, *a documented diagnosis is not the same thing as a documented special educational need*! A "diagnosis" is a medical entity, describing certain characteristics of a child. School districts, on the other hand, conduct educational evaluations to determine if the child's education is being impacted. If so, the schools then look to see if the child fits any of the 13 categories of disabilities making him or her eligible for special education or related services under IDEA. These are listed in Box 3.1. Even if you come to your school district CSE meetings armed with opinions from multiple experts, the district personnel may nod their heads, offer you sympathy, but deny services if your child's disability does not fall under the restrictions and guidelines placed by IDEA. It is not enough to show a diagnosis. It is not enough to show that your child's educational performance would *improve* with therapeutic intervention. I have no doubt that many of my son's peers would benefit from many of the interventions we are doing with Marcus. But the difference is, because Marcus has been classified as a student in need of special education services, interventions and accommodations are provided. By definition under the law, he would not be receiving an appropriate education without them.

Box 3.1 The categories of disabilities eligible for special education and related services under IDEA 2004

- Autism
- Deaf-blindness
- Deafness
- Hearing impairment
- Mental retardation
- Multiple disabilities
- Orthopedic impairment
- Other health impaired (i.e., having limited strength, vitality, or alertness that affects a child's educational performance)
- Serious emotional disturbance
- Specific learning disability
- Speech or language impairment
- Traumatic brain injury
- Visual impairments, including blindness

It is very important that your child's written evaluations include a *strong educational perspective*, and my experience is that not all evaluators are equally successful at doing this. You may need to include an educational psychologist or some other education-oriented specialist to help you demonstrate the relevance of your child's condition to the school setting. I find this to be an ongoing struggle for my own children. Because both my boys are very bright and high functioning in many areas, their special needs are less obvious than those of an individual who may be struggling more obviously academically. You may need to work with your evaluation team to present the educational significance of your own child's difficulties, to help turn your child's diagnosis into a condition recognized as requiring special educational support under IDEA or other legislation. If you are initially denied classification for services, it is sometimes worth pursuing further using an advocate or an additional consultant.

Our experience obtaining an evaluation for Marcus

My son, Marcus, was initially identified as needing further evaluation by our pediatrician at our well-baby check-ups. Our pediatrician referred us to a developmental pediatrics center at an area hospital, where we met with a specialist who identified his Asperger's Syndrome. After Marcus's initial diagnosis, I then called Early Intervention and told them what we had done, and that we'd identified areas of developmental concern for which we needed therapy provided. As is standard procedure, they requested that we obtain through one of their approved agencies, an additional, broader developmental evaluation to supplement our privately obtained, and more medically oriented one. We decided an appropriate evaluation team for Marcus would include a psychologist, a special educator, a physical therapist, an occupational therapist and a speech and language pathologist. Most teams are not this elaborate, but the multi-dimensional nature of Marcus's difficulties called for it: his difficulties with both fine and gross motor skills, coupled with his low muscle tone warranted OT and PT. His speech articulation difficulties called for a speech evaluation. The Asperger's diagnosis, with the pervasive developmental delays accompanying it, called for yet other specialists able to assess Marcus's cognitive, communication, and social skills. Sometimes individuals trained in one specialty, such as physical therapy, also review other related area concerns, such as occupational therapy (or vice versa). You have the right, however, to request that the specialist have particular expertise in your area of concern.

We had a second reason behind requesting such an extensive evaluation team for Marcus. Our personal experience with the developmental pediatric center had resulted in a pretty devastating diagnosis, posing a lot of emotional problems for us because it was so unexpected. None of the people we usually dealt with and trusted had prepared us for the possibility of such a diagnosis. We wanted to use this evaluation team as a second opinion on the Asperger's issues. I personally believed there was actually an adaptive reason behind many of Marcus's abnormal behaviors. I wanted specialists to look at the broader context of his behaviors to help us determine whether his difficulties were just isolated to speech articulation and motor concerns, or whether the broader (and to us more emotionally devastating) Asperger's concerns were truly applicable.

What if you're not satisfied with an evaluation?

Your first job, if you are unhappy with the evaluation you receive, is to stop and think about why you are not happy. Is it primarily an emotional reaction to news you didn't want to hear? That's understandable. I've been there too. Often an evaluator will orally summarize his or her preliminary findings, before composing the formal, written report. If so, you may have gone into shell shock, lashed out at the evaluator, made some initial attempts to understand—or perhaps all three. A knee-jerk, "shoot the messenger" response is probably one of the most common reactions to news you don't want to hear. My husband and I became so angry with one of my son's major evaluators, we walked out of the office vowing never to return. It truly is imperative that the evaluator takes the time to win your trust and to explain their findings to you carefully. They must help you deal with any initial emotional trauma so that you can hear what they are trying to tell you.

We went to Marcus's first developmental evaluation with no idea that an autism spectrum disorder was even a possibility. I still do not understand the aggressiveness of the diagnostician's attempts to initiate play with Marcus to assess his social skills. Marcus was a shy, easily overwhelmed three-year-old at the time. Basically sweet-natured and happy, Marcus tended not to interact with people other than immediate family. His speech was very difficult to understand by anyone other than me. The evaluation took place in a small playroom, at a clinic we had never been to before. Both my husband and I were in the room with Marcus, when the evaluator entered, followed by two other unfamiliar adults. Marcus was sitting on the floor, happily loading animals into a school bus. After greeting us, the evaluator got on the floor to join Marcus. The evaluator said a few warm words to Marcus, commented on his play, picked up a toy police car, and then immediately crashed the police car into Marcus's school bus while smiling at my son. Although my son didn't cry, he wouldn't interact with the evaluator afterwards. This was an entirely new type of play for my son, and over the next few days, I watched Marcus practice crashing cars in his own solitary play. The interaction did nothing to reassure me that the evaluator understood my son, or that he was getting what I felt was a representative picture of my son's social capabilities. Regardless of how we felt about his methods, however, the evaluator was very experienced with developmental disabilities. He completed his assessment within about 15 minutes, and turned us over to another individual, who completed a more involved test confirming the evaluator's initial diagnosis of Asperger's. The gentle, calming manner of the second evaluator did much to build rapport with my son. Her running explanations to my husband and me, and her willingness to respond to our questions, helped us to begin to accept the diagnosis that we were presented. Much of that rapport was later destroyed, however, when the office manager handed us a packet of materials collected from the Internet as an introduction to Asperger's Syndrome. The materials were informative, but complex and technical—quite daunting to the layperson. My training as a cognitive developmental psychologist helped me through this tough reading. As a parent, however, it was intellectually and emotionally draining to read page after page of the cognitive, social, and linguistic limitations and difficulties my son would experience as a result of his Asperger's. The reading certainly took a heavy emotional toll. When I read on the third page that our son could be taught to "mimic human behaviors," I literally screamed and slung the materials across the room. Was the author inferring my child was less than human because he has this disorder? I felt assaulted. I felt that I had trusted this developmental specialist's office to hand me parent-sensitive materials to help me understand my son's disorder, and instead they had ambushed me at a time when I was most vulnerable. Realizing how important it was that we get help for our son, I later returned to the materials and tried to see past the hurtful wording. This strategy often helps. Still, I think evaluators need to take very seriously the need to help parents be able to hear and understand their findings.

Several years later, my path crossed that of a social worker from this same clinic. She gave me a book the evaluator and his team had since put together, to help parents understand some of the more common diagnoses their clinic encounters. In the book, the evaluator acknowledged that it is always difficult to be the bearer of bad news to parents, and their office grapples with how best to fulfill this responsibility. No one means to hurt you. It is always difficult finding a balance between clinical descriptions, and descriptions that are more tailored for a parent's sensitivities. Even if we find the information hurtful, as parents we have the responsibility to try to hear the expert's message. On the other hand, it would help tremendously if evaluators kept in mind that we *are* parents, not mechanical information processors. These evaluation results are about our much-loved children, not impersonal clinical cases. Please, if you must hurt us, hurt us gently, point us towards help, and offer us hope.

Despite our emotions, however, the bottom-line remains: is the evaluation accurate? To answer that question, you'll need to look at a number of factors. A good evaluator will ask if your child's performance that day seems fairly typical, and will listen carefully to your response. The purpose of the evaluation is to get a good, three-dimensional "snapshot," in a manner of speaking, of your child. Your child needs to be healthy and well rested for this to be a good picture of your child's functioning. We've had to return to an area hospital for a second audiological test when Marcus's ears were blocked from a head cold for the first evaluation. His health status meant that we weren't getting a good measure of his typical functioning. In addition to your child's physical and emotional status on the day of the evaluation, you need to have a sense of how well the evaluator and your child got along. One would hope that a person trained in pediatric evaluations would have a good bedside manner with kids, but different kids have different personalities and different needs. Your child and the evaluator don't have to be best friends, but they do need to connect well enough with one another so that your child doesn't shut down. If that rapport is not established, the evaluator is much less likely to get a good read on your child.

I prefer, whenever possible, to eavesdrop on my children's evaluations. I might ask the evaluator to leave the door ajar, and I'll sit in the next room. Or I might ask if I can sit quietly in the corner. Of course, if the evaluator agrees to this, it's important for you not to distract the child or interfere with the evaluation. Now that my children are attending school, I'm often not even notified as to exactly what days my sons will be evaluated. Frankly, I resent the closed-door nature of the process. If I know that my child has particular behavioral, health, or energy concerns on a particular day, I would like to have the option to postpone a scheduled evaluation. I also like to be sensitive to my child's concerns, such as whether he is already having a rough day, or would be missing something very important to him. School personnel, however, tend to run on very tight schedules, and so you may have to make an effort to ensure your child's concerns are not lost amid scheduling concerns. At the very least, I ask that the school send a note home at the end of the day notifying me after the fact that extra testing occurred, so that I can anticipate resulting fatigue. This knowledge also helps me sense whether my child was likely to have performed typically on that day or not.

Realistically, sitting in on your own child's evaluation may not be for everyone. I have a professional background that makes me interested in seeing behind those closed doors. I've paid a price at times for doing so, however, similar to the emotional impact of being in a room with your child while he or she undergoes stitches or some other surgical procedure. It's painful to watch your child experience frustration or difficulty in a testing situation, and not step in to help. It hurts to look at them clinically, particularly when it is in a test situation designed to elicit their difficulties—in effect, designed to make them fail! So, I can't say to you that it is always better to sit in on the evaluation. I can say that it is my preference to do so, and I offer it as one option to explore. If I can't be physically present, I like to ask the evaluator to summarize what she or he did with my child, and how my child tended to react. After I receive the formal reports, I'll often ask for clarification, going slowly and carefully through the report. If the evaluator did not describe them, I'll ask for samples of questions used to reach various conclusions, and so I can get a sense of the skills tested. Be careful; what a specific test labels a set of skills might not match what you think it does! I'll read the reports carefully to see if the described performance matches how I would expect my child to perform. Again, your evaluator is offering you a type of snapshot of your child. If it doesn't "look like" your child to you, then you need to discuss with the evaluator what is bothering you about the assessment. They may be able to extend their evaluation to include other measures. Listening carefully to their responses to your concerns will provide useful information to you, even if you continue to disagree with the evaluator's conclusions.

When you take your child for an evaluation, whether for occupational therapy, physical therapy, speech therapy, special education, or whatever, the evaluator has a range of tests from which to choose. Individual therapists tend to gravitate towards one test or set of tests over others as a matter of theoretical approach, personal preference, and how useful they have found the particular tests to be for their particular purposes. Sometimes test selection depends on pragmatic concerns, such as what tests the individual has available to administer. The specific measures are usually objective in themselves, meaning that two different evaluators using the same measure should obtain the same results. However, the conclusions drawn might be different if a different test were employed. This is why any evaluation report must include a description of the measures used to obtain the results.

There may not be a single, right/wrong description of your child. One evaluator I consulted for Michael's fine motor skills used a contextual approach to evaluate him, while another used an approach that isolated particular motor skills. They evaluated Michael within three months of each other, and reached different conclusions as to his abilities and his need for therapy. The two evaluators didn't necessarily contradict each other in the sense that one had to be correct and the other incorrect. Rather, they used different instruments and weighed various characteristics differently, and this led them to different conclusions. I then had to decide for myself how much to weigh the differing reports in forming my own opinions.

Similarly, the speech evaluations for Marcus when he was in kindergarten and first grade, used tests that measured his articulation—how well he was able to pronounce certain sounds. His speech therapies were designed to address his articulation difficulties. General measures of language development showed him progressing within a normal range. Until, that is, his play therapist suggested that I ask the speech and language pathologist to administer a specialized test, designed to measure the pragmatic use of language in everyday problem-solving. Suddenly, the picture that emerged of my six-year, seven-month-old son was that on this one particular measure, his performance matched that expected of a two-year, eight-month-old child. I don't think you could get a more dramatic demonstration that one's conclusion will depend on whether one is using the right instrument and looking in the right place to spotlight a particular disability! Finding the right diagnostic tool made a tremendous difference for Marcus, because we could then modify his therapies to address specifically (and quite successfully too!) this deficit. *If you are not pleased with an evaluation, don't give up. You just may not have found the right diagnostic tool yet.* Clinical practice and standards evolve as we learn more about the diagnosis and remediation of various disabilities. You may need to check that your evaluator is using tests in line with the most up-to-date standards. Parents, disability organizations, and other professionals may provide information that can help if you need to try to fine-tune your diagnostic search.

There has been at least one instance of an evaluation in which I disagreed with the evaluator's conclusions. In this case, I did not question the evaluator's choice of tests, or even Michael's performance on the tests. My disagreement with the evaluator had to do with my sense that he was looking at only one of Michael's areas of difficulty, without an awareness of how known difficulties in other areas could be impacting this area of performance. The episode to which I'm referring was a formal evaluation of Central Auditory Processing functioning for Michael. The evaluation spread over a couple of hours, with breaks in between. The evaluator was wonderful about giving me feedback on Michael's performance as the testing progressed. About halfway through the evaluation, Michael's behavior changed. Until that time, he was showing no sign of Central Auditory Processing Disorders, but then suddenly the signs were there. The evaluator was ready to write those results off as fatigue, because they were inconsistent with how Michael performed when he was totally fresh. I understood and respected this sensitivity to test reliability concerns, in the same way that I recognized and appreciated the appropriateness of the frequent breaks between parts of the test. I had a different concern, however, and I offered the evaluator another possible interpretation of the inconsistent findings. The evaluator understood Central Auditory Processing Disorders, but he wasn't familiar with low muscle tone and how this can interact with attentional resources. I pointed out that, because Michael has low muscle tone, sitting itself could be tiring for him. Maintaining an erect posture, as required by the test, is effortful for him, even with frequent breaks. Auditory processing is also effortful for him. Michael is bright enough and motivated enough, that he's usually willing to exert the extra effort required to listen. When Michael gets tired, however, he has no extra resources left to compensate for his difficulty. It's a judgment call whether results from the "slightly fatigued Michael" provided an *inaccurate* or an *accurate* picture of his difficulty. As long as the tests were administered according to the age-appropriate procedures, I argued, the mixed performance was also a part of Michael's clinical picture. Although when he is at his freshest, Michael has the competence to compensate for his difficulties, the times when he is tired, over-stimulated, or not at his best are also an important part of his typical school day. Inconsistency is actually one of his symptoms and is a part of this disorder. After our discussion, the evaluator ended by describing Michael as having a mild Central Auditory Processing Disorder, and made a note in the final report that Michael varied as to whether or not it showed. He also suggested that we have Michael retested in a few years, to follow up on these results.

Box 3.2 summarizes your options if you are not happy with an evaluation. It is not uncommon to take several years, and multiple trips through the evaluation process before you have a *complete* picture of your child's disabilities. If the end result of the process is that you are still unhappy, and that you are not able to qualify for special education services, you may have to revert back to a wait-and-see mentality for a while. This, of course, is not the preferred outcome, but realistically, it may be what sometimes has to happen. I can reassure you, however, that waiting to find out more does not have to equate with doing nothing. In the United States, accommodations can often be put in place under a 504 Plan, so named after Section 504 of the Rehabilitation Act of 1973, specifying equal access and other civil rights of people with disabilities. Some parents may be tempted to follow this route, because it avoids having your child classified as a student with a disability. Some schools use 504 Plans well. You need to realize, however, that a 504 Plan does not have the same federal and state protections as does an Individualized Education Plan (IEP) under IDEA 2004. The No Child Left Behind Act of 2001 (NCLB) provides yet another set of educational mandates that can be used to your benefit. Wrightslaw or other legal advocacy resources can provide additional information on these. In addition, each state has a contact office for issues related to each of these laws. Useful resources at the end of the chapter can help you access these sources of information.

Finally, there often are informal interventions a parent can request as part of the regular educational process. One example is teacher signatures to a planner acknowledging that the child has listed all of that night's homework. The use of a timer to help with work completion, or the use of

---

Box 3.2 A summary of what to do if dissatisfied with an evaluation

- Think about the evaluation and its results. Include in this reflection a look inside yourself, at your own emotional responses and how they might be influencing you. Try to identify specifically what it is about the evaluation that concerns you. Is your unhappiness really just part of your own mourning that a problem exists at all?

- Share your concerns with the evaluator, either at the evaluation itself or in a follow-up visit or phone call. This is important to do in dialogue, because each of you needs to hear and respond to what the other is saying. Make a note of what the evaluator has to say in response to your concerns.

- Talk to others you trust, in order to get their perspective as well. If you are still concerned, request a re-evaluation or a second opinion. You may use the results from the first evaluation to fine-tune your second evaluation request, or to help you select a different approach or a different instrument to look at your child.

- Go back to your own research. Read more about what other possible diagnoses might exist for your child. Maybe you were looking in the wrong area. Maybe you had the wrong type of specialist. Maybe you had the wrong particular individual performing the evaluation.

- If all else fails, table it for now. Agree to disagree, and revisit the evaluation later. Maybe the passage of time and your child's continued growth and development will help clarify the issue.

---

a home- or school-based reward system to try to encourage a particular type of behavior are other examples. Generally speaking, teachers have a wide variety of educational techniques they can use to meet the individual needs of children, whether or not the children are identified officially as having special educational needs. True, the special needs acknowledgement opens a wider array of interventions to help your child, but it is not the only door to help. Trying a wider variety of basic classroom tricks may take care of your child's educational needs. If it does not, you are building a case for further intervention by collecting specific information on what has been tried, what works, and what is not working to meet your child's needs.

Your role in the formal evaluation process

Now that I've described the various channels that are open to you for obtaining an initial evaluation for your child, Box 3.3 summarizes my thoughts on the particular role we, as parents, need to play as we go through these formal channels. As you have seen, you are a vital participant in this process. Even though you are employing experts, it is important that you keep a questioning attitude toward what is going on, to be sure that what is done makes sense to you. If it doesn't, your search may not be over, and you may even have to call for additional evaluations, opinions, or assistance. Especially at the Early Intervention or the preschool levels, much of the evaluation is based on parent reports. Be as thorough and as honest as you can be. Now is not the time to sugarcoat over difficulties, or to resort to blanket overblown statements. Your input is important to providing an understanding of your child.

Box 3.3 Your role in the formal evaluation process

- Find out evaluation options and procedures. Initiate process both verbally and in writing.
- Decide what types of evaluations you will request and who will perform them.
- Schedule evaluation. Anticipate other tests that might be needed, and start scheduling those as well.
- Compile and keep comprehensive records on your child. Often you can save time by sending copies of your own instead of requesting additional copies from the original sources. Request to receive copies of all evaluation reports.
- Fill out developmental history and any relevant questionnaires, and keep copies for your files.
- Facilitate communication among evaluators, physicians, administrative agency, home, and school.
- Establish momentum and keep it going.
- Evaluate results: how well do they seem to describe your child and his or her educational needs?
- Start looking for the next step: do you feel pointed in the right direction to get help for your child?
- Recognize and manage emotions.

It's easy to get discouraged by the paperwork, or intimidated or disheartened by the evaluation process itself. Don't be! You may not be a professional, but *you are your child's best advocate. Helping your child is too important to leave only to the professionals!* Remember, the law is on your side. It clearly states your rights as an equal partner in making educational choices for your child's special needs. If you would like assistance with this process, you may wish to seek support from a parent/family advocate so that you don't have to go through this alone. Family support programs are available in every state and can be located through the resources listed at the end of the chapter.

Your role will often involve research—into your child's disability, into "best practices" in evaluation and intervention, and into your rights and responsibilities in the special needs system. You have to be able to tolerate uncertainty, while you keep actively searching for answers. You have to stay on top of things to be sure you understand what testing is being done on your child, and what were the results. Wrightslaw and other advocacy presentations often offer "Statistics for Parents" to help you understand the technical jargon and test scores. At some point, you are also probably going to have to wade further through the nitty-gritty details of the special educational process.

Not only are you chief cook and bottle washer, but you also are the official keeper of the records, and this important task can take up a significant amount of time and energy. Keep a log of your questions that remain unanswered, and the issues that are not yet resolved to your satisfaction. You must be willing and able to challenge findings and procedures that don't make sense to you. Above all, you should not be afraid to network and to ask for help or support if you feel like you're in over your head. You may not be a professional in the field, but you have your own important role to play.

Having our Michael evaluated: a work still in progress

In closing, I'd like to present one more example of obtaining an evaluation. This one also involves my son, Michael. It illustrates many of the steps I've discussed in this chapter. It has been difficult to get a handle on the complexity of Michael, and the diagnostic process for him has stretched over a period of nine years. During this time, he has bounced in and out of therapies (and sometimes back in again) as various evaluations have or have not shown that he was eligible for special needs interventions. We've tried a wait-and-see approach at times. We have had a variety of evaluations performed, and recently it has become clear to me that we're going to have to initiate even more. Being an advocate for your child looks like this sometimes. It means *never giving up*.

For example, over a three-year period, I began to suspect I needed to have Michael evaluated for Attention Deficit Disorder (ADD)/Inattentive Type, and for Central Auditory Processing Disorder. Michael had already been identified by the school as "Other Health Impaired," and received OT and PT services. However, for those three years, I kept noticing the same constellation of troubling characteristics. Michael seemed easily overwhelmed by loud noises, especially when coupled with darkness, as in a movie theatre. When having an "off" day, his common litany seemed to be "What d'you say?" He had trouble following any directions that involved more than two steps at a time. When directions were given to the entire class, he seemed oblivious to the fact that they applied to him as well. Picking up daily routines, such as the snack routine or the packing up routine, was very difficult for him. I found myself saying to him, "This is an always rule, not just one that applies today." Organization—in all its forms—was a complete mystery to him. At other times, he would simply "zone out" or stare off into space. I still haven't decided whether I'd describe it as retreating into a silent, empty inner space, or as fixating on thoughts so intensely that he screens out everything else around him. At any rate, these characteristics continue to be an enduring (and not always endearing) part of who Michael is. In some years, and in some situations, these characteristics are more dysfunctional than in others, and not only in school settings. I've even seen Michael zone out in the middle of a soccer game or a ski lesson. When I brought these characteristics up to my pediatrician or to my school CSE, they expressed concern. No one, however, initiated a course of action that would lead us to finding out what was happening with him, or what to do about it. Everyone seemed to keep with the "let's wait and see" approach. If I wanted more, I had to take the initiative.

Diagnosis of what is behind a set of behaviors takes time. In fact, it takes lots of time. To help speed up the process, federal law mandates that no more than two months pass between the time a child is referred for an initial special education evaluation and that evaluation's completion. But if outside or additional evaluators are needed, then the time may well be more variable and, unfortunately, more extended. In my experience, I've found that usually four months or more will pass from when I make the first phone call requesting an additional or outside evaluation, until the evaluation has occurred and an intervention begun. In fact, we endured a nine-month wait for a thorough neuropsychological evaluation completed two summers ago. The time delay gets compounded when, as is often the case, the particular evaluation you are requesting is not the only one needed. A parent must always be thinking ahead to see how scheduling can be overlapped or expedited. Do not count on the school district or the specialist's office necessarily to think of this for you. For example, when Michael turned seven, in first grade, I arranged to have him evaluated at a local hospital for a Central Auditory Processing Disorder. This particular evaluation needed to be coordinated with teacher and parent checklists, and a hearing screening at a specialized speech-and-hearing center. I also realized from past CSE discussions that Michael needed evaluation for ADD as well, and it did not appear that the school was going to perform these evaluations. If I had not known to overlap the scheduling of these tests, I could have easily wasted the entire school year obtaining the results for first one, and then the other. Particularly if you have waited to begin the testing process until your child is already floundering, this waiting period can mean a school year spent in unnecessary frustration, tears, and fatigue. I prefer to begin to push for interventions before my child has bottomed out.

The process takes time, and it takes persistence on the part of the parent to be sure that all the needed evaluations are scheduled and performed. I've learned the hard way never to let an evaluation form or a completed questionnaire leave my hands without making a photocopy for my own records. It is difficult to keep track of what types of evaluations, involving what specific tests, have been done for what children, on what dates. I have found that unless I am diligent about specifically requesting my own copies of test reports, particularly medical ones, often I will not receive them. Medical professionals sometimes feel that providing copies to your child's pediatrician is sufficient. Of course I want my pediatrician to be in the loop, but I want to be in it too. Unfortunately, tests get misfiled, information gets overlooked, and sometimes it's just a good idea to be able to look yourself for emerging patterns. No, I may not always understand the intricacies of the technical terms used. That's where the summaries provided by the professionals are useful. Usually, however, I can at least understand enough to get an idea of what questions to ask, and what to pursue next in getting the help needed for my child.

Your pediatrician can be a strong ally in your quest to understand your child's needs. She or he can also help you step back and look at the big picture emerging about your child's development, and guide you towards resources that the school district might not. Our pediatrician makes a point of scheduling extra office time for his patients with atypical developmental concerns. We meet at least once a year for these discussions. I schedule them through his office, and they are billed as developmental consults through our health insurance. After noting that Michael was not responding as we expected to the usual ADD interventions, my pediatrician suggested that the next logical step was to request a neuropsychological evaluation for Michael. There are very few specialists in our area qualified to administer these extensive examinations, which cover seven to nine areas of brain functioning. Furthermore, these neuropsychological evaluations are expensive, easily costing from $1800 (£900) to $2300 (£1665). Here's where I began really working the phones to get the information I needed. One of my main goals was to discover what the various types of providers were, and to see what names came up when I asked my pediatrician and other trusted advisors. I then went online to check the list of neuropsychologists participating in our insurance plan. Unfortunately, the individual in whom I was most interested was not currently accepting new patients, but her office called me back with a list of people they recommended, and described the specialties and relative training of each. Based on this discussion, I called my pediatrician again, to confirm the depth of evaluation he felt Michael would need. I wanted to know if someone familiar with some neuropsychological aspects would be sufficient, or if he felt we needed the more in-depth, thorough work-up done by someone with more extensive training. His confirmation that we needed the latter, further limited my choice. The person I preferred does not take our insurance, and accepts private pay patients exclusively. She also had a waiting list of over six months for appointments, so I added Michael's name to the list and went to work exploring what options I could open for paying for this evaluation.

My next goal was to keep the Committee on Special Education in the loop. I prepared a list ahead of time of the points I wanted to make when I talked to them about covering the cost of the neuropsychological evaluation. If I don't write them down, I risk getting flustered, forgetting important points, and weakening my own presentation. I decided that it was important for me to describe four things: what we'd done to date for Michael; why Michael's pediatrician and I both felt that the current interventions were not working; what we were suggesting to pursue next; and how I'd tried unsuccessfully to have insurance cover the suggested tests. I then called the chair of the Committee on Special Education to discuss my concerns. After asking a few questions for clarification, she said that my argument seemed quite logical, but that I needed to put my request formally in writing to the Pupil Services Team at my son's school. In our district, this team recommends whether or not funding for outside evaluators seems appropriate. She told me to be sure to include in my letter how the results of this evaluation would affect Michael's educational programming. In other words, an evaluation might give me more information about my son's learning style, but why should the school care about this? I needed to be clear about what deficit in his current educational program seemed to exist, and how the results of this evaluation would be useful in addressing those deficits.

Everyone who has looked closely at Michael agrees that there's something different about Michael's functioning. It just takes a lot of passes through the diagnostic net to find out what those differences are, and how they should be addressed. His compensatory strengths and the supportive environment we provide mean that he is often able to function quite well, with no disability evident. But then will come times of overload, when Michael's compensatory structures crumble, and he crashes. Personally, I am convinced that Michael also has an autism spectrum disorder, but that it is manifesting slightly differently than his brother's. We keep tweaking and modifying and increasing the interventions, but I think the reason we're not getting better results than we have with Michael is that we don't have the complete basic diagnosis yet. Maybe next year at this time, I'll finally feel like I have a handle on understanding Michael. Maybe his difficulties will always cycle through as more general executive processing difficulties. In the meantime, reminding myself that there may be biological reasons for his behavior helps me to control my own emotional reactions when I get frustrated with repeating the same things to him day after day. I'm trying to get help for both of us. As I told the school district in my letter, it isn't fair to treat this as a behavioral problem, treatable by providing the right reinforcement schedule, if instead it is a biological problem, warranting a more comprehensive, restructuring of his world.

Obtaining a thorough and accurate diagnosis for your child may take multiple cycles through the process to get a complete picture of the extent of your child's difficulties. This was certainly the case for us, and it also seemed to be true for most of the parents in a wonderfully comforting and encouraging collection of other families' experiences in the book, *Dancing in the Rain* (Stehli 1995). What's most important is that you start the process, not necessarily that you "get it right" the first time. The openness and the wide range of choices you'll be presented with can be intimidating. It may not be obvious what types of evaluations your child needs, or who should perform them. You're looking for reassurances and clear answers, and instead you're offered choices you have no idea how to make. Even worse, you're realizing that you don't even know enough to know what questions you should be asking. But do you know what? I realize now that fuzziness is normal and it's ok. In fact, the amorphous nature of the whole diagnostic process that I found to be so frustrating and so confusing when I began, actually has a positive side to it. The lack of "a" procedure also means there isn't "a" single route to obtaining a diagnosis. Until you've begun the process and started seeing what's involved with your particular child, you can't know which of a wide array of options might even be relevant to your situation. It's impossible to chart it all out ahead of time. A large part of advocacy for your child involves learning how to tolerate those ambiguities. You don't have to like it, but for your child's sake, you have to go out there and do your best with the various sources of guidance you encounter as you go along.

Before, during, and after the diagnosis: emotions!

I can't write a chapter on having your child evaluated without including a significant section on emotions, because you are going to have them—lots of them. No matter how you approached the process, or how certain you were ahead of time that something was different about your child, receiving the formal report unleashes a lot of emotional reactions that you might have put on hold until you "knew for sure." Your dominant emotion may be relief, that your concerns were justified. You aren't crazy in thinking things don't seem right. You now have black-and-white confirmation that they aren't. You didn't reach your current level of exhaustion from trying to meet the needs of a typical child, nor are you necessarily a less capable parent than your peers. But suddenly, upon receiving this confirmation, your child's diagnosis becomes very real. Maybe you are also relieved because, although the diagnosis feels bad, at least it isn't something "worse"—whatever our current emotional state would define as worse. Or perhaps your experience is more like ours, and you're feeling the opposite of relief—dismay and perhaps even fear—because the name for what you and your child are up against is much more serious than you expected.

Perhaps you are angry. I always keep that in mind when I consider how negatively I reacted to our first Asperger's diagnostic experience. Maybe the specialist wasn't really as inhumane as I remember him. Maybe this was also a case of wanting to shoot the messenger. "Dammit, there is a problem here and we don't want there to be, and so we're mad and it's your fault!"

I'm sure you are afraid. Your earlier fears have been confirmed, and now you feel like you're really heading out into uncharted waters. What's ahead for you as a parent? Even more importantly, what's ahead for your child? Your child needs so much, and you feel so inadequate. We all have memories of name-calling and other insensitive treatment of "different" children from our youth. Maybe we experienced this ourselves. We worry about how vulnerable our children are to such unkind treatment, simply because they are different. We're devastated that we cannot protect them.

There's the inevitable, even if irrational, guilt. Be careful. This natural desire to understand why, to re-establish a sense of reason and order in our lives may easily slip into the "blame game." Why is this happening to us? Whose "fault" is it? Did we/I/you do something wrong? Could this have been avoided? Why didn't we catch it sooner? (And perhaps even that dirty-feeling, soul-searching, "If we had known this was going to happen, would we have had this child?" Or, "Do we dare ever have another?")

There's almost certainly sorrow. We mourn. This news, this diagnosis, hurts. What happened to our dreams of our child's rosy, perfect future? We want so much for our child, and for ourselves. What does this do to our dreams?

Once you've ridden through the first (and probably even second and third) wave of emotions, especially the grief and guilt, you'll eventually realize it's time for you to start moving on to deal with the situation. Of course, there continue to be emotions—there always will be. Even now, ten years later, I'm occasionally hit with new emotional waves that sometimes overpower me. On the other hand, I have also found strengths I didn't know I had. Things I used to think I would never be able to do, have now become as natural and automatic to me as breathing. I've also met a lot of wonderfully supportive parents and individuals who have helped our family immeasurably. My experience is not unique, as I found in the emotional collection of essays collected by Stanley Klein and Kim Schive: *You Will Dream New Dreams* (2001). A companion volume, edited by Stanley Klein and John Kemp, is the 2004 volume, *Reflections From a Different Journey,* may also help by offering a different perspective. This may not have been the journey we expected, and it may take time to work through your emotions and expectations. That is okay. It is a natural part of the process. Emotions are personal reactions. We can control our actions, but we can't control the way we feel. We can't even reliably predict our emotions until we find ourselves in a particular situation.

Mark and I reacted differently from each other, and it took time for each of us to learn to respect and appreciate the other's reactions. My husband seemed to need more time to adjust to the situation, while I charged right in and dealt with it more actively. His reaction felt like avoidance to me, and I found it very frustrating. I had to remind myself that Mark is a different person from me. Perhaps it was enough that he trusted my judgment. At first, Mark didn't even want to hear about what I was finding out or planning to do. I tremendously resented the protective wall he hid behind, leaving me alone outside. Over time, Mark became more able to talk about our children's special needs. At first, I don't think he had the slightest inkling of what to do, and I think the responsibility paralyzed him. But over time, his behavior towards the children changed. I could see him modeling more of his reactions to them on how I treated them. Over time, behaviors supportive of their special needs became second nature to Mark as well. Although his support never has taken the interventionist tone that my own parenting style has acquired, Mark's parenting behaviors are encouraging and accepting—and never judgmental. I'm always on the lookout for what the children need help with. He focuses on their strengths. In fact, Mark is more likely the pillar of calm nowadays, when I become frustrated or upset.

In some ways, the task was harder for Mark than it was for me, because Mark found himself having to face his own past. The renowned pediatrician, Dr. Berry Brazelton (2006), talks about the ghosts from the nursery. By "ghosts," Brazelton means the experiences in our own pasts that come up to haunt us as we approach the task of parenting. Mark had lots of painful memories of how his own needs were inadequately addressed in childhood, back in the 1950s era of stern nuns, dunce hats, and rulers raised against a child who wouldn't perform up to expectations. I think in learning how to deal with our children, he first had to mourn the missed opportunities for himself.

Once we received the diagnosis and I got over my initial wave of emotions, I found this tremendous desire to fix my children's disabilities, coupled with an enormous sense of urgency. The fact that my children were toddlers and preschoolers contributed to this sense of urgency, I think. I felt that the more interventions I could do early, before my children began formal schooling, the more I could address their problems before the children themselves were aware of them. I worried about potential teasing and rejection from other children. I worried about later having to pull my kids out of classes for therapy, or dragging them to after-school therapies when they would want to be doing other activities. I also worried a lot about their self-awareness. At their young age, my children were not at all aware of having special needs. Their reality was the only one they knew. As preschoolers, they just accepted any therapies or intervention as "this is life."

Now, this many years later, I can re-examine that sense of urgency. I don't regret pushing as hard as I did in their preschool years. I think they were good years for our family, and for my children. When I see my children's strengths today, I think many of them result from the hard work we did in our earlier years. But I can also see another side to that sense of urgency. Some of the dragons that I was so anxious to avoid by tackling things early, turned out not to be the bad experiences that I thought they would be. Marcus's learning about himself is one example. I dreaded it so much at the beginning. I see now, however, that his self-knowledge has been constructed gradually over the years and is still evolving. Every accepting and supportive hour of his life has contributed to his self-knowledge. By time I had "the talk" with him about his diagnoses, the relatively low tone of his muscles and the Asperger's Syndrome were only pieces of the complex and capable person he is. They do not define him for himself, and we do not let those characteristics define him for others either. I've always found that a matter-of-fact attitude with my children about their abilities or disabilities, has always worked best. On those few occasions when he questions, "Why do I have to do this?" I respond, "To make you even better at (whatever the skill)." Or I might answer, "Well, you know how (whatever the skill or behavior) is hard for you? We're trying to help you with that." Those types of answers don't concentrate on weaknesses. Instead they concentrate on building strengths. My children are no different from any other person in the world, in that everyone has strengths and weaknesses, and I am quick to tell them this. As people, most of us define ourselves by those strengths, and not by those weaknesses. Recognition of one's differences does not have to be a self-esteem issue, unless it is pulled out of context and turned into one.

My husband deals with his emotions more privately. He does a lot of compartmentalization (thinking about the needs only when he has to), but I do not find him any less accepting of our children's unique range of abilities and difficulties because of that. In some ways, we make a good team this way. I'm always mindful of the needs; he's always focused on the normality. Sometimes I have as much to learn from his attitude, as he has to learn from mine. I've found that over the years, he has become much more willing to share information about our sons' challenges and triumphs with friends and close business associates. He is not only tolerating, but he is also openly encouraging my writing this book.

This may sound cold-hearted, but when adjusting to life with our children's diagnoses, I found it useful to look with fresh eyes at any person in my social world. When I felt I was drowning in being able to deal with our new knowledge of our children's difficulties, I found myself inwardly rating whether each person in my social world was constructive, destructive, or neutral to my struggle to adjust. I realized I really needed to surround myself only with those people who were supportive. I had no energy left for dealing with other people's negativity, even when those individuals were well meaning. I needed people around me who were willing to listen, who had faith in my judgments, who would give me support and sympathy as I struggled. I needed to identify and at least temporarily weed out those individuals who were "psychic poisons" to me. I might have to deal with them eventually, but while I was trying to get my balance in the world of special needs parenting, I didn't have the energy to deal with their issues.

Sometimes "their issues" took the form of denial, which also smacked of criticism of me. I think they wanted to reassure me, but what I *heard* was, "You don't know what you're talking about." Or, "You're over-reacting. You're too involved. You're too protective. You're too... too... too..." Sometimes I suspected that some of the individuals were trying simply to retain their own image of the world and their perception of how it works. Perhaps recognizing that my children had difficulties threw into doubt their conceptions of their own children? I don't know. Or perhaps they couldn't separate recognizing a disability from reducing the person to no more than the disability. Maybe paradoxically, they were trying to protect my children by resisting any discussion that there may be something developmentally "wrong" with them. Acknowledging and facing differences as natural is something on which, I think we, as a society, need to work.

What has *supported me* in my adjustment is having friends and relatives who are willing to ask, to listen, to empathize, and to try to understand. It helps me when people recognize that some of the things we're dealing with must be hard, and then support us in our lifestyle. My sons' special needs are there, and my family is working to deal with them. We need understanding and encouragement. We need a sense of connectedness to others, and we need patience and acceptance as we try to figure out how we can participate in our communities. I am frequently wrestling with people who either ignore my children's difficulties and needs, or who seek to isolate my children from opportunities because they can see only those difficulties and needs. I need people around me whose vision can include the complex richness of my children in both their strengths and challenges. Do we allow others to dehumanize and *disable* our children, or do we accept and *empower* our children? Every day I advocate for my boys, I choose the latter.

Useful resources
Your best, "one-stop shopping centers" for getting help within the United States

The National Dissemination Center for Children with Disabilities (NICHCY)

PO Box 1492
Washington, DC 20013
Tel: (800) 695-0285
Fax: (202) 884-8441

This national clearing house provides resource sheets organized by state. These include: state agencies serving or concerned with children with disabilities; disability-specific organizations; organizations especially for parents; and other useful organizations. The website is well-designed, informative, and easy to navigate. Plus, it is incredibly parent-friendly.

www.nichcy.org

Wrightslaw legal advocacy resources:

This detailed, web resource on the nitty-gritty of getting help for your children should be bookmarked on every advocate's computer. Its companion website of resources, FetaWeb, provides a wealth of connections to the details of how to advocate for your child. Invaluable for applying the major laws governing special education to your situation, it includes IDEA 2004, Section 504, and NCLB information. This website is updated frequently, and extends the information found in the book *From Emotions to Advocacy* (2nd edn), by Pam and Pete Wright (2006).

www.wrightslaw.com

A second resource, Yellow Pages for Kids with Disabilities, created by Wrightslaw and organized by state:

These yellow pages for kids with disabilities deliver exactly what you would expect. The listings are comprehensive, and updated frequently. Listings, sorted by state, include: educational consultants, psychologists, educational diagnosticians, health care providers, academic therapists, tutors, speech and language therapists, occupational therapists, coaches, advocates, and attorneys for children with disabilities. This site also contains state-by-state listings for special education schools, learning centers, treatment programs, parent groups, respite care, community centers, grassroots organizations, and government programs for children with disabilities.

www.yellowpagesforkids.com

4

What Next? What Does This Diagnosis Mean?

The evaluation results are in. In our case: hypotonia; scoliosis; Attention Deficit Disorder/Inattentive Type; Central Auditory Processing Disorder; Sensory Processing Disorder; Asperger's Syndrome; dysgraphia... Even if you were handed the diagnosis ever so gently, you feel as though you've slammed into a tree. Before, you had a child; now, you suddenly have a Diagnosis, with a capital "D." Where is your child in this new picture? What do these formidable labels mean for your life? This chapter is designed to help you with the process of learning what your child's diagnosis means. It will help you regain your perspective, to see past the label to how this particular condition is manifesting in your particular son or daughter. Beyond that, it will help you begin to see what you can do to help your child.

Let's start with a basic tenet for this chapter and for all that follows: *the special needs are something your child has. They are not the sum total of your child.* Your child is still the same person she or he was before being diagnosed. Your child still has his or her same abilities, his or her same personality, and all the million and one other characteristics that make your child a unique person. The disorder should not define your child. If it does, then that is a clear sign that you have lost your perspective. I wanted at first to title my book, *Becoming an Advocate for your Special Needs Child*, because it was so succinct and to the point. But my children are not a different species of children. They are still regular children underneath it all. It is just that some of their needs are different. *Becoming an Advocate for your Child with Special Needs*—or *Becoming an Advocate for Your Child*, period—is a much better title for this book. It is also a much better approach for you to take with your own son or daughter. Language shapes our thought. That's why people working in the area of special education focus so much on the language used. We need the focus to stay on the child, not on the disability or the special needs. The disability is only a part of the person who is my son.

That's the calm, big picture I tried to hold onto when we were given our first set of formal evaluation results. In the meantime, I began reading the sheaf of papers provided by the developmental specialist we had seen, and I tried to understand what "Asperger's Syndrome" means. I read lists and lists of all the things that would be difficult for my son as a person with Asperger's. I read about the social isolation, possible ostracism, and loneliness he could expect. I read how he would have difficulty identifying emotions (his own or those of others), reading body language, or decoding those social conventions and niceties that keep one from being labeled a "misfit." I read that he would be at risk for developing depression and anxiety disorders. Because of his difficulty understanding the perspective of others, he would have trouble understanding people's motivations, and the complex plots of novels might be beyond his grasp because of his difficulty piecing together cause and effect. The beauty of figurative language would elude him, and when confronted with problems in context, he would be a person who would probably not be able to see the forest for the trees. His would be a world where hidden patterns would stay un-inferred. His would be a literal world.

I don't know about you when you were faced with the initial, cold descriptions of your child's condition, but I wept. It was becoming painfully obvious to me that there was much I could not protect my child from, and I was terrified. The literature is going to try to provide a comprehensive list of all the things your child may need help with, and the problems your child may have to overcome. These confrontations are personally painful, so how do you accept this task of learning about your child's disability, while keeping the pain from overwhelming you?

Although this may feel like small comfort now, keep in mind that children vary tremendously in how a particular disability manifests, and how that disability interacts with their personality and with their life experiences. Yet the literature often collapses all possible severities and all possible manifestations into a single discussion. That's the purpose of the literature, to provide such encyclopedic coverage. The Internet fuels this, piling on article after article, some of which may not be accurate, and others may not apply to your child. Your task is to sift through this material until you understand it and can apply what is appropriate to your particular situation. As you do so, keep in mind that all you know are the past and the present—the future is still ahead. *Your ultimate purpose is to use this new knowledge to create the supports your child needs to be happy and healthy in the present, and to free your child to develop to his or her personal potential in the future.*

Donning your emotional armor as you work to master the cold, hard facts

To create the supports your child needs, you first have to build your knowledge of your child's disability. You have to wrestle with that ugly diagnosis until you truly understand what it means for your child, and for you. Blissful ignorance is a luxury that we, as parents of children with special needs, cannot afford. In fact, as we have already seen in the chapter on pre-diagnosis, ignorance is *not* blissful, either for ourselves or for our children. In the following sections, I reflect on what this learning process has been like for me, and I try to offer support and advice as you start your own research efforts. I also offer several strategies that will help you form a type of emotional armor, to help protect you when you are feeling most insecure and most vulnerable as you go forward with this task. Overall, my best advice to you is to *be patient with yourself.* Let's face it, when we overload, we shut down and no one benefits from our efforts, least of all, our families.

Acknowledge that learning is hard work and respect yourself for the effort

Learning can be an uncomfortable business. It's scary to admit your own lack of knowledge—especially when it is a lack of knowledge that is so important for your child's welfare. It is also scary to take the necessary steps into the unknown to remedy that lack. You're faced with new vocabulary and new concepts. You can't figure out how the pieces relate to one another or how they are organized. You discover that you had misconceptions and glaring knowledge gaps. You lose confidence in what you thought you already knew. You'll feel that the books and articles are just presenting an accumulation of unrelated facts—and ugly facts, at that. You can't see the underlying pattern yet, and you'll wonder how you'll ever make sense out of it all.

Mastering this new vocabulary, acquiring the needed facts, and organizing them into a usable, coherent story about your child that makes sense to you is an incredibly difficult task. One of the first steps you can take to help yourself with that task is to acknowledge that you are doing something arduous. If you acknowledge that the material would be hard for *any* beginner, you can be a little more forgiving of yourself. You aren't "stupid"—this is complicated new stuff, more important than any academic course you've ever taken, and you don't even have a nurturing teacher to guide you. Instead of feeling overwhelmed, try substituting a sense of pride in yourself for taking on the task of mastering this material. *Expect* it to be effortful, and pace yourself through it as you would any difficult task. When you sense that your eyes are glazing over and you're losing your ability to absorb what you're reading or hearing, just back off for a while. You can pick it up again when you're less tired and have had time to digest what you've read. No one said that this course has to be mastered in one sitting. If you stick with your attempts, keep coming back for more, and keep seeking until you find resources that make sense to you, you can start bootstrapping your knowledge to the next level. You will eventually build your understanding until you have mastered what you need to know.

Anticipate your own emotional needs

This course of material that you have made yourself responsible for learning is not just *any* academic material. It is material that is personally relevant to your child's well-being. There is a freight car of emotional baggage attached to it. In order to avoid being buried by that baggage, you'll need to allow yourself recovery time after your various intellectual forays. Compartmentalization can be a useful emotional defense. Remind yourself that you are a parent on a mission. This mission is not about you, or how you feel. This is about finding out what you need to do to help your child.

Of course, emotional distancing and compartmentalization can only take you so far, but it is very useful as you collect and organize facts. Then at some point, you are going to have to make a more intimate link. You must couple these factual descriptions with a very close look at your own child to see what seems to apply at this time, and what does not. At those times, it is important for you to recognize and accept that you are often going to have intense emotional reactions. It is only natural to do so. The best way to deal with this is deliberately to build in recovery time for your own emotional well-being. On days and weeks that I know I'm having to confront new aspects of my children's disabilities, I try to pamper myself in other ways. I might give myself down time, or schedule special treats for myself. I've taken up yoga, not only as a form of exercise, but as a way of relieving stress and centering myself when I am in danger of being pulled apart by trying to meet all of my family's needs. I look inside myself for signs of emotional and intellectual stress or exhaustion, and I try to limit the other things I expect from myself during these periods. There are only so many bowling balls that I can juggle at any one time, and I expect these confrontations to take up a lot of my emotional strength and resources. I can't afford total exhaustion or emotional burnout. My children need my parental involvement on a daily basis, and so I have to pace myself for a long-distance haul.

Use a peek-and-retreat strategy

Although it's important not to be blindsided by the future, I've found that I can't look very often at the wide panorama of symptoms, or time travel through a projection of possible future difficulties for my children. I get dizzy and lose my balance. I become overwhelmed and discouraged. What works best for me is to take a quick peek at what's ahead, and then retreat and act on what I can at this time. Then I repeat the process. That's what makes this peek-and-retreat strategy different from just running away or giving up. I am always getting back on the horse, taking another ride, and risking another fall. By risking those peeks into what's ahead of me, I get a sense of where I may eventually be going, but I give myself permission that I don't have to tolerate the dizzying view for long. I get a glimpse of where I might need to go, and then I put up my blinders and start the plodding steps in that direction. Note I said blinders, not a blindfold. Blinders are useful for horses, to keep them from seeing things that may spook them. Blinders allow forward motion without panicking at what else is around. They enable constructive focus. This peek-and-retreat strategy will help you to live one day at a time more effectively. It will help you set your priorities and then address those priorities, without being overwhelmed by all that may yet happen, or all the things that you aren't addressing at this moment. Peek-and-retreat will make your arduous task more manageable, while making it less likely that you'll be totally blindsided by unexpected terrain in the future.

The peek-and-retreat strategy serves another useful function as well. Over time, these brief exposures will help desensitize you to the intense emotions that this unfamiliar territory may raise in you. A quick peek is a safe way to start to familiarize yourself with what is ahead, without having to engage in the material for a prolonged time or on a deep level. We do this for our children all the time, when we try to help them face a necessary, but scary experience. We describe for our kids what to expect ahead of time, without dwelling on the rough parts. We might ease them into the experience—perhaps a first visit to a doctor or dentist or new school—by deliberately structuring that first experience so that it is short and as stress-free as possible. Why not use this same preview strategy for ourselves?

Finally, I believe that the peek-and-retreat strategy is the most appropriate one for dealing with your child's future. Your child is a living, developing individual. She or he is in a constant state of flux. Just as it's hard to picture the one-year-old toddler your newborn will become, it's hard at any stage to see the person your child will have become after the passage of any significant period of time. That's part of the wonder of development—a gradual unfolding and unveiling. A metamorphosis, if you will. Furthermore, effective therapies and supportive life experiences can open up entirely new possibilities for your child than those you are able to envisage now. Worrying in detail about what may be far down the road for your child may well be unnecessary worry. Peek to make yourself aware of what may be ahead and see how it may affect your current plans, but then leave more extensive worry about it for tomorrow, when you are better able to see if the worry is truly necessary.

Set your own pace and priorities

Once you start collecting resources on your child's disability, you may very well find yourself feeling quite intimidated by the thick stacks of dense materials you'll need to master eventually. I understand that feeling. I recently conducted some thorough Internet searches to learn more about effective social interventions with older children with Asperger's. I found so much dense, and sometimes competing materials, that I had to just print it off and then back away for a while until I felt more ready to read and try to absorb it. Now seems a good time to remind you, also, that even though this personalized (and personal) disabilities course may be one that you would never have chosen to take, you do have choice in how you go about it.

I used to guide a lot of independent research projects when I was a college instructor. The ones that were the most successful were the ones in which the student had a strong interest or a reason why they needed to master the materials. You, as your child's parent, certainly have that! As an instructor, I would then explore with my student, what specific questions they wanted to answer, and why. What were they trying to use the research to do? Then I'd usually guide my students towards some general books or articles to begin. These could be overview pieces, which described the topic in lay terms, or sometimes I would recommend a piece that personalized the research topic, by first showing what it looked like in everyday life, and then backing away for a more analytical view. My point is that there's no rule that you have to start with a particular type of text to build your knowledge. It doesn't matter how expert the text may be. If it is not written in a style or at a level to which you can relate, it will not be useful as a teaching tool for you. Start with whatever particular sources feel most comfortable to you. You'll discover that one source will then often lead you to another—sometimes at a similar level and sometimes at a deeper one. You can use a resource to which you've already connected, to help advise you where to look next.

Here's another secret. You don't have to read your material cover to cover. It's okay to dip in and out of it. In the beginning, you are trying to rough in an overall idea of the shape of the knowledge structure you'll eventually build about your child's disability. You're trying to get a sense of the general areas you might want to research. Then you can decide which ones are least threatening, or which ones are most promising for you to start with first. There are some cognitive advantages to multiple passes through the same literature. With any subject matter, your understanding of new material will be influenced by what you already know. As what you know deepens, so will your appreciation of the significance of the material you are currently reading. There's a certain amount of cognitive and emotional readiness to learn that has to happen before we can absorb new material. Sometimes our understanding will be limited because we haven't reached that state of preparedness—the time just isn't right for us to approach that particular material. Maybe tomorrow it will be, and so I periodically expect to go back over my children's files. I revisit my own bookshelves, or look over those at the local booksellers. I'm aware that as time passes, I've learned more and that I may be ready to gain new insights from sources I thought I'd already mined. Similarly, previously rejected sources sometimes look more inviting and useful to me at a later time.

Learn to tolerate the unknown

At one time I was upset because I felt I was uncovering important areas of my child's diagnoses that I thought other professionals should have identified for us. Whenever I encountered a new avenue of possible intervention, I became worried as to what else might be out there that I was missing. I confess, I still have those knee-jerk, fear reactions, especially when I stumble across things that have been around for a long time. I feel as though I've been neglectful of my parenting duties because I didn't even consider pursuing those avenues. I worry if I would have made the same choices if I had known about these other options earlier. Here's the self-talk I give myself at such times: instead of frustration or fear, a more adaptive response to my continual discovery of new aspects of my children's disorders could be *satisfaction*. Satisfaction? Yes, my own sense of feeling unsettled and discovering new things means that I'm doing a good job at the task I've set myself. I am learning more about my children and about the disorders they have. I'm uncovering new possibilities for helping them.

I accept now that keeping informed about my children's disabilities and their needs means that my home-grown knowledge will *always* be a work in progress. The truth is that any professional field has a lot of that same evolving, trial-and-error nature to it. Identifying developmental disorders always comes before developing effective interventions for them. A lot of what is accepted practice today was someone else's guesses and trials yesterday. I'm just adding to that evolving body of knowledge with everything we try with our sons—both our successes and our discoveries of things that don't work for them. The same is true for your own attempts with your child.

Enjoy the moment

No, I'm not talking about enjoying your experience as you learn about your child's disability. I'm talking about remembering to appreciate the entire individual that is your child. Delving too deeply and too long in the more academic aspects of the world of your child's disability, can make you lose your perspective on where you and your child are now, and what strengths and gifts you already have. My husband often reminds me of this. I don't recommend rose-colored glasses, but I don't believe in tunnel vision, focusing only on warts either. Your child is a wonderful, unique person. The special needs literature is about the disability, and it tends to focus on the negative side of that disability. Now is a good time to go back to your mantra: *this disability is only a part of the person who is my child.* You don't want the disability to define your child for others; please don't let it define your child for you! Box 4.1 summarizes my advice to help you keep your balance as you try to learn more about your child's disability.

Box 4.1 Emotional strategies for supporting yourself as you face the task of understanding your child's diagnosis

- Develop a supportive network. Don't be afraid to ask others for help. Protect yourself from "psychic poisons."
- Use a peek-and-retreat strategy. When you feel overwhelmed, back off and take time to absorb what you've already encountered.
- Prioritize what is most important and most possible at this time, and invest your energies there.
- Revisit materials again later.
- Be prepared for change. Nothing is set in stone—neither outcomes nor courses of action.
- Keep a running list of future avenues you may want to explore someday.
- Keep yourself emotionally healthy and pace yourself for the long haul.
- Accept that others in your close circle may have their own adjustment and learning process.
- Stay grounded in your love and appreciation for your child as a person, not a disability.

My boys and hypotonia: a personal example of learning what a diagnosis means

My pediatrician first used the term "low muscle tone" to refer to my son, Marcus, when he was a toddler. When I asked Dr. G. what he meant, he said it referred to the floppy state of Marcus's body. No, don't think rag-doll, but there was a laxness about the way Marcus held himself, and a lack of coordination in the way he moved. I thought I understood what Dr. G. was saying, but later when we started working with therapists, I realized I had a lot of questions. Did "low muscle tone" mean my son was weak? Is it something that can be strengthened with weight or other fitness training? Is it a permanent condition? I was searching for an understanding of the condition. I wanted to know what I could do to help my son with it.

On the Internet, I located a book called *The Hypotonic Child* (Boehme 1990), which described itself as applying to children with low muscle tone. I ordered the book, hoping it would help me understand. I was disappointed to discover the resource was a brief, technical manual written for the clinician and of very little help to me, especially as a beginning parent! The quote below shows an example from this text. The problem was that I could read the words, but I lacked sufficient background knowledge to be able to translate the text into my own words, or to even see in my own child what this description meant. I knew that "hypo" was the Greek prefix that was the opposite of "hyper," and so it would mean a state of having too little tone, as opposed to too much; but beyond that, I was at a loss. The term "hypotonia" is mentioned along with a number of other disorders, including cerebral palsy and Down Syndrome. Which of these might apply and which not? This text was clearly not the best place for me to begin as I tried to understand hypotonia!

> This material is designed to support the clinician in assessment and treatment of those children who exhibit insufficient muscle tone to sustain postural control against gravity. There are a number of ways of looking at the term hypotonicity. The quality of muscle tone may be associated with limpness or a feeling of heaviness when a limb is moved passively. On the other hand, I tend to observe the child during function, viewing the muscle as a spring. In order to move the skeleton against gravity, muscles stiffen. The degree of stiffness required to stabilize or move the skeleton is inadequate in the child with

hypotonicity. The child is unable to generate enough force at the joints to support the function being attempted.

Hypotonicity may be one of the characteristics of such nervous system dysfunctions as cerebral palsy, Down syndrome, and nonspecific developmental delays. Connective tissue disorders and metabolic, nutritional, and endocrine disturbances, as well as a variety of syndromes, can result in hypotonicity...

Efficient movement requires adequate postural tone. Adequate postural tone exists when the body has high enough muscle activation to maintain a posture against gravity and yet low enough activation to allow the body to move through gravity. Holding the head in an upright position while turning the head to visually scan the environment is an example of adequate postural tone to support function. Postural tone is changeable, and treatment utilizes the child's self-initiated activity to change tone. Automatic responses to changes in posture are stimulated in therapy. Using repetition, these automatic responses become available... (Boehme 1990, p.1)

I could not find more approachable material on low muscle tone, and so instead of reading, I built my understanding gradually through conversations with my boys' physical and occupational therapists. Although an "expert" might not be comfortable with my descriptions, I think I finally understand what hypotonia is, and what it isn't. At least I have a set of metaphors and connections that work for me. One of the most important realizations I made was that "low muscle tone" is more of a neurological condition than it is a muscular one. It only took eight years for me to make that connection! Yes, "working out" would help my sons' muscles to strengthen. Sports and sheer participation in physical activity would help build coordination. But equally important, I realized we needed to train my children's nervous systems to control their muscles differently. The neurological pathways with which they were born, were maladaptive for my children. We needed to help my children develop new pathways. Rather than muscular weakness, the basic problem was more aptly described as muscular control. Muscular actions that were automatic and almost effortless for a neurologically typical person, were conscious and/or effortful for my sons. The extra energy spent controlling their bodies, meant that my sons tired more easily than other children. Sitting erect is a good example of this, but there were many other examples of floppy, inefficient muscle usage that made life harder for my sons. Furthermore, low muscle tone affects much more than the physical domain! Let me explain.

One wonderful OT with whom we worked likened the human body to a marionette or string-controlled puppet. The OT explained that if the strings are left lax, the puppet flops, and cannot move. In a "normally" strung individual, the resting state of the strings is tight enough to hold the body parts together, so that the puppet is ready to move with the slightest twitch of the string when the puppeteer wants it to move. In an individual with low muscle tone, the puppet's parts aren't held in a state of optimal readiness. The strings are a little too lax, and the body becomes a little too floppy. When the puppet needs to move, the muscles first have to recover from this too lax state, and then perform the motion. For my elder son in particular, I could see how this laxness especially affected the beginnings of motions, which tended to be jerky and difficult for him until he was able to establish a rhythm. For example, if Marcus was going to do a set of jumping jacks (jumping to a position with legs spread wide, hands touching overhead, then returning to a position with feet together, arms at the side), or walk toe-to-heel along a straight line, he might flail around at the beginning. However, once his muscles become appropriately tightened and a rhythm could be established, he moved along fine.

The related term that I kept hearing in his OT and PT evaluations was "poor proximal stability." This translated into a weak center to his body, particularly his trunk and shoulders. Those parts of his body tend to be too floppy: his shoulders round and his whole body slumps forward when he is most manifesting this. When a child with low muscle tone sits on the floor, she or he tends to assume the classic W-sitting position, with the legs bent at the knees and turned to both sides of the body, forming the letter "W." This, coupled with the slumped upper torso, allows the child to brace him or herself for sitting. It is a very rigid position, however, and does not allow the child to readily shift balance from side to side, or from front to back. Aside from being hard on the knee and hip joints, W-sitting restricts quality of upper body motion, and so parents with hypotonic children learn to cue their children to "fix your legs" or to "sit criss-cross applesauce," (sit cross-legged on the floor) so that their bodies are better aligned.

Sitting upright at circle time, or sitting at a desk with his feet flat on the floor and both hands free to work, was (and still is) effortful for both my sons. At first, this used to be the case all the time. After years of therapy, I now see it in my eldest only when he is ill or fatigued. To compensate, he might stiffen or lock his entire trunk. Moving his arms or manipulating objects with his hands was difficult when he locked his trunk. Try bringing a loaded fork to your mouth without spilling, or cutting along the lines of a design drawn on paper with scissors, when *your* spine is slumped over, and you'll start to understand some of the physical ramifications of low proximal stability.

Another aspect of the low muscle tone condition has to do with reflexes. Understanding this aspect of his condition came much later for me. When infants are born, they have a set of reflexive movements that indicate good neurological development. These reflexes are automatic movements that our species developed as survival mechanisms. Over the first year or so of the infant's life, many, but not all of these reflexes are overridden during the course of healthy neurological development, and are replaced by movements that are under the individual's voluntary control. For Marcus, this was not the case. He still retained some vestigial, rigid reflexes that he should have "outgrown" and integrated into more flexible systems. The problem was that when he attempted more complicated physical movements, for example, those requiring coordination of the two halves of his body, with different body parts doing different things, the reflexes popped up and competed with the volitional movements. Not only did Marcus have trouble chewing gum and walking (patting his head while rubbing his stomach was out of the question), he also couldn't separate turning his eyes from turning his entire head. This sounds trivial, but it affected my active child throughout his day. He didn't use peripheral vision and so was extremely prone to tripping or bumping into things. He was often thrown off balance by his need to turn his whole torso to look at something while walking or running. Body parts that could operate separately from one another in a typically developed individual were locked into a relatively stiff tandem for him. Therapy involved helping retrain his body. We would isolate reflexes in a particular developmental sequence, and manually manipulate his body, having him practice physical motions to help his body learn to override those reflexes. Surprisingly, most of our work in this area was done with the vision therapist we consulted, and not the physical therapist or the occupational therapist.

(Sally Goddard's book, *Reflexes, Learning and Behavior*, 2002, is a useful resource on this process.)

When we first took Marcus for evaluation, one of his more obvious difficulties was the poor intelligibility of his speech. This too, was somewhat influenced by his hypotonia. Although Asperger's Syndrome meant he also had problems using language as a communicative tool, the hypotonia affected the forceful, fine motor lip and tongue movements required for clear articulation of speech sounds. At age two, my son could not blow a bubble, or move a piece of Cheerio cereal around his mouth with his tongue. He was late to develop the lip control needed to drink efficiently from a cup. Yet, six years later, due to the benefits reaped from comprehensive and skilled therapy, this same hard-working child was able to take up as his band instrument, the baritone horn—a medium-sized brass instrument in the tuba family. In fact, in sixth grade, he soloed his instrument in the "Star Spangled Banner" at a local high school basketball game!

It wasn't until Marcus was age five that I discovered how the low tone even extended to the functional use of his eyes. No one ever told me to expect this, although in hindsight, it certainly makes sense that muscular difficulties infusing the entire body would not suddenly and abruptly end at the cheekbones. What we learned is that a child can have 20/20 visual acuity, but still have vision difficulties because of ineffective use of his eyes. Functional vision involves several skills. One example is movement of the eye to use the entire visual field. If you think of the visual field as encompassing an entire clock's face, Marcus's field of vision was restricted to between 10:00 and 2:00. Marcus did not use his peripheral vision. He also could not separate the movement of his eyes from the movement of his head (or even the movement of his shoulders). This inability to operate the different muscular systems separately had a definitely negative impact on his hand–eye coordination, and affected both gross motor and fine motor movements. An occupational therapist helped us to make this connection. We then began vision therapy to address this aspect of his neurological difficulties. In case you are thinking that this may be useful for your own child, let me warn you that vision therapy is controversial in some circles. Some ophthalmologists, for example, argue that these are just splinter skills that won't transfer to real-life situations, or that vision therapy is a waste of time and money because the skills would develop on their own, given more time. Our personal experience is that over the course of the therapy regimen we completed over the next nine months, Marcus gained tremendously in his ability to use his eyes. At the start of a series of exercises, Marcus would not be able to perform the targeted task. One to three weeks later, after daily vision therapy exercises targeting the particular skill, he would have acquired the particular ability. We quickly began to see the benefits of this greater eye control in his everyday life. He soon stopped bumping into walls and falling, his Tee Ball (an introductory baseball-type game) and later baseball skills greatly improved, and so did his ability to track words across a page, or look from the board to his paper and back again. These were admittedly some of the most difficult therapy sessions to motivate and assist my child in performing, yet what a delight for parents of a child who faced other difficulties, to find a set of problems that could be "fixed" once and for all. (See Kaplan 2006, for more on vision therapy.)

Our own understanding of our child's disability affects our intervention choices. Developing a good understanding is important for helping you integrate the conflicting messages you may receive from different sources, and help guide you through later diagnostic "scares." You may have noticed that the technical discussion of hypotonia quoted earlier mentioned that hypotonia might be one characteristic of some nervous system dysfunctions, such as cerebral palsy (CP) or Down Syndrome. One therapist explained that low muscle tone is a cousin to CP, in the sense that both the individual with hypotonia and the individual with CP have neurological problems controlling tone. In thinking about CP, we tend to picture muscles and joints that act too tightly as opposed to too loosely. Understanding more about the relationship became vitally important to us, when an OT we'd employed for a one-time consultation for sensory integration issues, noted a spasticity in Marcus's movements. Although this was beyond the scope of her evaluation, she recommended that we obtain a neurological evaluation for Marcus, to rule out CP. We'd been working with a variety of specialists for three years by then, and no one had mentioned CP to us before! How could we be blindsided by this? It took another round of frantic phone calls and a visit to a neurologist an interminable six weeks later, before our fears were allayed and we confirmed that this part of the journey was a blind alley. The spasticity seemed related to trying to "jump start" his muscle system. Instead of a smooth transition into a physical activity, his body sometimes overcompensated the amount of effort needed to begin. His body may jerk to begin an action, and this surging musculature is awkward and sometimes difficult to control. Actually, after performing his neurological examination of Marcus, the neurologist couldn't understand why we were there to see him. "Clumsy child syndrome," he dismissively termed Marcus's condition. The phrase was, perhaps, apt enough, if meant to allay our concerns about cerebral palsy, but the neurologist's condescending tone and subsequent words moved beyond that reassurance, into aggressively stating that I was being too critical of my son. According to the neurologist, with the possible exception of the speech therapy, I was being too hard on Marcus. Physical and occupational therapy, he emphatically stated, were a waste of time. At best, they only hurried development of motor skills that would eventually evolve on their own. I wanted to respect the neurologist's expertise on the cerebral palsy question. However, his strongly voiced opinions on the value of other interventions were so counter to my experiences over the past three years, and so against the recommendations of the developmental experts I had consulted in other fields, that I was more than a little taken aback. This was one of my first experiences with the narrow attitudes and aggressive rivalries of some professionals, but then, that could easily fill another sub-chapter in itself!

As relieved as I was to rule out CP, I was initially very angry with the OT for alarming us unnecessarily. However, although I still question the casual certainty with which she bandied around such a serious diagnosis, I now realize that because CP and hypotonicity can be related conditions, it was not inappropriate for her to ask the questions. It took me several years, however, to reach this more forgiving perspective. The experience that helped change my bitterness occurred just three years ago, when an OT with whom we've worked for several years, warned me that children with low muscle tone were at greater risk of developing scoliosis (lateral curvature of the spine). She mentioned it to me in passing, after my younger son, Michael, needed physical therapy to treat back pain and a raised shoulder and hip, as part of the whiplash injuries he sustained in a car accident. When I informed our regular OT of Michael's injuries, she asked if I had ever had him screened for scoliosis, because it also often involved such postural abnormalities. Overwhelmed at the time with dealing with the ensuing therapies for both Michael's and my injuries, I filed this information away in my "I can't deal with this at the moment" mental file. I had to retrieve it a few months later when my older son, Marcus, came home with a note saying that the school's scoliosis screening indicated that further evaluation for scoliosis was necessary for him. Our pediatrician was not overly concerned with the screening results and was ready to just sign off that everything looked acceptable to him. This particular pediatrician, however, has, as one of his great strengths, the fact that he seeks input and listens to his patients and their parents. I mentioned I had a cousin who had to wear a body brace for scoliosis as a child. When I also reported our trusted OT's comment, our pediatrician agreed that an orthopedic consultation was reasonable. Three months later, we walked out of the next specialist's office with a definite diagnosis of mild scoliosis, and a new set of developmental differences to track.

What's the difference, other than mannerism and trust between these two OTs, the one who "alarmed" me with CP, and the other who "alerted" me to scoliosis? Frankly, in hindsight, it's hard to see the difference, except that one possibility ended up being correct, and the other was not. Both OTs were doing their job, sharing with me the impressions and knowledge gained from their experience. Raising such questions is probably always appropriate for a professional, if done with responsible care. But these questions are emotionally costly for the parent, in that each question sets off a new round of scares, and a new series of specialist consultations. You can't always determine ahead of time which possible leads are going to be accurate and which are not. It is important to be on the alert for all of them, for sometimes those warnings make early identification of correlate conditions possible. By the way, armed with this new discovery about my older son, and having developed a reflexively cautious nature, I scheduled a similar scoliosis check for my younger son, Michael, only to discover that he has an even more advanced spinal curve that had not yet shown up on any school or office screenings!

Current theories of intelligence recognize the importance of allocation of resources in brain functioning. We each have a limited amount of attentional resources available at any one time. The more distractions or fatigue we exhibit, the more effort we find ourselves putting into functions that should be on automatic pilot. This results in reduced resources to allocate to whatever higher-order problem-solving is at hand. My children, with their low muscle tone, are multi-tasking all the time. The automatic functions don't always come automatically to them. Sitting erect for extended periods of time drains them of energy and resources, leaving less for problem-solving or other tasks at hand. Luckily, both my boys are very bright and often have adequate resources to allow them to compensate, but as the taxing factors accumulate, even my boys show overload and start to shut down at times. Or, we have to take the time to re-energize my boys, by offering them brief breaks so they can move around and prime their nervous system, much as one would prime a pump, to be prepared for further exertion.

So, you see, physical disorders such as hypotonia affect much more than most people could possibly realize. When you have normal muscle tone, you take so very much for granted. An individual with abnormal muscle tone pays a heavy price, which is reflected in much more than just sports and gym class. Such is often the case for many disorders—you have to really understand the disorder to be able to see the totality of its implications for your child's life. Children with special needs often have multiple diagnoses and multiple disabling conditions that draw heavily on their attentional resources. By acquiring a deeper understanding of your child's various diagnoses, you as a parent are in a much stronger position to help your child in many areas of life.

Knowledge with a purpose: acquiring an effective understanding of your child's diagnosis

The preceding pages illustrate how complicated it can be to develop an effective understanding of even a "simple" diagnosis such as low muscle tone. Other diagnoses can be even more opaque. How deeply do you need to understand your child's diagnosis? How can you tell whether you know enough? I've given a lot of thought to this question, both as a parent of children with special needs, and as a professional who specializes in education and cognition. As you can see from my discussion of hypotonia above, the most important measure of my knowledge at any time was whether or not it was adequate to my needs. You don't have to be able to write books or journal articles on your child's condition, but your knowledge (or lack thereof) will form the basis of many decisions you will make about your child. Knowledge matters, and it is important that you build your knowledge to better equip you to meet your child's needs.

One of the most important functions for which I use my knowledge is communication. I need to be able to describe my son's developmental disorder so that others can understand how it affects my child. My knowledge has to be flexible enough, so that I can shape it to help people coming from different backgrounds and perspectives to understand what they need to know. To capture people's interest, I need to be succinct in the basic definition, selecting out that which is most important for a particular person to know, and then word my explanation in everyday terms so that people can easily grasp the essence of what I am saying. I need to give concrete examples of what I mean. Telling someone about the disorder is one thing. Showing someone what it looks like in my child and how it causes problems for him, hammers my point home. I need to be able to talk to the person very specifically, about what they could/ should do to help my child.

An equally important function for which I use my knowledge is to better comprehend the world as experienced by my children (which is often significantly different from the world experienced by others), and to try to help make this experience more positive. Frankly, I'm quite surprised by the extent to which I find that I need to take charge in this manner. I thought parenting a child with special needs would primarily entail finding the best experts available, and then just scrupulously following their advice. I was so wrong! Or at least so naive! I've been amazed to discover how important it has been for me to become a guiding expert in my children's disabilities. I am very fortunate to live in a progressive, receptive school district, but even so, a significant proportion of the interventions and supports employed with my children have been instigated by me. The school district is very good at implementing and assessing what is on the table. It is less good at recognizing the lacuna—the missed possibilities and innovations we could try. That has been my specialty. The school district deals with their past experience and what they know has worked in the past. My job is to envision what else could be possible for my child, and to advocate for it. Someone once said: "God is in the details." So are many of the things in my children's lives that make the difference between smooth days and tumultuous ones, or between blossoming and struggling. Many of these things lie in a sort of no-man's land, in which it is unclear where the responsibility for providing them lies. Part of my job as a parent is to patrol the borders and make sure that important factors are not overlooked.

Box 4.2 presents the characteristics that I believe are the hallmark of an effective understanding of your child's diagnosis. You don't have to know everything to begin speaking up for your child—all you have to do is ask questions, and test the answers against what you know of your child. Later, you'll cycle back through your understanding and go deeper into those areas that concern you the most. As your knowledge builds, so will your ability to ask questions and make suggestions to your child's therapeutic team. Acquiring knowledge is an important part of becoming an effective voice for your child. Add to that mix, good "people skills," diplomacy,

---

Box 4.2 Do I know enough? Characteristics of an effective understanding of your child's diagnosis

- Can you describe the defining characteristics of the diagnosis, in terms that are accurate and that other people can easily understand?

- Do you understand how your child's disability is similar to and different from other related or easily confused conditions?

- Can you apply the diagnosis to your own child, seeing which characteristics are currently present and to what extent?

- Can you put your child's diagnosis in perspective, describing both your child's strengths and challenges?

- Can you describe concrete examples of how those characteristics affect your child's daily functioning?

- Can you advise family, friends, teachers, recreational coaches, camp counselors, etc. how they can support your child in his or her daily activities?

- Are you aware of the general perception of the diagnosis that is prevalent in the mainstream population?

- Can you discuss currently perceived causes of your child's condition?

- Do you understand how different types of specialists approach your child's diagnosis—whether they even believe it exists, and their biases in treatment?

- Are you aware of the range of therapeutic options—both mainstream, and "alternative therapies"—that are possibly applicable to your child?

- Are you aware of the educational concerns facing your child, and the best current practices for addressing those concerns?

- Have you developed an understanding of the diagnosis appropriate for sharing with your child?

persistence, and determination, and you'll become a much more effective advocate for your child.

There are many types of resources you can use to build your knowledge of your child's diagnosis and special needs. Some suggestions are listed in Box 4.3. Ideally, the person who performed your child's formal evaluation will give guidance to at least get you started. But whether or not that is the case, a first step is to start collecting resources and asking questions of professionals until you can start to understand the diagnostic label itself.

Box 4.3 Sources of information about your child's disability

- Network with other parents.
- Ask your pediatrician.
- Whenever you consult a new therapist or specialist, ask if they know of others in your area who work with this population or this condition.
- Schedule consultations with therapists or professionals specifically for the purpose of learning about the condition.
- Read.
- Periodically browse through the special needs section of your local bookstore.
- Check the Internet for relevant websites.
- Subscribe to relevant parent periodicals or e-mail newsletters—these will often summarize new developments in the field.
- Check the bibliographies of interesting books and articles you read, and follow that trail to other valuable resources.
- Attend conferences—speakers are informative, it's wonderful being around a community of concerned individuals, and you are often exposed to new books/resources.

When you're trying to understand your child's diagnosis, it is wonderful if you can find individuals that you can talk to about your child. Never underestimate the importance of dialogue in building understanding. When you're talking to someone who is knowledgeable about one or more aspects of your child's condition, you have the opportunity to test versions of your understanding. You have the chance to build your knowledge, to test its limits, to clear up misperceptions, and to confirm your intuitions. You also have an opportunity to acknowledge privately some areas as things you evidently should understand, but do not.

I do have one strong piece of advice for you. When you have meetings or telephone consultations with other people about your children and their needs, take notes on what they say! As I watch other parents try to come to grips with their children's special needs, I'm stunned by the way people don't use this simple learning strategy. Trust me, when you talk to professionals about your children, you may not be understanding as much as you think you are, and you certainly won't remember the details of the things you're likely to hear during rapid-paced conversations. In some respects, you are like a student who has heard the teacher present a novel concept. You may *think* you understand the gist of what the teacher is saying, but then the teacher leaves the room or sends you home to complete the assignment on your own. Suddenly, when you actually try to tackle the problems yourself for the first time, you realize the gaps in your knowledge—the things you've already forgotten, or the things that you realize you didn't understand well enough in the first place. Learning takes more than superficial listening. It takes active participation and time to absorb. So, take notes on these conversations you have with professionals! Write down their explanations and their reasoning. Your notes can later help you sort through what seems credible to you, and what leaves you doubting or unsatisfied. I also tend to take notes on things I learn and ideas that come to me while I am reading. At least with written texts, you always have the option of re-reading, but a misremembered and unrecorded conversation is simply lost. My years as a researcher and an academic have made me a very thorough note-taker during conversations and consultations. However, I often slip into my own personal shorthand or find myself so involved in dialogue, that I'll find my written records are sometimes quite abbreviated, cryptic, and hard to decipher later. I've learned that, soon after an important conversation or consultation, I need to sit down and reconstruct everything I can remember that was said. If you do so, you will gain a permanent record, which you can then consult later, when the words might take on different meanings to you.

A lot of terms related to special needs diagnoses may be used in a different way in our everyday life and culture than is meant by the technical descriptions you encounter. Words *do* mean different things in different contexts, and so you need to explore these possible other meanings as you try to come to grips with understanding your child's diagnosis. Also, some words are bandied around incorrectly in our society. Some of the things you *think* you know about your child's diagnosis, may actually be *misinformation*. Be alert to this possibility as you explore your child's diagnosis with the relevant professionals. If you're not sure, ask!

You also need to be aware of how the media is presenting topics related to your child's condition. I'm often disappointed with the depth of coverage of Asperger's in the mass media. Eventually, I realized that my disappointment was often because I am hoping to learn something new from the media presentation, and I usually don't. But perhaps when I'm disappointed by what may feel like superficial media coverage, I should realize that mine is not the only knowledge that matters. Every time *Newsweek*, *Time*, or *The Today Show* focuses on a disability such as Asperger's, it brings that disability into the public eye and helps to educate the mainstream population about its existence and its many faces. Every "Did you see the news last night?" water-cooler conversation helps make my child more real to others. Awareness is a first step towards acquiring further resources, accommodations, sensitivity, and acceptance. I recently read *Aquamarine Blue 5* (Prince-Hughes 2002). A recurrent message in these essays is that the biggest problem these students faced was not the difficulties and limitations posed by their physical or mental condition. Rather, these individuals saw their biggest problems as being in society's rigid expectations and assumptions that the "norm" was the only legitimate way of being. Opening the public's perception to other ways of being and experiencing the world, matters.

Mass media presentations often include a significant focus on the causes of the disorder. This is logical. If a magazine, newspaper article, or television or radio report is going to present a disorder as something that can affect your child or someone you know, it is quite natural for people to want to know what causes it, and what the chances are of it ever affecting their families. My husband and I were told from the beginning that our boys' low muscle tone was probably a genetic condition, present from birth, and so I never really worried about the causes of it. Current theories on the causes of autism spectrum disorders are more complicated.

I think that cause and prevention questions are important to ask. But personally, I have not found much solace in pursuing them. The current scientific perception is that autism spectrum disorders, such as Asperger's, are genetic in nature. Alternative views, however, are that autism spectrum disorders can be triggered (or perhaps even caused) by dietary factors, such as gluten, or the presence of thimerosal, a mercury-based preservative recently banned in the MMR vaccine given to children. At some point, I made the choice not to pursue the implications of those possible explanations for my own children. I had my hands full with other choices I had made, and given my children's already picky eating behaviors, I could not bring myself to expend the energy for the dietary struggles necessary to explore whether diet was a contributing factor in our case.

More recently, I attended an incredibly persuasive presentation by a developmental neurologist who argued that the recent rise in new cases of autism spectrum disorders might actually be our bodies' response to all of the environmental neurotoxins to which we are exposed. I'm glad that there are consumer advocacy groups exploring the possible toxicity of vaccines, and pushing for the removal of unnecessary risks to children. I sometimes add my voice to various advocacy efforts. Awareness of those issues is certainly a part of well-developed knowledge of your child's diagnosis. You need to be at least somewhat familiar with those issues, if for no other reason than that other people will ask you about them. It'll be up to you, however, to decide the extent to which you want to invest energy and resources into pursuing causal questions.

The next step in developing your understanding is to figure out how the diagnosis applies to your particular child. Does your child exhibit all of the defining characteristics? If not, which ones apply? Does your child show mild, moderate, or severe degrees of each characteristic? How about the diagnosis overall? Does your child exhibit a mild, moderate, or severe case overall? When we received his diagnosis, we were told that Marcus has a mild case of Asperger's. The evaluator elaborated that, at least for now, his functioning was impaired on two of the three dimensions characterizing Asperger's: pretend play, and pragmatic language use. She did not note significant impairment on the third dimension, executive functioning, at that time. I am absolutely certain that if we had Marcus re-evaluated four years later, he would show significant impairment in that realm. Executive functioning—planning, organization, and self-evaluation—certainly has taken on increased prominence in terms of expected school performance as he progresses through the grades. Even when you have an initial handle on your child's disability, it is difficult to tell how that disability will play itself out at different ages and in different situations. The literature available on a particular condition may give you broad guidelines, but seeing what that actually means for your child takes time and experience, and frankly will sometimes involve just waiting to see what does or doesn't develop. Willey (1999), for example, in her autobiography, *Pretending to be Normal*, describes times of her life when her Asperger's Syndrome characteristics were more apparent, or interfered more with normal functioning than other times. As Willey puts it:

> "If one thing is certain in the AS (Asperger's) world, it is simply that the diagnosis means different things to different people at different times in their lives. Put another way, AS affects individuals in varying degrees and in varying ways. This reality can make it quite difficult to suggest a pat and foolproof summary of how others can lend effective support". (p.161)

Even when you have developed strong supports, they need to remain fluid enough to accommodate the developmental and environmental changes that comprise your growing child's life. In Chapter 6, I will revisit this question of how the characteristics of a disability, the needs of a child, and the supportive responses of therapists, schools, and parents, will need to evolve over time. I will use Marcus and his diagnosis of Asperger's Syndrome as an example. Coldly and clinically stated, a diagnosis can be quite intimidating and overwhelming. Presented in the context of a child's life, with supportive accommodations provided to foster growth and development, the diagnosis shrinks to much more manageable proportions. Instead of overwhelming one's perspective, it becomes just another set of individual characteristics that need to be addressed to parent *any* child supportively.

What to tell your child about his or her diagnosis

Telling our sons about their disabilities was an emotional bogey monster that I dreaded for years. However, it turned out to be relatively easy to do within the context of our lives. For those of you who have already handled the "birds and the bees" question with your children, this is probably the closest analogy I can think of to what this experience was like. I always was matter-of-fact about my children's genitalia and gave direct answers to their questions about reproduction, letting their interest be my guide as to what I told them. I took this same approach to talking to them about their developmental differences. My boys' knowledge of their diagnoses evolved over time. Therapies were a part of our lives since my oldest was three, and so they accepted them as natural and seldom questioned why they had to occur. The understanding in our home was that every person has things they can do well, and things they need to work on. The therapies were presented as things to make them "even better" at whatever the activity was, or if the child acknowledged having difficulty with a skill, we would present the therapy as a way of getting others to help us learn. It wasn't until my son, Marcus, was in fourth grade (usually ages nine—ten) that I talked to him about why *so many* things were difficult for him. I told him he had been born with a difference in the way his brain was wired. This difference meant that some things were easier for him than for other people, but that he would also have to work much harder than normal to try to be good at other things. The disability was not presented as a limiting factor, but rather as an explanatory one. The disability explained some features of the past and present; it did not necessarily predict how good he could be or what he could or could not do in the future. In one essay on her website, www.disabilityisnatural.com, Kathie Snow describes disability as "a body part that works differently." I love this matter-of-fact description, and have found this attitude useful for talking with my sons.

I don't think there is a specific age at which you should have the disability discussion with your child, any more than there is a set time for other value-laden discussions. For me, the middle/late elementary years just seemed natural. Around this time I noticed my boys starting to eavesdrop more and more on adult conversations. Their world starts to broaden. Until this age, it is easy to duck questions one is not ready to answer. A fourth grader, on the other hand, is much more savvy and persistent. If a parent chooses to try to duck an issue with an older elementary child, she or he is more likely to end up in the world of half-truths and evasions—not a good example you'll want to set if you want to show your child they can talk to you about a-n-y-t-h-i-n-g. Fourth grade was a year in which Marcus's interests in the world beyond childhood toys started expanding. The literature he read branched out into accounts of people conquering adversity, and people from different walks of life. Somehow it seemed quite logical that I would have to talk to him matter-of-factly about the non-existence of Santa Claus and the existence of Asperger's in the same two-month period. Fourth grade also was the year in which my youngest and I began discussing his ADD more. Our school was surprised when they discovered my sons already knew about their diagnoses, but it seemed to me that my boys had more of a right to know than anyone. The thought of sitting them down at age 16 or so and revealing a "deep, dark secret" just never felt right to me. I don't think the revelation was devastating to him because his disability had always been a natural part of the way we lived. On the other hand, Michael, true to his more outspoken personality, tried arguing with his teachers that he couldn't be expected to sit up straight because he has scoliosis, and he couldn't be expected to remember instructions because he has ADD. I think this excuse-giving is one of the things people fear, but I found that it was easy enough to address: I simply told the boys that just because something was harder for them, that didn't mean they didn't have to do it. Their diagnoses just told us there was a logical reason why some things might be harder and might need a little extra attention and effort.

When I had "the talk" with Marcus, his biggest question was, were there other kids like him out there? In response, I asked our play therapist to help us approach another family with a child with Asperger's, and to facilitate and supervise several meetings between our boys. Even four years later, he is still—like most adolescents—exploring how he fits into the social world, and what are the limitations, skills, potentials, and interests he possesses. I'm glad I've laid the basis for his understanding over so many years. In seventh grade science, he began reading about genetic disorders, and again I could see his mind trying to sort through how Asperger's fits in with the genetic traits and diseases they discussed: is it like eye color? Is it like sickle-cell anemia? What language do you use to describe it? Is it a disease? A disorder? A disability? A defect? An abnormality? I still cringe every time people use the colder/harder words, because I don't want him to think of himself as "defective," but I can't protect him from the language. I can only help him understand it in a more complex sense, especially when it is used as shorthand to compare his situation with what is "normal" or with what is "typical." I can see that now he is also ready to learn more of the specific details of Asperger's. My job, once again, will be to help give him a context for building his understanding of these characteristics as only some of the many characteristics that make him a unique individual.

It takes a while for each of us to absorb the realization that any disability has many faces, and a given individual's personal experiences and personality are also reflected in those faces. As with any group of individuals, some of the people who share a diagnostic label are going to be people we like, and others are not. Some we will see as similar to us, and others we will see as very different. While at an amusement park in Ontario, Canada two summers ago, Marcus tapped on my shoulder and pointed to a group of adolescents wearing identical, red tee shirts, bearing the logo "Autism Awareness Day Camp." For the most part, these were kids more noticeably on the autistic spectrum than Marcus. I could see Marcus's fascination—and anxiety—as he again tried to figure out how he fit in with this group of individuals. I've begun to use books to explore Asperger's Syndrome with Marcus (for example Jackson 2002), and to invite discussions with him about his experiences and various characteristics of his diagnosis. Asperger's Syndrome describes a set of characteristics, some of which do cause Marcus difficulty, but I don't see his self-esteem as being dictated by his diagnosis. (See Dinah Murray's *Coming Out Asperger* 2006, for a thoughtful collection of essays on the issues involved in telling your child and others about his or her diagnosis.)

There's always tomorrow

In case you haven't figured it out from all the discussion above, learning about your child's diagnosis is a never-ending process. Contrary to popular belief, knowledge isn't a static thing that you "achieve." It is fluid, organic, and growing. The professional, scientific understanding of your child's disability changes as new discoveries are made and new insights gained. You need to keep up with that science. But your child changes as well, and so you will often need to "hit the books" again, to see what they offer about the new challenges facing your child as she or he grows and enters new phases of life. Openness to learning and active pursuit of knowledge must become a way of life for you to advocate effectively for your child. But that's okay. Once you get over your initial emotional reactions to facing the hard facts about your child's diagnosis, and start to build a rudimentary understanding of what his or her diagnosis means for your child's life, you'll realize that you *can* do this. It's just a matter of taking that basic approach to learning you've already employed, and applying it again and again. You're bootstrapping your knowledge, constantly moving it ahead from the base you've managed to build so far.

At the beginning, it's obvious that you don't know enough to help your child. Your sense of being lost shows you that you have a lot of learning to do. When you feel as though you understand your child, when you can anticipate his or her needs, and you feel capable of dealing with the challenges you see—that's a sign you've prepared yourself well and have a solid knowledge base. Then you can coast for a while, and enjoy having a good handle on things and a supportive net in place. When you see new challenges looming ahead, see your child consistently struggling, or realize that you're starting to feel lost or out of control in your daily functioning with your kids—that's a sign you need to find out more. Your life with your child will help guide you as to what direction you need to go.

5

Beginning Therapeutic Interventions for Your Child

Once you have a preliminary grasp of your child's diagnosis, it's time to start moving forward to do something about it. After all, that's why you started this whole process: to get some help for your child. One of your first decisions will be what therapist(s) will work with your child, and where and when will these therapy sessions take place. Your research into your child's diagnosis should have informed you about the range of approaches used in working with your child's particular type(s) of disabilities. To a large extent, which options you pursue will depend on the recommendations you received, your own preferences based on your understanding of your child's disability, and pragmatic factors such as whether you are using external funding sources, therapist availability, scheduling issues, and personality fit between a therapy/therapist and your child and family. In the following discussion, I will briefly discuss some of these concerns, which are summarized in Box 5.1. Later in this chapter, I will discuss how to investigate other types of supports for which your family may be eligible, including specialized equipment, respite care, family training, environmental modifications, and financial supplements. Your goal is to create a multi-faceted framework that supports your child throughout his or her day, and in as many areas of his or her life as are needed. You will always need to take an active role in determining what route to follow to best meet your child's needs while fostering his or her competence and independence.

Box 5.1 Questions to consider
when choosing a therapist for your child

- What type(s) or subtype(s) of therapist do you need?
- Do you plan to go through an agency, or put together your own list of independent practitioners?
- Who is responsible for paying the therapist(s)?
- What administrative approval or medical prescription, if any, are needed before therapy begins?
- Who will serve as case manager, to coordinate communication between the therapists, and to oversee administrative and procedural issues?
- How often will the therapy occur?
- Where and when will the therapy sessions take place?
- Does this particular therapist feel like a good fit to your child and family?

Selecting and scheduling therapists

As I discussed in Chapter 3 describing the special needs process under IDEA, therapeutic interventions are free for children under 21, provided that you can document your child's disability and specific educational need. I refer you back to that chapter on the administrative aspects of entering the special needs network for different aged children. Just as different administrative entities provide procedural guidelines for selecting evaluators, they also have guidelines for selecting therapists. In many instances, especially for school-aged children, therapy will be offered at the child's school and will be provided by school personnel. In other instances, the school district or county will present a list of therapy providers they will agree to employ at their expense. These may or may not meet the total extent of your child's needs, however. Although we have been very pleased by the options provided through these free channels, at most stages of my children's lives we have opted to supplement school-approved therapies with other interventions obtained through health insurance reimbursement or covered out of our own pockets. It will be up to you to research what is readily offered, and what less-advertised options are also possible.

Pragmatic constraints, such as availability will certainly influence your choice of therapist. When Marcus was first diagnosed with Asperger's, the evaluators recommended that we pursue Floor Time therapy, a social and language developmental approach developed by Dr. Stanley Greenspan. Unfortunately, ten years ago such therapists were not available locally and, due to the frequency of the therapy needed, I did not even consider locating such therapists elsewhere and taking my child to them for services. The good news is that there is usually not only one recommended approach to working with a particular child.

Nowadays, when I need a new therapist, I start working the special needs grapevine where I live. When I do, I often find the same set of names keep popping up as being the "best" in our area. I then call one or more of them to check availability. I always ask to speak directly to the particular individual, even if it means asking them to call me back. As I describe my child and our concerns, I'm already listening as well, to get a sense of the therapist's personality and approach. I might ask if they would be available or who they personally would recommend. I almost always come away with a shortlist of one to three names. When encouraged to do so, referring individuals will often describe the relative strengths of the people they'll list for you, and the differences between what the various individuals can offer. They will sometimes also describe personality or treatment styles so that you can better judge which may fit your own situation. It may take a chain of phone calls before I finally reach an individual who is available to work with my family, but at least I know I am following a quality chain, based on personal referrals. Especially when you are dealing with therapists who work with preschool-aged children, you may find that an individual's caseload is temporarily full. Explore how long it would be before they anticipate an opening. To engage a good therapist, it may be worth a wait of six weeks or so. Or if time is more critical for you, you could ask to be put on a therapist's waiting list while you investigate other possibilities. The therapist's year certainly has its own rhythm, with the late winter and spring months probably being the most tightly scheduled, and so the hardest time to be added to a therapist's caseload. Year-round therapies are assumed for children in Early Intervention. Services are usually reduced during the summer for preschool-aged children, unless you are just beginning services or can make a strong argument that regression would occur without continuing the usual therapeutic frequency. Unless your child qualifies for a special program, school-aged children usually do not receive summer services through the school district.

If your child is going to receive more than one type of therapy, you will need to decide whether to contract with a single agency to provide all of the therapists, or whether you are going to put together your own itinerant team. I had particular individuals in mind, and so I chose to do the latter, but it is time-consuming and more difficult to coordinate services in this way. You may want to request a service coordinator to assist you. Some agencies incorporate therapies into their own, integrated school settings. Others contract to send therapists to the location of your choice. Whichever route you follow, you need to ensure that communication between the therapists occurs regularly. If they are not able to speak to one another easily, you must be the one who keeps everyone apprised of what is going on. Occasional team meetings or telephone conversations can help, but also I found it useful to employ a therapy communication book. In it, each therapist recorded a few notes on what they were working on and their observations about my children's progress. My children's teachers and I would also enter questions, comments, and concerns in this communication book. Informal discussions held at the beginning, end or during therapy sessions can also be useful, but participants need to take care that the discussions do not undercut the child's actual therapy time. I often attended my children's therapies, and so I used these informal discussions extensively to learn about my children's progress and to share information and observations with others.

Different therapists will specialize in different aged children. This is natural because the therapy job is actually very different with different developmental groups. I usually advise people who are first starting therapy through Early Intervention, to try to find a therapist who can also treat your child when they age out of EI, at age three. This way, the same therapist can continue into the preschool years with your child. At least in the United States, you will usually have to switch therapists to local school personnel once your child becomes school-aged, but one of your goals is to have as much continuity of care as possible—provided, that is, you are pleased with the therapist. You are always free to change therapy providers if you feel that a relationship is not working out, although such a change can be tricky to negotiate if you are using school district personnel. When transitions between personnel are necessary, push for some form of communication to ease the transitions. If possible, it is a good idea for the old and new therapists to meet each other. If that is not possible, sharing information about what work has been done to date and what the old therapist would recommend for the future is a good idea, whether or not the new therapist continues with the same approach. Although I am not an expert in these fields by any means, I like knowing what the therapist is trying to accomplish, and why. Such frequent and open communication helps me become more of a participant and makes it easier for me to evaluate how I think things are progressing and what changes I would like to see occur.

In choosing therapists, I have found the particular degree held by the individual to be less important than their experience and openness to learning more. I remember once being informed that a physical therapist I was considering engaging, tended to split her treatment visits with a partner, who was a physical therapist assistant. Wanting the "best" for my child, I was initially quite concerned that someone without an advanced degree would be directing and conducting at least half of my child's therapy sessions. Naive me! Although training is important, competence can take many forms, not all of which require a degree. I wanted the best, and I got it: the team ended up being incredible, and I found that I gained valuable insights from each member.

Selection of location for the therapy to occur depends on pragmatic concerns such as space or equipment availability, and bigger picture concerns dictated by the philosophical approach and goals of a particular type of therapy. In the United States, there is currently a trend for more naturalistic therapies, especially with children below school age. By naturalistic, I mean that instead of bringing the child to a clinic, there is an effort to embed the therapies into the child's natural life, using materials readily at hand. This is considered to be especially important for younger, pre-school-aged children, and has the advantage of easing transfer of skills to the child's everyday life. Primary grade children often receive therapy through "push-in" programs, in which the therapist comes into the child's classroom. Alternatively, "pull-out" programs, in which the child is pulled out of their classroom and brought into a special therapy room, are often used when there are privacy concerns, and with older elementary children. Speech and language therapies usually occur in separate, quiet spaces; for my boys, for example, articulation exercises were often woven around playing board games. Conversational or social skills may need a small-group meeting area, but could also entail a push-in approach. Pull-out programs or therapy in a clinical setting is also useful when equipment needed is not readily available in a classroom or home setting. My sons' physical therapy programs often involved swings, trampolines, and other pieces of large equipment. Unfortunately, dedicated therapy rooms are not a high priority for many daycare centers. Especially during their preschool years, my children spent far too many sessions receiving therapy on the floor of a hallway or a coatroom. You'll have to be flexible, brainstorming with the therapist about what location(s) seem best for meeting your child's therapy goals. You may even have to start a campaign with your school district or your child's daycare, to convince them of the desirability—and sometimes even legal necessity—of providing an appropriate site for your child to receive services.

Parents are often worried about stigmatizing their child, by making it obvious that the child is receiving therapy within the school. I'm not particularly worried about this issue. At least in our elementary school, so many children are pulled out at different times for special lessons or different types of work with specialists, that the traffic flow is a natural part of the school day, receiving no special notice. Again, if your child is going to be stigmatized, I believe it will more likely be due to your child's natural behaviors than to any recognition of the fact that they receive therapies in a school setting. I do give thought, however, to my child's preferences. When/if your child reaches an age that she or he becomes self-conscious about receiving "special" attention, then this is a different story and certainly needs to be a factor when planning therapeutic interventions. Given the way American public schools are run, I wouldn't expect this to be a concern until the upper elementary grades, at the earliest. My most recent experiences have been at the junior high school level, when adolescents are very concerned with self-image and fitting in. Here I find that school personnel go to great pains to protect student privacy, but accessing needed services without calling unwanted attention does continue to be an issue for my young teen.

Especially if you have a choice of therapists, you will need to consider the fit between the therapist and your child's personality. Therapy is difficult enough for all concerned without having to deal with a therapist you or your child do not like, or a therapist who is not enthused about his or her job. This is horrible to have to say, but do look for someone who seems to understand children, and who uses encouragement and positive reinforcement for motivation, instead of more negative approaches or a "let's get this over with" attitude. My own experiences have been positive but, unfortunately, I have observed other interchanges between therapists and children that certainly did not echo the emotional tone I would want my children to experience. My children have always worked hard in their therapies, but because the therapists were adept at knowing when and how much to push, and how to embed their therapies within games and fun activities, motivating my children was seldom an issue. When deciding upon which therapist to engage for your child, it is wonderful if you can watch the person in action if at all possible (although due to privacy concerns, you will need to ask for permission to do this). Another possibility is to interview them or watch a sample interchange with your child. A friend of mine, who home-schools her four young children, interviewed quite a few therapists before she was able to find one who was comfortable with her family's values and the way her home was structured.

Not all therapists can work well within the context of a child's environment, and not all school or daycare placements are open to allowing "outsiders" into their classrooms. As archaic and wrong-headed an attitude as I find that to be, it is still one you may occasionally encounter. I rejected one private school placement for my son based on their resistance to the idea of having PTs, OTs, and speech therapists coming into their classroom. The Montessori preschool I eventually located for my second son had to be convinced that opening their classrooms to therapists would not interfere with their own sense of mission. Having a child with special needs does not rule out an academically rigorous or enriched school or daycare situation. It does mean, however, that you need to look at how to support your child in such an environment, and at the school's willingness to work with you in that regard. You, your child's therapists, and your child's teachers or care providers must operate as a team, working together to support your child's growth and development. A willingness to communicate, to learn from one another, and to respect each other's contributions is critical for this team. If you don't have that, I would advise you to seriously consider a change unless you are willing to be in constant struggle, fighting for your child's rights and needs.

Scheduling therapies is not a trivial concern—for you or for your child—and setting an optimal schedule takes deliberation and thought. I mentioned earlier in this book that at the height of our therapies, we had 17 therapy sessions between my two boys scheduled every week! Needless to say, this started me off in my present-day habit of keeping a large calendar, and of being very deliberate in our selection of additional activities for involvement. Before you begin imagining an unpleasant, regimented life for your child, I want to be quick to say that you shouldn't think of this as a world of sterile appointments. If you've chosen your therapists well, what your child will have is a world of lots of one-on-one, often fun attention. You and the therapists will become experts at "hiding the peas in the applesauce," to use an analogy from my toddler-feeding days, and you will become great at creative approaches to embedding therapy practice in everyday activities.

In setting up your child's therapy sessions, you must take into account your child's energy levels. Put bluntly, although a good therapist will make the experience as pleasant as possible for the child, she or he is definitely asking the child to "work." She or he will be pushing your child, asking your child to try new things, to do things that are difficult, that tire your child, or that sometimes even feel uncomfortable for short periods of time. For everyone's sake, schedule therapy sessions at a time of day when your child is emotionally and physically refreshed and ready for these challenges.

Sometimes your child's primary therapies will be provided by the school, and you have little choice in who delivers the services or where. But even so, there are requests you can make about scheduling. When Marcus began receiving therapy through our local school, he was only in kindergarten for a half-day (actually only two-and-a-half hours at that), and I felt strongly that he needed this classroom time for peer interactions and for experiencing kindergarten itself. The school agreed with my concerns and offered an extended day to accommodate his therapy. Twice a week he would stay an extra hour to have his speech and physical therapy sessions. Because the occupational therapist worked with Marcus on a push-in basis, helping him with activities to improve his fine motor skills within the context of the classroom, I agreed to have the OT sessions occur during the school day.

When you have scheduling concerns, help your school district understand your concerns. In our case, I explained that both physical therapy and occupational therapy included goals that not only helped my boys build strength in the long term, but that also helped them function in the hours immediately following therapy by physically priming their bodies for attention and for gross and fine motor activities. I requested that these therapies be provided on alternate days, to maximize the spacing of the benefits they provided. Not all of my scheduling requests have been granted, although I do feel they were at least seriously considered. When I delayed Michael's entry into kindergarten for a year, the responsibility for his therapies still transferred to our local school because he had reached that magic "kindergarten-eligible" age I mentioned earlier. Although the school district declined my request to provide the transportation from his private preschool, they were willing to work with me to schedule his therapy first thing in the morning, so as to minimize the disruption to Michael's day.

One thing to keep in mind is that your child's peers will be continuing with their regularly scheduled activities while your child is taken from the classroom for therapy. You and your therapist need to be sensitive to those instances when your child is being pulled at a particularly difficult time for your child to leave (an exciting special event, for example). You will also need to ensure that your child's transition back into the classroom goes smoothly, and your child is not left feeling lost or confused about what she or he missed, or should be doing upon return. Rejoining a class already in progress can be especially difficult for children with organizational concerns. Plus, you will need to put a mechanism into place to make up for missed work. This has periodically caused problems for us, when my boys would come home tired from their school day, yet still have make-up work to do, in addition to their regular homework. People sometimes forget that therapies can be tiring in themselves, and that we are asking our children to do even more than children who don't receive services. Close communication between parent and teacher can provide feedback and address any overload issues that arise. Reduced workload or extended deadlines are sometimes appropriate solutions, and may even be written as an option into your child's IEP. We seldom employ it, but I usually have an understanding with my sons' teachers that I will use my parental judgment to intervene when I feel my son has reached his limit.

Whenever possible, I encourage you to attend your child's therapy sessions. I know we are all over-scheduled, and it is very tempting to use the therapist's time as an opportunity for you to get something else done, perhaps in another part of the house. Please think twice before doing this, at least on a regular basis. Admittedly, some children seem to work better with their therapists if their parent is not nearby. This is a question you should probably raise with the therapist. If it is better for you not to be involved, try at least to be where you can eavesdrop on the sessions. I prefer actively watching the sessions and sometimes joining in myself. You will be amazed at the things you will learn about how to help your child by watching the therapists, and your regular presence makes ongoing communication between the two of you much more likely to occur. When therapy sessions occurred during the course of the school day, I sought and received permission to attend one of each type of therapy session at least once a month. I believe that my willingness to watch, learn, and reinforce the various therapeutic techniques, has been a key element in my success in building a strong, cooperative team. There's a big difference in how you are treated if you are seen as "in the trenches," observing and working along with the professionals trying to help your child, as opposed to being seen as distant, uninvolved, or unreasonably critical of the therapy team.

Recognizing your role in the therapeutic intervention process

Once you have a team of therapists working with your child, you finally have some help in place, but I must stress that your work is nowhere nearly done. The second half of this book continues a discussion of the roles I encourage you to take as a team member in addressing your child's needs. For your child's benefit, you need to become a sort of paraprofessional yourself.

Therapists serve multiple roles. One is to provide direct, hands-on interventions with your child. They also serve as a consultant teacher to others who work with your child, including you, the parent. Not only did this help the application and transfer of newly learned therapy skills into my children's daily activities, but I also brought problems I noticed to the therapists and asked for their help addressing them. The therapist–parent partnership has definite benefits to all parties.

One way to develop your partnership is by attending your child's therapy sessions as often as you can. Alternatively, you can ask for regular, periodic consultations with your child's therapists in which you ask them to describe what they are working on with your child and to provide a list of supplemental activities for you, or brainstorm with you things you can do to reinforce or extend this developing skill into your home life. Although seeing the therapist in action is always useful, I think the key to any meaningful extension beyond the therapy room is frequent communication in some form of a two-way dialogue, instead of just a brief written record. The latter can have a tendency to become dry, impersonal, and technical. On the other hand, some form of dialogue provides the opportunity to elaborate, to clarify, to check for understanding, and to offer your own ideas to the therapist based on your knowledge of your child's interests and activities. To me, there's nothing like regular chats, every two or three weeks, even if they're short phone conversations.

I didn't "do therapy" with my children at home. Rather, therapy informed the way I did life! Many of the toys and games I played with my children were selected to have fun while enhancing a particular skill at the same time. Time and energy are precious, and so I budgeted our time and energy so that many of our activities had a dual, or even triple purpose. For example, walking the dog was an often-used time for embedding therapy activities into a necessary part of our day. While holding the dog's leash in one hand, I might pull the boys in a wagon while they happily blew bubbles into the wind (a fine motor activity that helped with both speech therapy and occupational therapy). Or while we all walked the dog, I'd play "Simon Says" with my children to encourage physical activity and motor planning: "Simon Says walk on your tippytoes. Simon Says walk on your heels. Simon Says walk heel-to-toe. Now Simon Says try it backwards. Skip!" The boys (and, occasionally, even I) might dress up in Halloween costumes while we walked, or carry balloons or pinwheels to maintain their interest or to reward their efforts. As a parent of a child with special needs, you too will need to become incredibly inventive in finding better, more therapeutic ways of "doing life." The next three chapters explore parenting and home life issues more thoroughly, with many examples from my own family. My philosophy has always been one of learning how to "walk the walk" of meeting my children's needs. Then I find I am more listened to and respected when I "talk the talk" to others about what I think should be done.

Your close involvement with the therapy process is also important to help you develop a plan for educational supports and services, and to be able to monitor how well this plan and the people involved, are meeting your child's needs. This is such an important topic that I have devoted two chapters, Chapters 9 and 10, to its discussion. Monitoring is not necessarily critical or distrusting. Rather, I've always seen it as a means of providing feedback, trouble-shooting, and solving problems as they arise. It is vital that you establish a working partnership with your child's therapy team. In this context, your willingness to learn from the therapy team and to assist them in creating your child's Individualized Education Plan goes a long way towards defusing negative reactions. No, you don't have to work side by side with the therapists, but you do have to put some effort into staying a connected, informed member of your child's therapy team.

Just as when you were first learning what your child's diagnosis means, you will need to pace yourself, prioritize what is most important to you and your child at a given time, and gradually adjust your life. As I became more and more familiar with my children's disabilities, I found that I had parenting decisions to make that were beyond those expected in the world of everyday parenting. I found that I also needed to redefine my notions of what everyday parenting meant in order to better accommodate the reality of my children's needs. As I learned more about my children, I learned more about how their disabilities might manifest and what I could do to help avoid or alleviate difficulties. It became evident to me that becoming more involved, and helping my children master the skills they were lacking would be a major step towards creating happier, more independent children. At the same time, I realized that by putting more concentrated efforts into helping my children develop the abilities to do for themselves, I would eventually lessen my need to have to stay close to help them or to do things for them. I used therapists and other professionals to assist me, but I also did significant work with my children on my own. "It's not my job" was an attitude I could not afford to take. In fact, I found that expanding my notion of what was and wasn't "my job" has had immediate benefits to both my children and myself.

Hooking up with other types
of supportive resources

This section of the book is a short, but important one. In 1996, the options I was offered by our school district and by our county's Early Intervention program revolved solely around types of therapies. But therapy and educational modifications and accommodations are not the only types of resources to which your child's evaluation and diagnosis may open doors. Other federal and state programs offer a variety of other supports for which your child may be eligible. For example, your family may be eligible to have the medical and pharmaceutical expenses reimbursed. Respite care, in your home or at centralized locations, to relieve family members for several hours a week—or even overnight—is often a much-prized option. It is also an option of which I remained ignorant throughout my children's preschool years, or I certainly would have applied for it! Recreational camp fees may be covered, and your child's disability may make your family eligible for housing supports. Funds may be available to assist with environmental modifications or adaptive technologies necessitated by your child's disability, and funds are also possible for family education and training.

Eligibility and application processes vary from program to program, and so I cannot describe them here. Unfortunately, even now I find that learning about the available programs involves about as much sleuthing as learning about treatment options for my sons' disabilities. I have been frustrated to discover that there is no single website or agency that links them all together. State dollars are often used to buy into these programs, and so what is available to you will depend on where you live. In my home state of New York, for example, my children would not be eligible for Medicaid, because our family income is too high. However, New York State offers a Medicaid Home and Community-based Waiver, designed to support the care of children with disabilities in their homes and local communities. My children may be eligible for this program, despite our family's income. However, I have been told that to find out, I will first need to apply for Medicaid and be rejected, and that it is not uncommon to be rejected for the Waiver the first time one applies—persistence, and evidently the use of a knowledgeable case manager who best knows how to work the system, makes the difference in final approval. (See also Mercado 2006, for one determined mother's account of learning how to maneuver through the system.)

The Useful resources at the end of the chapter list the various agencies that you should investigate. Some of these programs are basic entitlements, which means they must be provided to you, no matter what, if you are eligible. Other programs are more supplemental, and are often dependent upon available funding. The cynic in me suggests that perhaps this explains some of the secrecy that surrounds the programs. Families who have been approved may be hesitant to share this information with others, for fear of jeopardizing their own supports. More usually, I think, it is difficult to discover the whole array of options because of lack of communication between agencies. What is available really does vary depending on what federal, state, or local initiatives are being pursued in your area. Personally, I would love to see more coordination between agencies, and perhaps a resource clearing house or network developed to guide families and service providers. Parent to Parent and Families Together are two non-profit organizations that may be useful in helping you navigate available options in your area. Even if you choose not to explore various avenues such as Medicaid or programs and supports available through the Office of Mental Health, it is useful to know what might be possible if your child or family's situation should change in the future. There is an age restriction for qualifying or applying for some programs. Talk to other parents to learn from their experience.

Useful resources
Other supportive resources to investigate

To locate particular contacts in the United States, you may wish to refer to the state resource guides provided by the National Dissemination Center for Children with Disabilities, at www.nichcy.org. The types of supportive resources include:

- Your state's Department of Vocational and Educational Services for Individuals with Disabilities (VESID).

- Your state's Office of Mental Health.

- Disability-specific agencies are a good place to contact—these often now serve more than the particular population for which they are named (e.g., United Cerebral Palsy, Easter Seals, and

The Arc, formerly known as the Association for Retarded Citizens).

- Parent to Parent organization in your state.

- Families Together organization in your state.

- The Social Security Administration, for SSI (Social Security Income), SSDI (Social Security Disability Income), and Medicaid and Medicaid Waiver Services: www.socialsecurity.gov.

- Your state's Developmental Disability service offices: www.disabilityresources.org/DD.html.

6

Marcus and Asperger's Syndrome

An Example of How the Manifestation of a Disorder (and One's Parenting Role) Can Change Over Time

You may have a diagnosis for your child now, but what can be done to help your child? After all, that's the crucial issue, isn't it? Not knowledge, but action. The literature available on a particular type of disability may give you broad guidelines as to what your child will need. But each child is an individual, and seeing what that disability actually means for your child takes time and experience. Even when you have an initial handle on your child's disability, it is difficult to tell how that disability will play itself out at different ages and in different situations.

In the pages that follow, I'll use my son, Marcus, as an example to show how his Asperger's Syndrome has manifested at different stages of his life. As his needs changed, so did the focus of his therapies and the nature of my own interventions to help him cope better with his world. As I read back over the clinical list of characteristic difficulties of autism spectrum disorders, presented in Box 6.1, I realize that Marcus has indeed encountered many, if not all of them. I no longer have any doubt that Marcus has Asperger's Syndrome. Sometimes he struggles with it. At other times, it recedes into the background. But as much as I was terrified and overwhelmed when I first read the description of Asperger's, I have found that when encountered within the context of his personality and his life, the autism spectrum characteristics have been nowhere near as damning as presented in that first cold list. Yes, they are there, and they sometimes present difficulties we have to deal with, but they also include strengths. His Asperger's does not define his life. I think one reason it doesn't is that we have learned enough about the diagnosis to also learn how to live—and live well—with it. His is a good life. In the paragraphs that follow, I will look at some of these defining characteristics of an autism spectrum disorder, within the context of a specific child, mine, and a real life, ours. Developing and personalizing your understanding of your own child's disabilities is the task you will be facing as well.

Box 6.1 Characteristics of Asperger's Syndrome, an autism spectrum disorder*

Asperger's Syndrome is a neuropsychological condition that affects social and emotional interaction. It is a developmental disability, which means that a child is born with it, and it affects development through-out life. The American Psychiatric Association's *Diagnostic and Statistical Manual of Mental Disorders* (4th edn) (DSM-IV 1994) looks for impairments in the following five areas:

- impaired communication
- deficits in socialization and social skills
- restricted interests
- unusual responses to stimulation and environment (sensory integration difficulties)
- repetitive or odd patterns of behavior.

Early indicators tend to include:

- lack of eye contact
- lack of joint attention (defined as attention to the same item or topic as another person)
- lack of reciprocal conversation (engaging in verbal turn-taking)
- atypical sensory/motor processing.

Other characteristics include:

- difficulty identifying important global concepts and elements of tasks (difficulty seeing the forest for the trees)
- difficulty processing auditory information (visual learners)

- difficulty generalizing skills—skills need to be taught separately in a variety of contexts
- difficulty sequencing information or steps in a task
- difficulty transitioning between different activities
- difficulty with time concepts and time management
- atypical and/or uneven academic, social, or emotional development (for example, high functioning in some academic areas and low functioning in others)
- difficulty picking up on body language, emotions, proper etiquette, or the unspoken rules of behavior
- rigid adherence to rules—a black-and-white interpretation of the world
- difficulty identifying and understanding the point of view of others
- a literal interpretation of language.

Children with autism spectrum disorders are also at higher risk for depression or anxiety.

This description is compiled from discussions of Asperger's presented in The Puzzle of Autism *(National Education Association 2006) and* Asperger Syndrome and Your Child *(Powers and Poland 2002), see also Attwood 1998, 2006.*

As an infant, Marcus's most obvious needs were emotional. He was easily over-stimulated by people and experiences, and very hard to comfort. Marcus had a tremendous need to be swaddled and held. He did not respond well to rocking, but did to bouncing, walking, back thumps, and other deep pressure input. Our biggest challenge as parents was to try to anticipate his sensory meltdown triggers, so we could avoid them. In the first year of life, infants develop the ability to regulate their emotions. So, to some extent, our working to help soothe Marcus was simply normal infant parenting; but the usual comforting behaviors didn't work very well for us. We didn't know yet about Marcus's Asperger's Syndrome. We didn't understand why so many of the social bonding experiences that are soothing for other infants, were stressful for him. When nursing him, I learned that he wouldn't look into my eyes, although he did focus on my mouth and lower face. Sucking did seem to calm him, and we kept many pacifiers scattered across his crib, to help him self-soothe. It was not uncommon to find him with one in his mouth, and several others clutched in his hands. We were careful to have his Huggy Bear and his musical dinosaur to help him sleep. Barney, the purple dinosaur, provided a gentle, safe, predictable world, in which Marcus would anchor himself for the next several years. Books were always a strong interest of Marcus's, especially books with beautiful language and predictable cadences: *Good Night Moon*; *Jamberry*; *Mr. Brown Can Moo, Can You?*; *There's a Wocket in My Pocket*, and *A Day with Barney* were quickly established as favorites even in his early weeks of life. Beyond that, I confess my memories of his needs in infancy are not exceptional.

The parenting world began to change for me with the advent of mobility and speech, because then some of my child's more obvious differences began to emerge. It was hard work to keep Marcus safe, due to his tendency to climb, coupled with his poor balance. His weaknesses in communication started causing problems for us. He had severe articulation difficulties. Around this time, I noticed that he would start repeating himself again and again, stopping only if an adult repeated back to him what he had just tried to say. Marcus didn't seem to even try to use pointing or other pragmatic techniques to express his wants. These communicative limitations are very common in Asperger's, but again, we didn't know about the Asperger's until Marcus was almost three years old. All we knew was that, as parents, we had to work very hard to try to second-guess or interpret what Marcus wanted. My husband, Mark, still sadly remembers a night when the two were home alone, and Marcus turned on him, tearfully pounding on Mark's chest because he could not understand what Marcus was repeatedly trying to say. Marcus's desire to be understood was very much there, and we found ourselves increasingly dealing with a frustrated child, unable to get his body to do what he wanted it to do, and unable to ask us for help effectively. Sometimes the frustration would be expressed as anger, and at others by a withdrawal and passivity. He definitely was not a full participant in the social world going on around him. I constantly had to seek ways to reach into his world, and to try to help him bridge the distance into ours. My parenting skills were more and more taxed. I was doing everything I knew how to do, but it wasn't enough. Here is where entering the world of Early Intervention, and therapists and therapies became invaluable. I wish I could have initiated it even earlier—we needed the supports so badly.

When the course of normal development would lead children to master self-help skills leading to greater independence, Marcus again encountered many frustrations. His low muscle tone and poor coordination interfered tremendously with his ability to do the things he wanted to do. Yet he had a typical toddler's desire for independence, especially in feeding and dressing. Frustration, followed by withdrawal tended to be his norm, and I hated watching his world become smaller at a time when other children were branching out. Speech therapy worked to help build oral motor strength and control, which helped with his many articulation errors. Occupational therapy helped develop his hand strength and fine motor skills, such as manipulating small objects, or using thumb and forefinger together in a pincer grasp. Occupational therapy also worked on the button, zipper, buckling skills needed for dressing and other self-help activities. Physical therapy worked to help trunk and shoulder strength, motor planning, and coordination. Therapy swings helped develop his sense of balance and his awareness of his body in space. Occupational therapy and physical therapy together worked to help develop more adaptive sensory integration processing, through the use of weighted vests, joint compression, and skin brushing to build up his tolerance to common stimuli his nervous system was unable to handle. (See Kranowitz 1998, *The Out-of-Sync Child*, for more information.) In addition to the usual childhood necessities, the diaper bag I carried for his younger brother was crammed with therapy toys, including puzzles, whistles, bubble-blowing toys, or button-controlled water tube games. These novelties not only kept him entertained; they helped incorporate therapy practice in our daily life.

Marcus's one overriding fascination was "trains," and he would become quite animated over them (again, not at all uncommon with children on the autism spectrum). Our weekends were spent chasing trains in the car for him to watch, visiting trains for him to ride, going to stores so he could play with their Brio displays, finding train puzzles for fine motor development and teaching his ABCs, finding train songs and train videos—we even called the stitching on the front of his underwear "train tracks" to distinguish the back from the front when dressing himself. Trains were his obsession, and our friend. We will always be indebted to Thomas the Tank Engine and the Island of Sodor for providing a social bridge between his interests and those of other children his age.

By preschool, Marcus had more marked difficulty entering into social interactions with peers. The give and take of social communication is hard enough when a child is talking with a competent adult who can anticipate much of what the child is trying to say, but communicating in the world of child-peers with their own limited ability to take others' perspectives, adds additional levels of complexity. Marcus didn't know how to initiate and sustain play with other children, although he was certainly interested in them. An adult was often needed nearby to translate Marcus's words to others, to provide a running commentary to help Marcus understand what was going on, and to cue him how to respond to interactions attempted by others. As a parent, I made extraordinary efforts to schedule play dates (and gross motor practice) for Marcus at local neighborhood or McDonald's playgrounds. His interactions still tended to be parallel play alongside other children, instead of the more interactive play I'd see in his peers, but he enjoyed the company of other children nonetheless. Videos featuring the gentle world of the puppy, Spot, started to broaden his social world, coupled with the *Kidsong* video series—again wonderful, predictable videos portraying children singing and acting in related activities and inviting him to join in.

Marcus struggled with transitions, such as arrival to daycare, and moving from activity to activity during the day. He needed a great deal of "pre-setting," in which we'd give him advance notice of approaching transition times. He often needed one-on-one, physical guidance to get him started on the next activity. When I dropped him off at preschool, he'd usually just circle the room unless someone helped him settle into an activity. He was interested in the playground equipment, but needed a lot of physical assistance to navigate it or the tricycles successfully. Motor skills that other kids develop easily had to be explicitly taught him, from pumping his legs to make a swing move, to climbing up and down stairs by alternating legs. It was incredibly time-consuming to schedule and coordinate his therapies, and to attend as many sessions myself as possible so that I could carry over the therapy techniques into the rest of his day. But it was also clearly worth the effort. Wherever we were, I would watch Marcus to determine where his interests lay, and then work with teachers and therapists to help him obtain the skills to be more successful at those activities. I let him go wherever he wanted on the playgrounds we visited, but hovered nearby to give the extra hand needed to keep him safe as his physical world broadened.

By the time Marcus was school-aged, his physical self-help skills were still limited by his body control. He continued to be very messy and disorganized. He was extremely susceptible to over-stimulation, and the noisy bustle of typical publicly funded school classrooms provided no shortage of that! The need to follow a classroom schedule with its many transitions was extremely taxing, especially for a child whose physical skills made him slow to complete tasks, but whose Asperger's makes it imperative for him to seek closure before beginning another activity. Although Marcus had near-normal visual acuity, he had almost no functional peripheral vision. Navigating the halls meant frequent bumps into walls and other people. We began vision therapy with a private practitioner, to help him develop his visual range and eye–body coordination skills. Negotiating stairs, or climbing on and off the bus, were major challenges to Marcus, again due to his limited awareness of his body in space, poor balance, difficulty coordinating his feet, and poor ability to monitor and assess his own behavior for safety. Watching Marcus move often felt more like watching an accident waiting to happen. Kindergarten routines such as snack time, and packing up and unpacking for the day posed tremendous organizational obstacles. Even holding his body erect during group time sitting on the carpet was tiring for him. Therapies continued to focus on improving speech articulation, and developing gross motor and fine motor skills. I stayed in close contact with therapists and teachers. My world was one of monitoring what was going on, trying to anticipate what would be expected of him, and helping him rehearse in a safe, unpressured environment so he could better perform on his own when the time came. I coached him to develop skills I saw he needed to participate with his peers or to follow his apparent interests, such as riding a bike or playing Tee Ball. I was constantly monitoring and analyzing, and often would ask therapists for guidance or for direct intervention when I saw basic skills that seemed to cause him problems.

Marcus's Asperger's meant that his pretend play skills were quite limited. He didn't seem to have internalized schemas of everyday settings and events, and so he couldn't "play fireman" or "pretend to be a cowboy." For him, that sort of play meant just physically manipulating the supporting props, rather than playing a character or role, or even making the verbal sound effects that other children would make. He couldn't engage in a pretend dialogue, or create an impromptu script to act out in play with another child. When asked to tell a story, he had no concept of producing a beginning, middle, and end, and this lack hampered him during writing assignments at school. He also had a very limited sense of his own emotions. Although he *felt* things intensely, he didn't have names for what he felt. Helping Marcus learn to interpret his own internal, emotional landscape, was a first step towards helping him develop the ability to infer and interpret the emotions of others. We started intense play therapy with an independent psychologist. Her job was to help him develop these emotional and social dimensions, and to help him develop his sense of self and his sense of others. (See Shub and DeWeerd 2006, *Ready to Learn*, for a companion approach for use in the classroom.) From simple identification of the body language associated with various emotions, the play therapist helped us move to role-playing, in which Marcus would act out, from different perspectives, the social scenarios that had floored him during the week. The play therapist also helped Marcus develop a sense of the structure of stories, and the give-and-take form of conversations. Speech therapy expanded into language therapy, in which we worked to help Marcus to develop conversational skills, and to understand figurative language, jokes, and the subtle meanings and pragmatic undertones of speech. I started watching movies with him, providing a running commentary on what was going on because Marcus didn't seem to understand how plots connected the scenes together. I also started reading and explaining the comics to him, so he could "get" the humor. We started collecting joke books and other funny books—yes, I read the entire *Captain Underpants* series aloud until he could manage them on his own. It was a wonderful victory for us when Marcus starting "getting into trouble" conversing with peers and clowning around in the classroom, because it meant that he had become aware of the social world, and was trying out different roles to be a part of it. We were fortunate to have supportive teachers who understood and supported Marcus in these early attempts at reaching out to his peers.

Parenting meant working hard to do his therapies with Marcus, trying to provide motivation, rewards, and encouragement, and always trying to make all this work as fun as possible. I think I did a good job with that. He almost never complained about the therapies he needed to do. This was the time when I myself was most overwhelmed as a parent by his needs. He had so many needs! Even with the help of all his therapists, it was hard to feel like his needs were being adequately met, and we still had his younger brother to tend, to help flourish, and to guide through his own set of therapies.

By age nine, homework became our albatross. Marcus is very bright, but needs a lot of support during homework time. Many of his needs during elementary school were exemplified by our experience at home-work time. Distractibility was only part of the problem. I'm not sure that he was actually more distractible than any other nine-year-old. The bigger problem was that whenever he encountered the least difficulty, it seemed to derail him. He didn't have a large repertoire of problem-approach strate-gies. He tended to go totally passive when he encountered a problem without someone there to help him, and he didn't seek help on his own. Providing support for Marcus at age nine meant I had to make extreme efforts to be nearby to notice when he was starting to flounder, and to help him over those little humps before he got derailed.

The types of academic tasks that were difficult for Marcus in third and fourth grade included even fairly mechanical tasks such as copying sen-tences/problems from the board or from his textbook. When writing is difficult and fatiguing for you, you can imagine what an ordeal copying becomes. The problem avalanched when he had to read or interpret what he'd just written. His writing was hard to read, and poorly organized per-ceptually on the paper, yet his sensory integration problems meant that he could not easily interpret the resulting visual confusion. The problem was worse for mathematics, which often requires precision in symbol forma-tion and alignment. Inadequate instructions floored him, especially when the assignment was not a massed repetition of a familiar task. "Mixed review" assignments, because they shift back and forth between several skills with little warning, were quite a challenge for him. As worksheets and textbooks provided more and more information on a single page, the chances of getting visually lost in the page-maze increased. He'd often leave out entire rows of problems—not out of laziness, or even out of fatigue (which would have been quite understandable), but because the problems got lost in the visual confusion that he experienced. When it was homework time, I always had to be in the same room as Marcus, and it was important that I check over his shoulder often, to ensure that he under-stood what each assignment was asking him to do. Homework took him long enough to complete, and I certainly didn't want him to have to complete it *twice* because he set off on a wrong path early on.

Despite the perceptual difficulties encountered in math assignments, Marcus's intuitive math reasoning abilities carried him through. In the primary grades, this caused a problem for a few years, when his teachers began stressing following a particular procedure for solving a problem. In his desire to please, Marcus "turned off" his own intuitive math style, with an actual accompanying drop in mathematics understanding! It was several years before he began using his more natural math sense regularly again, melding it with the requested solution process. His incredible visual memory continues to serve him well in spelling, but other parts of the language arts continued to cause difficulty. Rebus problems (for example, finding the word that sounds like a picture), word associations, and identifying multiple meanings for words—the typical enrichment activities used to focus the elementary school child on their spelling words—were very difficult tasks for him. Writing on demand about an assigned topic was very stressful, because he had trouble generating ideas and developing them into a coherent whole. His therapists suggested we ask his teachers to announce the next day's theme ahead of time. This way, he could brainstorm a network of basic ideas (sometimes with a little prompting) when the time pressure was not on him. He could then work to flesh out that initial structure in class. Concept maps and thematic webs helped him tremendously. (I've since encountered *Inspiration* software that does something similar.) He gradually became more and more independent and adept at developing a story or an essay on his own. However, the frustration and fatigue from the physical act of writing, started to affect his composition assignments. We noticed that he would deliberately write as few, brief sentences as possible to minimize his fatigue, instead of working to develop his ideas into a more complete presentation. I would sometimes help by scribing his stories for him at home. The school was ready to reduce the number of sentences required for his assignments. I felt, however, that he needed the experience of developing an idea across a full paragraph, and so I requested that we look for a different solution. Eventually we trained him to use an AlphaSmart™, which is a very basic, portable word-processor that allowed him to keyboard his longer assignments. Occupational therapy helped him learn keyboarding skills ahead of his peers. Keyboarding was an obvious help for him, and it was easy to convince his teachers to allow this option once we showed them the improvement in the richness of written products produced by this method.

Leisure time and free choice activities—always a delight for most of us—can be stressful for the child with Asperger's Syndrome, and Marcus was no exception. Marcus liked to play, but he was very uncomfortable with the lack of structure in his free time. At one time, I made a list for him of the various activities that I knew he enjoyed, so he could choose something from this menu for his playtime. I still will go through similar lists to help him identify his preferences before his friends visit, or when we have a longer than normal period of unstructured time ahead of us. As he says, coming up with ideas of things to do is hard for him sometimes. Without such structure, he becomes passive and shuts down, or cycles aimlessly for long periods of time. By third grade (usually ages eight—nine), he and his friends had developed a repertoire of usual playground activities for recess time at school. The stress of recess lessened for him because he could usually find a group who would welcome him into an activity he enjoyed.

Beginning around third grade, we added the ongoing project of interpreting for him playground and other social incidents with his friends. You hear a lot about facilitated language with children on the autism spectrum. I guess in our case, I worked a lot on "facilitated friendship." Marcus gradually moved beyond his fascination with trains, and developed strong and enduring interests in such popular fads as Pokemon™, and later Yu-Gi-Oh!™ Magic—The Gathering™, BeyBlades™, and of course video games. Give a boy a Game Boy™ and he is an instant magnet for other children, wherever he goes. At school, Marcus found a circle of boys who shared his strong interests, and we turned our home into a frequent gathering place to pursue those interests. We developed a tradition called Friend Friday, in which each of my boys selects a friend, or sometimes two, to come home with us on Fridays and play until suppertime. A steady group of four or five friends developed for each of my two children, and these boys still continue to rotate through our home on Friend Fridays. Marcus and these core friends gravitate towards one another in the playground, in the lunchroom, and at other unstructured social times at school. On Friend Fridays, I bake favorite snacks, eavesdrop on what is going on, and surreptitiously intervene or make suggestions if Marcus seems socially stuck. Although children with Asperger's have marked social deficits, often so do other children. These deficits become more pronounced as they move into a social world less under direct adult supervision, and as they are encouraged by adults to attempt more of their own social problem-solving. Bossiness, tearfulness, bullying, disappointment, competitiveness—there are a lot of emotional challenges elementary school children face every day, in themselves and from their peers. I find that many children can benefit from a little adult assistance in developing appropriate ways of keeping their emotional equilibrium. As Marcus became a skilled reader, I started exposing him to books and stories highlighting children's social situations and problems, and we began watching sitcoms and other television shows together. When our local community center offered a series of group counseling sessions on assertiveness training, and on building positive self-images, I enrolled both my sons. We continued to work to develop physical skills in a variety of team sports, so that Marcus could better hold his own in the playground. PT helped with ball throwing, strength, motor planning, and balance while kicking a soccer ball Surprisingly, he became a child who could cross back and forth between the more athletic social group, and the more cerebral one, and be accepted by either.

By mid-elementary school, the physical challenges of getting dressed were no longer difficult for him, and I could finally buy him clothes with zippers, buttons, and belts without these posing major impediments. He'd improved on putting one toy away before starting to play with another. He'd learned to put his eyeglasses down in the same place all the time. He'd done an excellent job assuming good care of his pet guinea pig, and helping with the family dog. However, the organizational challenges of brushing teeth, replacing the toothpaste cap, rinsing the sink, putting dirty clothes in hamper, and closing drawers after opening them—totally overwhelmed him. Eating continued to be an ordeal. His sensory difficulties meant he has extreme aversions to a number of different textured foods. He would gag when pushed to eat a food outside of his comfort zone, and this gagging was reflexive and not manipulation on his part. At age nine, he was such a messy eater that his teachers asked if anything could be done to teach him to keep his snack area clean. He still needed constant cuing to use silverware, to position his chair and body directly in front of his plate instead of somewhere down the table, to use his napkin instead of his sleeve or his shirtfront, and to monitor his eating area for tidiness during his meal. I consulted with OT to help him with some of these problems, such as developing a more appropriate utensil grip or assisting with a better table posture. Our play therapist helped him by role-playing good and bad table manners, and by having him critique her meal performance as well.

In fifth and sixth grades (when Marcus was ten and eleven), I started noticing more of Marcus's personality and creativity emerging. He decided to run for classroom treasurer, logically strategizing that all the popular kids were going for the more prestigious, presidential position. He independently developed his own campaign, and won the election! When the sixth grade produced *The Legend of Sleepy Hollow*, Marcus (again independently) chose to audition for the role of pirate. Then later, he developed for himself the body language and voice intonations he would use to deliver his lines. In characteristic autism spectrum fashion, he sometimes needs suggestions on ways to mesh his own performance with the movements and words of others—whether it is in the context of a band ensemble piece, or the smooth flow of dialogue in a scene in a play—but I am incredibly impressed with his ability to come up with ideas that would elaborate or enrich a production. By sixth grade, he even celebrated occasional sport successes. Although he tired easily on the soccer field, his dogged determination resulted in his making several important soccer goals.

When Marcus was eleven and in sixth grade, the school discontinued his therapies. He still maintained the services of a shared aide to help him with classroom organization, which continued to pose significant difficulty for him. A resource room teacher acted as a consultant to his classroom teacher, to help identify pockets of difficulty and suggest modifications to support him in classroom participation. He needed help keeping his desk clutter manageable. He needed extensive cuing on managing the flood of paperwork entailed in his classroom assignments. I confess that by the end of sixth grade, we still had not developed a sustainable method of efficient portfolio organization, so that he could quickly locate needed classroom materials or his completed assignment, but miraculously he always managed eventually to find and hand in his work. Color-coding systems helped, but he tends to move slower than other children and will fall back onto stuffing papers indiscriminately when he becomes anxious that he will be late for class.

By sixth grade, Marcus had developed the ability to work independently, pacing himself efficiently through the list of nightly assignments written in his homework planner. This was a welcome development, because the homework load had become significant by this time (easily two hours most nights). He needed help pacing himself through long-term assignments, but I do not think he was any different from his classmates in this regard. He usually remembered on his own to practice his musical instrument, and was able to evaluate his own progress learning a particular piece of music.

Most of my interventions for Marcus between the ages of 11 and 13 consisted of organizational coaching, helping him with higher-order thinking skills, social debriefing, helping him manage his energy, and guarding him from emotional and sensory overload. In sixth grade, we realized that the noise and confusion of the school bus had become an intense stressor for him, and so I began driving Marcus to and from school. We also began using medications in fifth grade to help him manage his attentional needs and to help lessen his fatigue. Marcus has always tended to shut down or become irritable or sensitive when overwhelmed. Around this time, I began monitoring his emotional status more carefully, because Marcus began to show signs of anxiety, peeling his fingernails and the pads of his fingers until they bled. He would sometimes hyperventilate at night, worrying about possible social situations that might arise with one of his peers (a friend, actually), the next day. His sensitivity to food textures still caused problems at home, but by grade six he had broadened his repertoire of acceptable foods so that his food pickiness in public was not significantly more pronounced than that of his peers.

Although Marcus was able to complete his homework independently, I found I still needed to read over his assignments, to check for trouble spots in his understanding. Learning how to develop his answers completely for science labs, or to show his work in the way the math teacher needed, probably posed his biggest academic challenges. Here is where my training in cognitive development and education came in very handy, but an alternative solution is to request resource room or academic skills help for your child. The tutoring I did with my boys usually had to do with meta-cognitive tasks—those tasks involving project planning and evaluating results. Because taking the perspective of teachers is difficult, I worked with Marcus to develop the skill of evaluating his larger assignments against grading rubrics provided when assignments are given. He became quite skilled at accurately rating his work against a list of explicit criteria. In sixth grade, because so many of the projects or problem sets involved multiple steps, we added the routine of re-reading the entire problem after finishing his answer, and checking to make sure he had completed all the parts mentioned at any point in the assignment's description. The reality of schools, we've discovered, is that sometimes important information is given in what we would call the "prologue" or introduction to an assignment, and is not in the main body of the instructions. Going over the entire assignment information again, after Marcus thinks he has completed the assignment, has helped with the quality and completeness of his work.

I've also worked with Marcus a great deal to develop his writing. I coached him to complete multiple drafts of an assignment, spreading his work across several days so that he would have time to rework and develop his ideas. I taught him to proof his assignments by reading them out loud—he has a very good ear for identifying when a sentence doesn't sound right, and he takes pride in his creative expressions. The resulting pieces often carry his own trademark twist—he is an interesting writer. With Marcus, a little bit of intervention has always gone a long way, and it is very satisfying to watch him gradually start to generalize the strategies to new assignments. Sometimes Marcus and I discuss the wording of assignment questions. For example, what does it mean when an essay question asks him to "discuss the impact of writing on the development of civilization." How much discussion is enough? One teacher had concluded from reading Marcus's test essays, that Marcus "was not cut out to be much of a writer." In response, I asked the teacher to provide us with copies of a few perfect score answers to the same questions, and I went over those model answers with Marcus. "Oh, I can do that," Marcus said. And he has, ever since.

By sixth grade, Marcus had become much more aware of his social world. He had an active circle of friends, and he showed the ability to reflect on his own personality traits and values, as well as those of his friends. It became easier to get him to talk to me about what was going on at school, and we got into a habit of debriefing his social day, discussing his observations and interpretations. By sixth grade, he had developed a large enough social problem-solving repertoire that I seldom needed to propose solutions. Rather, my role switched to serving as a sounding board for him as he voiced his own observations and frustrations. His sixth grade teacher told me that he had a reputation as a fair and helpful mediator with his peers, and he is an absolutely wonderful social interpreter for his brother. We talk about the plots of books he reads, and the social situations that come up in the movies and television shows he sees. Marcus has become adept at interpreting complex comic strips, and spent months of allowance acquiring the complete *Garfield* and the more historical *Tintin* graphic novel series. He still needed occasional help figuring out cause/effect or emotional nuances, but he has developed a fairly sophisticated schema representing the social world. By the end of sixth grade, he began expressing an interest in more abstract concepts, such as alternative universes, or the concept of social justice.

Last year, Marcus started the new challenges of junior high school (secondary school), at the same time that we began to lessen some of his more obvious educational supports. We enrolled Marcus in advanced math and science classes. Although these are faster paced and more challenging, we believed they would be welcome challenges for our son, who is often bored with the slower, repetitive nature of regular classrooms. Frankly, the types of things that cause him difficulty are the same in regular classes as in advanced, and so we decided that we would just have to learn how to deal with them in the newer environment. Unfortunately, the school into which he transitioned is not set up to provide academic supports in the advanced classes, and because we were not willing to sacrifice band practice or the exploratory courses his peers regularly take, his supportive network is not as strong as I would like. My role as Marcus enters secondary school, is becoming one of helping the school to develop a model for students who are academically advanced while also dealing with a disability (also called "twice exceptional" students). Because seventh grade (usually ages twelve—thirteen) was Marcus's first year since kindergarten without the assistance of a shared aide, I increased the amount of academic supervision I provided Marcus. Adjusting to advanced math classes, when many of the other children had previous advanced math preparation, posed our biggest academic challenge in seventh grade. He had particular difficulty learning how to show his work in the manner that the math teacher wanted. Some units were easy for Marcus; others were more difficult. For example, he had problems computing the areas of various geometric figures because he would have trouble visually deciphering the diagrams, or he would get confused as to which formula to apply. Marcus has a wonderful visual memory for how to spell words. His strong memory also serves him well when learning facts from social studies and science texts. He reads such texts once, and then seem to be able to visually recall what he read. On the other hand, he tends to voluntarily read novels at least twice, because I think it is more difficult for him to draw connections and determine the relative importance of various events.

Cumulative mid-term and final exams were another new experience, and Marcus impressed me with his independent drive. He has incredible perseverance and determination, and a very strong work ethic. He may eventually melt into exhausted tears, but he almost never complains, even during difficult times when several weeks go by with nightly four-hour homework sessions. Our hard work paid off. By the last quarter of seventh grade, Marcus had raised his grades to all As, and was listed on the high honor roll. We decided to add an advanced placement in English for eighth grade, although, like many parents of children in advanced secondary school classes, I am increasingly torn between the positives of his intellectual engagement, and the negatives of the pressure he feels from his workload. He crashed again at the start of eighth grade, and after six weeks is still adjusting to the new teachers and expectations. We remain optimistic about the eventual outcome, remembering where he ended up by the end of last year after similar struggles.

Organization became an increasingly significant problem with the addition of junior high school scheduling and changing teachers and classes. Although Marcus was now able to tolerate the noise of the school bus, I picked him up in the afternoon for the first seven weeks of seventh grade, so I could check that he had recorded and pulled together everything he needed for homework for each of his classes. Planning his time was another area in which Marcus needed a great deal of help. Juggling the different assignments, pacing himself through self-study packets and long-range assignments, and filing his work into appropriate folders, continues to require assistance from me throughout the school year. The other, unexpected difficulty is a social one, emanating from his relationship with his teachers. Junior high school gives effort grades. Marcus's body language and poor organizational skills make it difficult to judge his attentiveness and effort. The advanced classes in which he is enrolled, have high expectations for the amount of "extra effort" they consider normal. Teachers will announce they are holding after-school study sessions, but Marcus does not realize the importance of attending them, both for checking his understanding and listening to the teachers highlight the sorts of information they deem most important. Yet he will be frustrated when the wording of tests floors him. Those unwritten social and academic expectations continue to ambush him, but we are working on identifying and coming up with proactive ways of dealing with them.

Fatigue and exhaustion is our most recalcitrant problem. The school bus picks Marcus up at 6:50, and school dismisses at 2:20. Sometimes he stays after school for additional help with math or science. He has little free time during the week, as homework and band practice regularly take two or three hours a night, which evidently is typical for students in his classes. For the first six weeks of eighth grade, when Marcus was most struggling with the transition adjusting to his new teachers' expectations, homework was more often taking four to five hours nightly. Marcus feels too pressured and tired to continue his involvement in extracurricular sports, although he misses them. He does seek out new interests, and has joined an after-school German club and an art club when his schedule permits. He participates weekly in an extracurricular Jazz Ensemble, working towards a high school achievement award in music.

Social dynamics are difficult for Marcus in junior high. In seventh grade, the children from Marcus's small elementary school merged with students from five larger elementary schools, presenting a new range of social possibilities and challenges. Because I no longer knew all of the children in his social circles, it was harder for me to help him unravel new social dynamics. His lunchroom encounters with one boy in particular caused him a great deal of anxiety, and we eventually asked the school for help. In a natural extension of the puberty-talks that our school offered in fifth and sixth grade, I started working with him on self-awareness, including helping him identify and work on those idiosyncratic mannerisms that could cause him social difficulty in this larger social world. He still has the support of his Friend Friday buddies, and I was thrilled to watch him develop a new friend on his own by the end of seventh grade, even chancing a sleepover at his new friend's home. School psychological counseling sessions have been added, to help him navigate the more complex peer situations of junior high. Marcus becomes stressed by rough-housing and foul language. Unfortunately, the secondary school environment does not lack for either, especially in the hallways and the lunchroom. He began shying away from summer sports camps for this very reason. Extracurricular field trips still pose a social challenge for him, when he tends to sit alone because he is not comfortable approaching others who are not close friends. Despite Marcus's tight time schedule in eighth grade, we have recently enrolled him in an after-school social skills group that meets bi-weekly at a local disability center, to help him develop his social coping repertoire. Communicating his needs to teachers who expect independence from adolescent students, instead of parental intervention and translation, has posed some significant challenges for us this year. The experience has underscored my realization that I need to work more with Marcus, to help him develop self-advocacy skills.

It is an exciting and scary time for us, as we look to see what new experiences might lay ahead. Looking back over the past 13 years has also been *very* affirming. It makes me appreciative of the developmental challenges we have met, and the wonderful successes we've had. Marcus has developed strengths I'd never imagined. Even better, he is earning respect and appreciation of those characteristics from others. He surprises us with his observations, and his unique sense of humor. Our son is quite a boy! And our Michael is carving out his own, equally individual path.

7

Your Parenting Role, Part I

Promoting Positive Behavior and Reducing Misbehavior in Your Child

I believe that good parenting of any child is always based on understanding that child—his or her personality, capabilities, needs, and drives. Your child's diagnosis provides an essential piece in building that understanding, and it will almost certainly have implications for the way you'll parent your child. In this chapter, when I speak of "parenting," I'm referring to the way I treat my children on a daily basis—those seemingly mundane decisions I make about discipline, activities, homework, and meals. As will become fairly apparent, I believe that the quality of our children's lives is as affected by those small choices that we make daily, as it is by the more programmatic decisions that we make once or twice a year when dealing with doctors, specialists, and school IEP teams.

With special needs or without, I believe that all children want to feel good about themselves. They seek and enjoy approval from those they love. They want to feel valued. They want to be competent and independent. Like all children, those with special needs may need assistance from others in figuring out how to accomplish those things. In particular, their disabilities sometimes complicate their ability to understand the situations in which they find themselves. Their disabilities may also limit the range of competencies available to them to accomplish their goals. My children's developmental differences have especially affected three areas: the degree to which they need assistance acquiring competencies that other children would develop earlier or more easily; the degree to which they need structure to support their behavior; and the degree to which I have to demystify the world for them, translating hidden expectations and conventions into a form my children can recognize and understand. In this chapter, I will illustrate how understanding your child's needs translates into providing structures in your home life that can minimize difficulties and support the development of better behaviors. The following chapter discusses helping children develop other competencies.

Structuring your home life to support your child

One of the main factors contributing to a happy, competent, well-behaved child is the child's home environment. Whether we're talking about success as meaning staying out of trouble or success as accomplishing one's goals, there is much that you, as a parent, can do to set up your home life so that your child's success is more likely. In today's fast-paced society, many of our homes are not "user-friendly" when it comes to children in general, much less when it comes to children with special needs. Even adults are more likely to be successful at attempted tasks if we are well-rested, free from distractions, understand what is expected of us, and are given adequate time and support to accomplish our goals. Yet, as parents, we often inadvertently set our children up for failure by not providing those same supports in the daily living tasks our children attempt at home. We don't make behavioral expectations clear, we allow our children to become over-tired or over-stimulated, and we ask them to perform in distracting circumstances or at a pace that is unnatural to them.

My children have executive processing difficulties, as do many children with autism spectrum disorders, ADD, and other types of learning disabilities. Executive processing includes behavioral planning, impulse control, allocation of attention, and monitoring the quality and consequences of one's actions. Providing external structure is key to helping children with executive processing difficulties to compensate for their weaker internal controls. Structure helps them bring order to their internal disorder. Structure also helps them bridge the gap between their internal worlds and the expectations of the outside world.

An important place to start when looking at the structure of your home is *how time is managed* and how this impacts your child's behavior. Poor time management leads to tired, stressed parents as well as tired, pressured, over-stimulated children. Many of the battles in our home come from my boys being on a different timetable from my own. From my perspective, of course, mine is the right time—the time the rest of the world expects—and theirs is the time of La-La-Land. Mine is the world of clocks ticking inexorably away, marking when school will start, appointments begin, and assignments are due. Their time seems set to some internal clock and is measured by whether or not they feel ready to move on to something else. Clashes between the two time systems mean that pressures mount for all of us.

Both my boys need extra time and cuing to bring their current activity to a close, and then assistance to refocus and start on the next activity. One good way to help my children with time management is to give them time estimates and warnings of how long it will be before they need to stop one activity and move on to the next. I usually provide ten-minute and five-minute warnings, and to help my children internalize these, I stick to them. Without follow-through, our warnings become some sort of verbal ritual that we as parents do for some mysterious reason of our own. I couple these warnings with occasional reminders to the boys about the passage of time. Sometimes I actually set a timer and place it in the boys' sight. This takes some of the reminder responsibility off me, and puts it onto the timer. Use of the timer also helps defuse or deflect any emotional frustration about being rushed, because it makes the "enemy" the timer and not the nagging mom.

Unfortunately, even providing advance warnings of transitions may not be enough for some children. More specific clarification may be needed. For example, I've begun to suspect that "We're leaving in five minutes" means something different to my children than it does to me. To me, the words mean they should be totally ready to walk out the door in five minutes. To them, the words seem to mean, they'll need to stop what they are doing in five minutes, and then start getting ready to go out the door. It's amazing how much extra time those last-minute preparations consume, while I wait at the door, car keys in hand, fuming. I often find I also must clarify what exactly I mean by "Be ready to leave." I have to say explicitly that I mean turn off the video games and lights, be sure you have gone to the bathroom, have your shoes on, and get your coat and whatever you need to take with you for the ride in the car and for our final destination. Furthermore, I still need to cue each of those items individually, unless I tape a detailed list on the front door for the boys to consult. Michael's executive processing deficits mean that even repetitive routines are difficult for him to establish, often requiring more obvious cuing for a long period of time before they become automatic. It is important for me to recognize that this is a problem for Michael in many areas of his life, so I can stay focused on helping him, instead of taking it personally and venting my frustration at him.

My attempts to provide structure are complicated by the fact that Michael processes oral instructions much slower than is typical as well. What this means is that for multi-step directions, he is often still processing the first step when the second step is given, and so he misses or is confused by the rest of the message. Shortening or slowly repeating the instructions helps, but even when I write the steps down for him, he also has trouble organizing his actions to perform the various steps in order. These executive processing problems necessitate a lot of repetition and correction to deal with his resulting confusion, as well as close monitoring to ensure that he has successfully completed all parts of the instructions.

The times I've been more successful, with Michael in particular, are when I've given him a detailed visual schedule showing him specifically what I need him to have accomplished by a set time. Box 7.1 presents a sample "Get Ready for School" schedule that I used in third grade, to help him take responsibility for pacing himself through our morning routine.

Box 7.1 Michael's "Get Ready for School" schedule

7:40	Come downstairs:
	fully dressed
	hair combed
	glasses
7:45	Start eating breakfast
8:10	Stop eating
	Start putting on:
	shoes (or boots)
	coats and gloves
8:20	Get backpack and walk out door to wait for bus
8:27	Bus arrives

The book, *Visual Strategies for Improving Communication* (1995) by Linda Hodgdon, includes many examples of visual aids presented in a wide variety of formats to help children establish and keep to a routine at home or at school. This is one of the hallmarks of parenting a child with special needs: the types of support tools that you usually associate with classrooms have infiltrated our home, sometimes discreetly, sometimes less so. Lists, progress charts, reward stickers, labeled bins—not to mention therapy tools as games—have been a part of our lives for years.

My boys' disabilities mean that they also have other structural, environmental needs. The personality and diagnoses of both my boys mean that they have a strong need for consistency. Autism spectrum disorders are notorious for that. Change is very stressful for these children. They need a lot of extra support dealing with the anxiety they experience in unfamiliar situations, and explicit guidance as to what to expect and how to perform. Also, both boys have a strong need to be able to predict what is coming next, and they do not bounce back easily from disappointments. I often rehearse with them what is going to happen that day. I am careful to check for their understanding, to ensure that their expectations of what is going to happen during the day are realistic and match my own plans. In addition, since Michael's form of Attention Deficit Disorder is primarily of the Inattentive Type, he zones out on me occasionally. I can never assume, even if I say his name before speaking to him, that he is attending to what I am saying. He misses out on a lot of my oral previewing of our upcoming plans. To compensate for this sporadic inattention, I must seek explicit confirmation that he heard me, interspersed with checks on what it was he thought he heard. Or, I sometimes post color-coded sticky notes (blue is for Marcus and green is for Michael) on our pantry door, indicating what special activities or tasks the boys can expect on a given day of the upcoming week.

Mental and physical fatigue often causes difficulties in my home, and structuring the pace of our life to accommodate my children's fatigue levels is important for avoiding problems. Their low muscle tone not only affects the ease and efficiency with which they accomplish motor movements, but it also affects the energy they have to expend for supposedly restful activities, such as just sitting erect. My children's neurological systems are different from typical, and this is an additional source of fatigue for them. My boys spend mental effort blocking out distractions and sensations that are effortlessly handled by typical neurological systems. At times, my boys drown in a whirlpool of social, cognitive, or even sensory confusion. They also spend more effort trying to untangle social situations and implicit expectations that are easily understood by neurotypical individuals. The accumulated expenditure of all this additional energy fatigues my children, sometimes to the point of tears. It is my job as their parent, to *structure* our world for them to make it more manageable, and to help *filter or eliminate stressors* that are too great for their systems to handle. For example, during sixth grade, I found that it helped Marcus in his school day tremendously if I would just take the time to drive him to and from school every day. The loud and unregulated nature of the elementary school bus ride seemed to be attributing to meltdowns at school and home. This was one stressor that was easy enough to circumvent, leaving him more energy for social navigation during the school day. The one advantage of the early start of the junior high, is that the morning bus is much quieter—the kids are too sleepy to make much noise!

My children were born with lower tolerance thresholds, and less well-developed monitoring systems to warn them of impending overload. As their parent, I help teach my boys the self-monitoring and coping skills that they desperately need and will probably not acquire on their own. I will often tell them when it looks to me as though they are getting too tired or over-stimulated, and suggest they take a break or give themselves some quiet time. It is also my job to help them avoid being over-scheduled. As valuable as extracurricular activities are, we have to choose our commitments carefully, with their energy limitations in mind. The scheduling issues become even more intense if one must arrange therapy sessions outside of school hours. All children need time to just chill at home, spend quality time with their families, and play with friends. As I mentioned in Chapter 6, although "down time" is certainly needed for my children, too much unstructured, free time is actually a stressor for my eldest. He needs suggestions for activities, and often co-playing at some point. Otherwise, he tends to retreat to reading or to video games. Nothing wrong with either of those activities in themselves, of course, but when that is all his imagination suggests for him, he needs my assistance to broaden his activities and develop skills and interests in additional areas.

```
┌─────────────────────────────────────────────────────────┐
│              Box 7.2 Summary of structural               │
│        modifications to meet my children's needs         │
└─────────────────────────────────────────────────────────┘
```

Child's Need	Proactive Structural Support
Consistency and predictability	Establishment of routines Schedules (oral or written) Pre-setting; rehearsal of expected events Checks for child's understanding of schedule or planned activities
Difficulty with transitions	Advance warning of transitions Extra time allotted Training on transition expectations Physical presence of a monitoring adult
Slow movement, slow processing, and trouble following multi-step directions	Extra time allotted Shorter instructions Repetition of instructions Written or pictorial lists Checks for understanding Monitoring of compliance
Sensory, physical or mental fatigue	Monitor for over-stimulation Slow down pace of life Build in recovery/down time Select extracurricular activities carefully Teach self-monitoring and allow for self-directed breaks
Misunderstood expectations	Explicitly teach expectations Provide checks for understanding Slow down speech Use of lists Consistency

Box 7.2 summarizes my children's various needs I've discussed so far in this chapter, and the structural modifications we've made in our home life to try to accommodate those needs. Although time management concerns are a major part of these modifications, it is not only in the temporal domain that I find my children need structure and assistance. *Cuing, close*

monitoring, frequent checks for understanding, and frequent feedback are essential to keep my children on track and to help them learn to internalize the external structural supports I provide. My greater involvement initially, leads to greater independence later, and is well worth the thought and effort it requires.

I have found that when my boys are appropriately and adequately supported in their daily lives, things run much more smoothly, both at home and at school. Everyone is happier, and there are fewer behavioral issues to resolve. In fact, I see the issue of providing appropriate supports to my child as actually one of taking a proactive, preventative approach to discipline and to behavior management. The structural supports—or lack thereof—in your home life are likely to be directly related to the level of conflict due to behavioral issues in your home. When your child misbehaves, she or he is often responding to something in his or her environment, and good environmental supports encourage positive behaviors.

Understanding misbehavior

Most children want to think of themselves as "good," and they want approval from adults and from their peers. I base most of my interactions with children on the assumption that children really would rather be good, if given an environment that makes sense to them. In other words, children behave the way they do for a reason, and that reason usually is *not* that they want to get into trouble. Children *behave*; it is just when the behavior does not match what we need or want them to do, that we label their behavior as *misbehavior*. I believe that if you can identify the reason behind a particular (mis)behavior, then you are more likely to address the misbehavior effectively by directly addressing its cause. Understanding will help you see misbehavior as a puzzle to be solved, instead of a battle of wills. Even those instances when it appears that a child is being deliberately difficult or hurtful, often have another side to them from the child's perspective. As you learn to read the situations and identify the likely causes of particular misbehaviors, you'll gain the ability to prevent many of them. Then everyone will benefit from the smoother, happier home life that can result from this more proactive approach to (mis)behavior.

One of the first things you can do to address misbehavior is to look for patterns in its occurrence. My own children actually seldom outright "misbehave," but rather they are more likely to melt down or shut down. Close observation of my boys over time showed me that those times when they most often had difficulty were actually fairly predictable. Their trigger points are listed in Box 7.3. Recognizing that these are the most usual precipitating factors for conflict in our home is a powerful tool for me as a parent. It allows me the opportunity to try to avoid them through putting better home structures into place. Although there is not a direct one-to-one relationship between the triggers and my children's needs presented earlier (Box 7.2), it is clear that not meeting the needs makes my children more vulnerable. By acknowledging the patterns, I can draw on past experience to determine what the best solution is.

Box 7.3 Predictable triggers to behavioral issues in my boys

- Over-excitement
- Fatigue
- Sensory overload
- Unfamiliar situations
- Tight schedules; time deadlines
- Transitions between activities
- Unannounced errands or schedule changes
- Frustration with task or with others
- Sense of injustice or sense that someone meant to hurt them

---

I also have certain trigger points, when I tend to expect more from my boys than they are able to provide, or when my tolerance levels are lower than usual. For example, Box 7.4 lists those times or situations when the children are most likely to push my own buttons, leading to negative responses such as snapping or "yelling" on my part. You might find it useful to make a list of triggers to your children's emotional meltdowns, as well as the patterns you see in your own vulnerable times. Again, awareness can lead to a proactive approach to discipline, by helping you learn to structure your home life better, to prevent behavioral issues from arising. For example, although I am trying to work with my children on time management, it is important for me to remember when setting my own schedule, that my children's slow pacing and disorganization are as inevitable as traffic and stoplights. I must take extra care to accommodate that pace into my own schedule and my own organization. Understanding and awareness can also help you adjust your expectations and filter your emotional reactions.

Box 7.4 My own trigger points for when I may be least tolerant of my children's behavior

Certain times of day:
- early mornings
- when we are getting ready to leave for school, church, or an appointment
- bedtime (when I am ready to be "off-duty" for the night).

My behaviors most likely to cause a problem:
- trying to fit in too much
- fatigue, stress, or illness.

Children's behaviors most likely to push my buttons:
- ignoring my instructions so that I need to repeat myself or "puppet" their actions
- passivity in regard to problem-solving
- prolonged focus on disappointments, injuries, or perceived slights.

When I know that we will be dealing with factors that tend to lead to behavioral issues, I take extra steps to redirect that potentially negative energy into a positive channel. For example, highly competitive board games or video games sometimes over-stimulate my children, so that they are wilder, argumentative, defensive, or prone to tears. Similarly, there are certain of their friends whose play styles differ enough from my own children's style that inappropriate behavior is more likely to occur when these children are together. I don't eliminate either the games or the friends, but I have learned to oversee play a little more carefully in such instances, to monitor the arousal issues. I may shorten the activity, or intervene with suggestions to change the competitive nature of the activity into teamwork, or try to channel the energetic play into more acceptable avenues. For instance, when my children developed a fascination with swords and weapon play, at first I used paper towel rolls or aluminum foil-covered cardboard to fashion "safe" swords for them. When that was no longer sufficient, I finally gave in and created a "weapons bucket" in my home, but I also created targets to tape onto the walls, doors, or windows. Some might be bull's-eyes, some might be life-sized drawings of knights, and some might be cardboard block towers. I coupled this with providing walkie-talkies, canvas tents, costumes, spy gear, and laser-tag guns and vests. My point was to take the seemingly unavoidable fascination with fighting, and work with it to show them how they could play safely and cooperatively with it. There are explicit rules for "play fighting" in my house, and the most significant one is to "listen to each other's words." If someone calls a "time-out," you must give it. If someone complains that they feel ganged up on, you must come up with a solution. When energetic battles are in progress, I make sure that the door to the basement is open, so that I can overhear whether the children are successfully negotiating their play. I want my children to be practicing good behavior, and so monitoring them, giving them feedback, and guiding them over snags can help them learn to do this. Proactive supports make it much less likely that misbehavior will occur, or when it does, it can often be quickly redirected, rather than merely punished after the fact.

When children's behavior falls short: reacting to (mis)behavior

When I look at misbehavior, I start with certain assumptions about the child—any child, not just one who may have a developmental disability. One of my first assumptions is that *inappropriate and inadequate behavior is due to inaccurate or incomplete understanding of what behavior is expected.*

Making the effort to determine how the child is reading a situation helps me see what corrective action we need to take to ensure that it doesn't happen again. Starting with the child's understanding and building from there is a valuable approach for correcting misperceptions. "Oh, I didn't know that…" is a frequent response from my children, and one that I accept as descriptive, signaling that explaining more fully should resolve the problem behavior. If the limits are clear and understood by the child, then I find that I have to intervene less later because I am offering the child the opportunity to manage himself. Teaching the limits and expectations takes some extra time, but it is worth it.

My second assumption about my children's misbehavior is that *if a child knows what appropriate behavior would look like and misbehaves anyway, then I need to look to see what is getting in the way of the child being good.* Usually it is because the child is so caught up with their current emotions, that those feelings obscure their view of anything else. Although my children could produce the appropriate behavior if they were calm, they are acting from a state of non-calm. In this case, I'm especially thinking of misbehavior due to the child's lashing out from anger, frustration, or fear. Part of helping the child learn to behave well, involves helping the child learn how to channel those negative feelings in an appropriate manner. So again, my response to my children's misbehavior also often has a teaching component to it. We discuss what is going on. When I say, "discuss," I truly try to elicit their perspective and take seriously their concerns about the way they were feeling. Helping children learn to manage their own emotions is an extremely important tool in creating positive behavior. I think most children could benefit from more supportive work in conflict resolution, anger management, and healthy responses to disappointments and blows to self-esteem. In our household, emotions are taken as a reality. They don't have to dictate behavior, but they do have to be recognized, respected, and dealt with.

Finally, my third assumption is that *once behavioral expectations are clearly set, the child needs support in behaving well.* If she or he does misbehave, I skirt the issue of "blame." Instead, I focus on the simple reality that the positive behavior I need is not happening, and I look for what I can do to help my child practice good behavior in this situation. This support is usually in the form of closer supervision on my part, which helps my children recognize earlier and more clearly where exactly their behavior is getting off track. Close monitoring allows me to reinforce good behavior, and to teach or redirect when I can see the child hitting a snag. It is much easier to rectify misbehavior if you catch it early, when it is just beginning. Then you can be very specific about where the child's behavior is going wrong. Instead of more global rewarding or punishing after the fact, I can use cuing and feedback to guide the child's behavior towards more positive channels. The end result is that more of our time is spent practicing good behavior, and less is spent correcting bad.

These three assumptions about the nature of misbehavior lead me to approach good behavior as a skill to be taught. By "teaching," I don't mean lectures on the rules of good behavior. Although providing a few, summary rules can be useful reminders to our children of how to behave, good conduct is much more involved than can be captured by a list of rules. For me, good behavior is a complex subject matter, just as "mathematics" involves much more than just addition, subtraction, multiplication, and division. To illustrate my point, imagine how difficult it would be to program a robot to behave like a human in the wide range of social situations children encounter every day. Good behavior involves being able to read a situation, having a repertoire of behavior patterns available, and knowing which of many competing reactions would be appropriate and which would not. Good behavior involves dealing effectively with one's emotions, channeling them into appropriate outlets. Good behavior involves social negotiation, inhibiting impulsive responses, and being able to monitor one's impact on others. Teaching good behavior is less amenable to a rule-governed approach, and more amenable to a learn-as-you-go apprenticeship. Yes, we teach by direct instruction, but also by modeling good behavior ourselves, and by giving feedback to our children about the appropriateness and inappropriateness of their behavior as it occurs. If good behavior is a set of skills that need to be learned, then misbehavior is a mis-step or an error that needs correction and redirection. Bad behavior is a problem to solve. So, how do you take a problem-solving approach to bad behavior? Box 7.5 outlines the basic steps.

Box 7.5 A four-step model for dealing with your child's misbehavior

Step 1   Intervene to stop the current episode of misbehavior.

Step 2   Redirect the child towards positive behavior.

Step 3   Determine what, if any, consequences are needed to help the child learn good behavior.

Step 4   Parent reflection: is a pattern developing? Do I need to be doing anything differently to help my child behave well?

Interrupt the misbehavior

When misbehavior occurs, the first step the parent should take is to stop it. You must interrupt the child's current behavioral path, preferably as soon as it starts. *Later*, you can use that pause in action to try to redirect the child towards more positive or appropriate behavior. But at this point, you are not concerned with trying to ensure that the behavior doesn't happen again. Rather, we are only dealing with the fact that the child is starting to spin out of control, and we must stop the momentum of that spiral and get the child back onto neutral ground. A warning glance or verbal reprimand is often sufficient. When it is not, an enforced time-out might be useful. Your purpose at this time is to help support the child's ability to reclaim control of him or herself. At the same time, you are providing valuable feedback to your child. Your child obviously isn't recognizing that his or her behavior is inappropriate. By calling a halt to it, you point this fact out and give your child a chance to make a different behavioral choice.

Sometimes parents confuse this first step of *interrupting* the misbehavior with *punishing* the misbehavior. When the child is in the middle of a misbehaving spiral is not a good time to choose a punitive reaction to the child's misbehavior. A time-out removes both child and parent from a potentially escalating situation, ensuring safety, while allowing everyone a chance to cool off and reflect on the situation. You may be surprised by the degree to which the child can regain self-control on their own, once she or he is removed from whatever situation provoked or allowed the misbe-havior to occur.

Sometimes, especially with younger children, you may find that you'll actually have to sit with the child to enforce the time-out. Calming children during a meltdown is especially difficult when they have an autism spectrum disorder, because they often do not understand the emotions they feel, and they do not know how to soothe themselves. Sometimes to assist the child in achieving calm, you will need to add an additional step of empathic response to their emotional turmoil. Never underestimate the power of a cuddle, or the healing that the words, "I'm sorry that you are so upset," can provide to help the child in his or her efforts to regain calm. Acknowledging negative emotions is one of the first steps towards helping the child learn to deal with them—especially for a child who is confused by emotions in general. Once acknowledged, the child may need some help in getting the emotions calmed and under control again. To make this process clear, it is a good idea to tell the child that when he or she is cooled down, you'll be happy to talk with him or her about what happened and why. Remember, this is a cooling off time for *both* of you, so it is not a time for you to be ranting angrily at your child.

Redirect your child

The second step in responding to undesired behavior is to attempt to redirect your child away from what he or she was doing, and towards more positive or appropriate behavior. What, still no punishment yet? No. Remember, your discipline goal is to establish positive behavior, and so *that* needs to be your focus and your priority. Here is where I listen to the child's description of what happened and what led up to it. I might debrief what I saw happen, sometimes offering alternative interpretations. My son, Marcus, sometimes doesn't realize that what he did was inappropriate, and so this simple concrete explanation is often enough. At other times, I will offer alternative reactions that the child could have displayed once the situation started. It is not enough for the child just to understand what was unacceptable about the situation. She or he also needs to know how to avoid it next time, if something similar should arise again. Helping the child consider alternative responses can help them establish their own behavior problem-solving toolbox and help them take steps towards greater self-regulation.

Is a behavioral consequence needed?

Now, only in my third step of responding to undesired behavior, do I consider what consequences, if any, are needed for the situation. I take my cues from my child. Is any further action from me even necessary? Remember, my goal is not to punish. My goal is to teach good behavior! I find that I seldom need to use punishment to reinforce my points. We don't use punishment in regular teaching/learning of skills, do we? Instead, we may re-teach, ask the child to try again, and use consequences that are logical and reinforce the learning we are trying to establish.

When I do have to use specific "punishments," I keep in mind that the goal of discipline is to reshape the child's behavior. The short nature of most immediate interventions gives the child a fairly quick chance at a fresh start. (A "do-over" as kids say in their games!) No one likes to be backed into a corner and trapped there—it's natural to seek a way out. Avoid power plays between your child and yourself. Instead, put the focus on the behavior itself, so that you and your child are a team, working together to help him or her learn good conduct. Give thought to your own responses as well. Moderating the emotional aspects of your reactions is especially important when dealing with an impulsive or out-of-control child. Remember, your disciplinary intent is to give feedback and to teach, not to join in an out-of-control spiral.

Parent reflection

The fourth and final step in a more problem-solving approach to training good behavior is an important, yet often overlooked one. This step is to look for patterns of behavior over time. Individual behavioral incidents will arise when a child tries something new, experiences new situations, or when behavioral expectations are not clear. Both parents and children are operating on a trial-and-error basis when there is no prior experience. We try something, we see what happens, and we adjust future behavior accordingly. But when the same type of situation arises again, what happens? Has the misbehavior been replaced by more appropriate behavior? If not, then it is time for you, the parent, to re-examine what you are doing. You have the advantage of being able to analyze patterns and take charge of change.

I mentioned earlier in this chapter the ways in which I have tried to put numerous supports in place to help my son, Michael, in our ongoing struggle to get him out the door in a timely fashion. The fact that we're still experiencing these struggles, however, is a clear indicator to me that I'm not doing enough. Or rather, it indicates that I'm not doing the *right* thing. The primary thrust of my interventions with Michael, have been to *prevent* Michael from being late. My work, however, seems to be having some inadvertent side-effects. By insisting that he be on time, even if I have to do the work for him, I am inadvertently shielding him from experiencing what happens when he is late. Michael's missing the bus he wants to catch, and having to ride with me instead of with his friends, is one example of a natural consequence. Another example of a natural consequence is facing "being yelled at" by his teacher for coming in late. If for some reason the natural consequence is not an acceptable choice for me, perhaps because I have to be somewhere at a particular time myself and cannot afford the consequences of his dallying, I might design another negative consequence, but one that seems logical for the situation. For example, I might suggest that maybe Michael is moving so slowly because he didn't get enough sleep the night before, and so I will enforce an earlier bedtime for a while until he gets the morning routine more efficiently under control. Or I might note that since it took Michael 90 minutes to get out the door, that is how much time we need to allow by getting up earlier (ouch!), until we can reduce the amount of time required. Or I might tell my children that since their being late cost me extra time off my day, then they owe me compensatory time doing chores or errands to make up for it. I've also tried praising smooth mornings, and giving them a sense of accomplishment when we are successful. If I notice that I'm in a rut, and none of the other interventions are working well with one or the other child, I may finally switch to a straight punitive response, such as no TV or video games tonight. I am most likely to switch to straight punishment when I feel that my children are not making a serious effort to improve, and I want to increase their motivation to break the cycle and to work with me. My children's behavior will tell me if I have found effective reinforcers for training their behavior.

Box 7.6 presents some "dos and don'ts" of effective use of discipline techniques. I take a teaching perspective to behavior management. I only use punishment if it seems absolutely necessary to motivate my child's memory or compliance. In other words, I tend to use punishment only

---

Box 7.6 Guidelines for effective discipline

Dos

- Recognize and reward success!
- Make your expectations clear.
- Consider whether a consequence is even necessary.
- Remember the goal of consequences is to help teach good behavior.
- Be specific about what behavior is being punished.
- Be specific about the nature and duration of any punishment.
- Have a range of consequences available to you, and use less severe ones when possible.
- Listen to your child's perspective, and make a strong effort to be fair and logical.
- Follow through on the consequence you chose.
- Offer a child a fresh start afterwards at good behavior.
- Judge the effectiveness of your punishment by the degree to which it shaped later behavior, not by the signs of remorse.
- Change your response to your child's misbehavior if you see a pattern developing or persisting.

Don'ts

- Don't punish if it isn't necessary.
- Don't punish out of anger.
- Don't back your child into a corner with no way out.
- Don't turn the punishment into a battle of wills.
- Don't increase punishment because of an apparent lack of remorse.
- Don't back down from your responsibility to teach good behavior.

---

for repeat offenses. Overuse of punishment—especially harsh consequences—can lead to learned helplessness, in which the individual gives up on learning the behavior you desire. To avoid this and to keep the individual engaged in trying to learn, it is a good idea to reward success. I don't think parents tend to do this frequently enough: positive or compliant behavior is too often ignored, and parental attention is reserved for negative behaviors. "Catch 'em being good!" is strong educational psychology advice, and it works equally well in the home. If you need to couple positive reinforcement with negative consequences in order to eliminate undesirable behaviors, behavioral psychologists offer guidelines for this as well. Keep punishments brief whenever possible—remember, the goal is to stop the misbehavior and get the child started again on positive behavior. Don't bring out your most severe consequences at the beginning, if a lesser consequence will do the trick. For example, banning TV or video games for only one day may make one's point just as effectively as banning the entertainment for a week. More serious and extended consequences are for those events that seem to be more persistent patterns. Although it is fine to let your child see that his or her behavior made you angry—after all, your emotional reaction is a type of feedback to the child about his or her actions—never punish out of anger. Always wait until you have calmed yourself before deciding upon a behavioral consequence. You have multiple goals when handling your child's misbehavior, and one of those goals is to model for your child how to deal responsibly with negative emotions! That's why a cooling off period to give the adult time to think things through as well is sometimes desirable.

Behavioral psychologists are wonderful for helping us to recognize destructive or ineffective parenting patterns. Some parents may choose to seek professional help in learning how to adjust their parenting styles to improve their children's behavior. Dr. Phil McGraw has a popular television series, called *Dr. Phil*, here in the United States, applying behavioral analysis to parenting. Many parenting guidebooks identify some of the more common ways in which parents inadvertently play into their children's bad behavioral cycles, and offer constructive solutions to help parents break these cycles. Haim Ginott's *Between Parent and Child* (2003) is one that comes readily to mind. I refer you to one of these resources for detailed applications of behavior management techniques to concrete situations.

What I find the behavioral approaches lack, however, is any interest in understanding where the negative behaviors are coming from, or what needs they are fulfilling for the child. Instead, they focus solely on reshaping the problem behavior and redirecting it towards appropriate behavior. In the case of a child with special needs, my own personal belief is that this approach may need modification. Because their disabilities affect the way our children interpret and react to their environments, we as parents need to take those differences into account when we correct our children's misbehavior. General parenting and discipline principles still apply, but an extra step may be needed to apply them appropriately, and the general parenting manuals offer few or no clues as to how. At the end of this chapter I list some books I have found useful for understanding and reframing the misbehavior of children with disabilities. Of these, Dr. Martin Kutscher's book, *Kids in the Syndrome Mix* (2005), in particular, offers a wonderful annotated resource list. *Positive behavior support* is one therapeutic approach that takes seriously the function that misbehavior plays in the lives of children, and that seeks to help children devise more prosocial ways of serving those same ends. I recommend parents of children with recurrent behavioral issues to consult with such a therapist. IDEA states that school behavioral interventions for children with disabilities should begin with a *functional behavioral analysis*, which collects further information on the circumstances surrounding the child's misbehavior.

To give a specific example of how my child's disability affects my discipline techniques, I don't see the point of insisting on direct eye contact when you are trying to discipline a child with Asperger's Syndrome. Actually, I think a lot of people have trouble making eye contact when they've disappointed someone or when confronted with someone else's anger. For a child with Asperger's, eye contact is a severe challenge in itself, even in situations that are not emotionally charged. Requiring my son to look me in the eye while I scold him, stresses him and significantly interferes with his ability to hear the message that I am trying to deliver. By insisting on eye contact, I may *think* I am getting my son's attention, but in reality, I may be so *overloading* his attention that he can't hear what I am trying to say. Similarly, I need to be careful as to how and when I use touch—what I may *intend* to be a calming touch on the shoulder of my child, may be *seen* as an aggressive act.

Furthermore, when my children violate acceptable standards of behavior, I am slow to assume it is a deliberate violation. For example, understanding what behavior is appropriate in a given situation and what behavior is inappropriate is not easy, especially for Marcus whose disability involves difficulty deciphering social situations. I often have to deconstruct situations for him. I have to spell out exactly what he did that "got him in trouble." I tell him the logical reason behind the behavioral rule.

Sometimes, he gets into the conversation and tells me about another child doing the same thing and not getting in trouble. I take these conversations seriously, and instead of the pat answer about not following lemmings off a cliff, I usually help him explore what was different about the friend's behavior or the comparative situation. Often it is a question of timing for him—by the time he gets around to doing the clowning around behavior, the teacher has noticed the group and is sending out "the warning eye," which he doesn't know how to read. Other situations in which my boys become confused are actually questions of what degree of behavior is acceptable. His friend may have taken the silliness to step x; Marcus hypes it up a notch to step $x + 1$. Helping both boys understand which of those invisible lines are okay to cross, when, and how far, is not easy.

I am also extra careful about when and how I touch my children when they are misbehaving. Of course, nowadays in our culture, physical hitting is not acceptable with any child, but I also try to be especially aware of my child's need for physical and psychological space. When Marcus was younger, sitting on the floor with him and wrapping my body around him to swaddle him during time-outs was very calming for him. It gave him the message that I was not rejecting him, even as I tried to help him get himself back under control again. I spent many time-out periods on the floor with him. Now that he is older, touching him is more likely to inflame the situation, especially if he is already revved up and over-stimulated. I have learned that leaving him alone and giving him space to regroup is especially important for him now that he is older.

After disciplining my child, I am aware that his sense of social interactions is very different from mine, and so I have learned *not* to look for obvious signs of contrition from either of my boys. My boys tend to shut down emotionally when they are scolded, and I would be making a big mistake if I were to escalate my own reaction until I broke through their seeming lack of a reaction. I've learned that I need to wait until the opportunity to misbehave repeats itself, and then I will be able to tell from my child's actions whether or not I got my message across earlier. I've also learned to watch both my boys after a disciplinary incident. They tend to be much harder on *themselves* than I was, and both are prone to placing blanket character judgments on themselves. ("I'm a bad person" or "Nothing I do is right!")

Make sure that your feedback provides a clear message to your child, and that the message received is the message you intend. This is especially important if your child has executive processing difficulties, and has trouble analyzing situations, or seeing the connection between actions and consequences. *Our children's behaviors tell us whether or not our behavioral interventions are working.* If not, the task falls back on us to try to analyze why, and then to try something else.

My children are sometimes inept at reading body language and other social cues. This means they also have trouble reading the disapproving or warning glances I send their way. I have to remind myself that they can't always interpret my "evil eye" and so I sometimes have to make a joke or otherwise specifically point out that I am sending non-verbal feedback their way. Michael tunes out the world so often, I insist on some sort of verbal utterance that shows he heard my correction. It may be useful to work out a specific warning signal with your child, at least to alert them that they are being given a warning that their behavior is being inappropriate. Michael has developed his own solution: he'll just outright ask me if what he heard from me was a sigh of boredom or annoyance or fatigue. Although sometimes disconcerting to me, his direct questioning approach is very effective. His expression of concern with my reactions helps defuse my emotions. It also gives me a chance to confirm or correct his reading of the behavioral situation.

Fostering our children's character development, teaching them good values, and helping them learn how to make good behavioral choices independently is one of the most important tasks we have as parents. Your own values will determine what those words mean for you. My goal in this chapter is to offer a perspective and some tools to help shape and nurture your child's behavioral development. Whatever your basic parenting style, I believe that looking at the world from your child's perspective matters. Considering his or her understanding of what behavioral expectations you have and the factors influencing your child's behavior can provide invaluable information to use for helping your child establish the habits of good behavior and self-control. The ultimate test of our success will be the degree to which our children internalize the behavioral standards we try to set for them, and the degree to which they make good behavioral choices when they are no longer under our direct control.

Useful resources
Books about understanding discipline from the perspective of a child with a disability

Greene, Ross (2005) *The Explosive Child: A New Approach for Understanding and Parenting Easily Frustrated, Chronically Inflexible Children.* London: Harper.

Hieneman, Meme, Childs, Karen and Sergay, June (2006) *Parenting with Positive Behavior Support: A Practical Guide to Resolving your Child's Difficult Behavior.* Baltimore, MD: Brookes Publishing Co.

Kutscher, Martin (2005) *Kids in the Syndrome Mix of ADHD, LD, Asperger's, Tourette's, Bipolar, and More! The One Stop Guide for Parents, Teachers, and Other Professionals.* Philadelphia: Jessica Kingsley Publishers.

8

Your Parenting Role, Part II

Increasing Your Child's Competence

In the previous chapter, I discussed structuring your child's environment to try to eliminate common causes of misbehavior. I also presented some general parenting guidelines for behavior management and discipline. Although I highlighted discipline issues because they are such an obvious concern for many parents, it probably became pretty evident to you that my personal philosophy is that behavior management is actually only a small subset of a more important issue. Our biggest focus as parents is to help our children develop those emotional, social, physical, and intellectual competencies that will allow our children to become more independent and better prepared for whatever activities they choose to do.

But isn't that the job of your child's therapists and teachers? Well, yes, that is one role performed by their therapists and teachers. The fact that there are professionals working with my children removes a great burden from me. But, employing such outside help does not release me from my responsibility to roll up my own sleeves. These experts can work with you, modeling for you how to help your child. Watch some of your children's sessions, and consult with the therapists about what you could be doing to extend their efforts to your home setting. But even more important than learning how to extend therapeutic practice, I encourage you to shift your focus: your observations of your child's life can actually guide your child's therapists in their work with your child. You then can use your child's therapies as an avenue to improving your child's life at home and at school. For example, our therapists suggested certain goals based on their knowledge of normal developmental progressions. I suggested other goals based on my awareness of my children's needs. My child and I were spending significant time with experts every week. Why not use them to help us with those things that most challenged us? My choices might be those issues that are major sources of turmoil in our home, difficulties that I see eating up a lot of my time, energy, and attention, or those skills that are frustrating for my child or causing him problems in his daily life. My focus might be on learning how to climb stairs efficiently and safely; putting more food and drink in the stomach and less on the floor; pumping a swing or pedaling a tricycle; or tying shoes, buttoning buttons, snapping snaps, and zipping zippers so he can dress himself. Gains in these salient areas would provide immediate benefits to him, and free me to support him in other areas. Realizing this, I simply spoke up and asked for help.

The benefits of the addition of this parent-driven strand to therapy seem so obvious, you would think that it would be a natural part of the goal-setting process. But it is not. Therapists don't often think to elicit our views, and we don't think to initiate requests for specific assistance or suggest goals on our own. Our culture stresses the importance of listening to the experts and following their advice. We forget about the importance of being involved in a *dialogue* with experts, and asking for their advice on the things that bother us, instead of just the things they want to tell us. It has taken a while for this parent-driven approach to become second nature to me, but now I always make a point of stepping back periodically, to think about my children and what *my* goals for them would be.

Once I started thinking like a therapist (and a fully involved parent) and viewing my child's life with an eye towards how we could help him in the things he does every day, a wide vista of possibilities opened to me. I realized I could use many of his daily activities as ways of enticing him to new challenges. Practicing and working on skills didn't have to wait for therapy time to roll around. I could showcase particular toys and activities around the house, selected with the goal of tempting my son towards practicing a specific skill. Of course, when I placed him in those challenging situations, I also had to accept the responsibility of being around to lend a helping hand as needed. Otherwise, my children would simply back away, towards the familiar and the easy. Kids are often learning the most when they are doing a project with just a little bit of adult help. Then they can work slightly past the level of competence they could manage on their own.

Scaffolding more capable performance

My approach is very much guided by a psychological concept developed by the Russian psychologist, Vygotsky, popularized in the 1960s. Vygotsky's notions first applied to theories of intelligence, but they have tremendous implications for education and developing competencies (Vygotsky 1978). Vygotsky wrote of a child's "zone of proximal development"—a term he used to describe the area that is just slightly beyond what a child can do independently. He used the term to describe the next logical level for a child's skills to progress, as evidenced by the child's ability when supervision and guidance is provided. Vygotsky called this performance-enabling support, "scaffolding," meaning that the adult/assistant is providing the framework on which the child's own activities can build. The adult is not doing the activity for the child, but is providing support with the parts of the activity that are proving difficult for the child, much like training wheels help the child learn the balancing skills necessary to ride a two-wheeler independently. Scaffolding can make the difference between giving up on a task, and having a successful learning experience.

Scaffolding can be a direct helping hand—much like the supporting hand on the bicycle—or it can be indirect, provided in the way you structure the task for the child. When working with a child who is trying to complete a jigsaw puzzle, scaffolding might take the form of gathering together a group of more obviously colored or patterned pieces for a child to fit together. In building a Lego model, scaffolding might involve taking over some of the evaluative functions, checking each building step closely after the child has attempted it. Or it might mean positioning his or her model so that it is easier for the child to compare it to the example shown in the instruction booklet, perhaps guiding their attention by pointing to the particular part they need to examine. An outline, concept map, or checklist would be other examples of scaffolding.

Scaffolding should be used to build more competent behavior. Ideally, it is not a permanent structure or permanent support. Judging the appropriateness of scaffolding involves treading a fine line. Won't he or she learn to depend on the support? Possibly, which is ok if that is what he or she truly needs. But if you begin to suspect your child is not doing things he or she could do for him or herself, then it is no longer supportive scaffolding. Instead, you have located an impediment to his or her development.

Distinguishing the two is very tricky. It isn't always black and white. Sometimes it is a judgment call, and you may find yourself in disagreement with others. Sometimes both sides can be right: my Michael *does* have the ability to monitor the quality of his own performance, or plan ahead and follow through on that plan. However, it costs him a great deal to do so and he cannot sustain the effort indefinitely. Therefore, my providing reminders or doing parts of the task for my son helps him. It is only by closely watching his later attempts, that I can see whether my intervention is helping him develop the skill, or getting in the way. Does he seem to be learning and is he trying to take more responsibility for himself? The trick is in recognizing when and how gradually to fade out those supports, to move the child towards independent performance of the task.

Sometimes you'll need to take a more obviously instructive role in teaching your child. For example, I had to add in a lot of direct instruction to my own boys' attempts to ride their bikes. I had to explain and demonstrate to them about steering, handbrakes, footbrakes, and the importance of keeping moving. My boys were trying to treat their bikes as though they were just larger tricycles—and the training wheels had not disillusioned them of that notion. Our physical therapist helped me to understand what some of these sticking points were. For example, she suggested starting them on a bike that was actually a little too small for them. This size allowed their feet to reach the ground more easily if they needed to stop. She also said that they needed more of a bend to their knees, to get a forceful pedal push, and so the smaller bike helped provide this as well. Before every bike ride, I would remind them how to use the pedal brakes to stop the bike. Without this cue, my boys would take their feet off the pedals and try to stop their bikes by dragging the tops of their shoes on the ground. I broke the bike-riding task down into its component skills of steering, balancing, pedaling, and stopping, and I worked with my boys on each of the skills separately, providing scaffolding by doing for them those things that they weren't ready to do. I also used modeling, direct instruction, cuing, and closely supervised practice to help them advance their skills. Later, when they moved to slightly bigger bikes, I had to add in the concepts of how to use handbrakes and gears.

Training more competent behaviors

I find that I often have to break down complex tasks for my boys, demystify the hidden steps, and help them practice one part of the task at a time. I'm sure you've heard that parents are the child's *first* teachers. Actually, this part of parenting may well be a *lifelong* job, made all the more important if your child's special needs means that she or he learns in a different way from more typical children. My training as a psychologist and educator make it second nature for me to break down tasks into the different skills they involve (like bike riding), or teach and check the sequential steps, one at a time (like building a Lego model). If you watch your children closely, you will be able to see what they understand. Their actions will also give you important clues about what they don't understand, and where they need help.

Box 8.1 lists a step-by-step process for training more competent behavior. In the paragraphs that follow, I will use some examples from my children's homework performance to illustrate how you can use this same approach to helping your child learn. I use this approach for school tasks, but also for sports or physical skills, social difficulties, and behavioral problems as well. Once you have a process for approaching problems, you can always pull others in to help you with the steps. Sometimes a quick question to the teacher or a therapist is enough to do the job.

Homework time often poses a challenge for many parents, and this is all the more true for families with children with special needs. If you find yourself like me, sometimes "bracing yourself" for the homework ordeal, remind yourself that this is an opportunity to peek into your child's mind. Homework offers you the chance to see what your child is getting out of his or her school day, and it offers your child a second chance to learn those things that passed him or her by. Teachers use homework as checks on the individual child's understanding, and as opportunities to practice and reinforce the day's lessons. When it comes to homework time, even children without special needs often find that they didn't understand the day's lesson after all. There may have been a mismatch between the way the teacher presented the information, and the way a particular child needed to have it presented. Or your child may have missed part or all of the instruction because she or he was called from the room or something else happened in the room that drew their attention. Finally, what the teacher says doesn't always match what the child hears. We are always filtering and

---

Box 8.1 Increasing your child's competence

- Describe the problem as specifically as you can.
- Identify the skills the task seems to require.
- Analyze the child's performance to more fully describe where the child is and is not having problems.
- Form a hypothesis about what is causing the error.
- Re-structure the task to avoid the troublesome part if it is not crucial to the task.
- Teach your child one-on-one to address the error specifically:

  Allow plenty of time, so no one feels rushed.

  Break down complex parts into simpler steps, and work on one step at a time.

  Direct your child's attention to the areas causing him or her difficulty.

  Make the implicit, explicit: use direct instruction and modeling to teach.

  Use supervised, guided practice, with immediate and specific feedback about the child's own attempts.

  Put the most practice on those areas most needing remediation.

  Employ appropriate reinforcements and rewards, especially at the beginning of learning, and fade out reinforcers only gradually, as performance improves.

  Do not move to independent practice until practice is perfect.

  Be aware of the power of your presence to support learning.

- Evaluate progress and repeat the process above, as needed.

---

interpreting information, and sometimes we do so inappropriately. The teacher may have erroneously assumed your child possessed some pivotal background knowledge needed to make sense of the instruction. When you throw into this mix the fact that your child has some additional, atypical needs that the teacher might not have taken into account when presenting a particular lesson or assignment, you can see why it is especially important for you to check in with your child at homework time. Your child doesn't have to tell you what they learned today; their homework will show you.

Why didn't your child speak up and say they didn't understand the lesson? One possible reason is that it is difficult to speak up and admit you don't get it—especially if it looks like your peers do, or if it is obvious that the teacher wants to move on to something else. But also, kids aren't always good at recognizing that they don't understand. Haven't you been in situations in which you *thought* you understood what you were supposed to do, but it wasn't until you sat down and tried to do the task yourself, that you realized you were stumped? Teachers try to get a sense of their class's understanding, but that is not the same thing as checking the understanding of each individual child. Unfortunately, when time is tight in a classroom (as it usually is), there isn't always time to have each child try a few problems while the teacher is around, or for the teacher to check that every child is on the right track. So, this is where you step in.

"But," I hear you say, "I'm not an expert in the subject matter!" You often don't have to be. Keep in mind that *good teaching is as much about understanding the child and the child's thought processes, as it is about knowing the subject matter at an expert level.* You have the advantage of being able to work one-on-one with your child. You can see first-hand what seems to be difficult for your child. You can then re-teach the child yourself, engage a tutor, write the teacher an e-mail or note, or direct your child to ask the teacher for help on that particular problem. Your eyes and your diagnostic skills will help the teacher be able to re-teach the material in a way to address your child's problem specifically.

Sometimes you may discover as you work alongside your child, that it is not the skill itself that is causing your child the problem, but the physical way that the task is presented. Marcus is easily visually confused, and for years, he wrote larger than other children. Math worksheets were his particular downfall. There were too many problems on a page and they were too close together. His columns were often not neatly aligned, and it was difficult for him to tell what numbers should or should not be included in calculations for a particular column. When he couldn't fit his work into the space provided, his calculations often flowed into the space reserved for other answers. This visual jumble made re-checking his work almost impossible to do. When I realized that these factors were making his math much more difficult for him than it needed to be, I began recopying his math worksheets onto notebook paper. I wrote the numbers larger and left much more space between problems than the formal math sheet would allow. When columns were the problem, his OT suggested we turn the notebook paper on its side and use the faint blue lines to indicate where each column should go. There is even a special notebook paper available, with slightly raised lines if your child needs tactile clues for a guide. Whenever my child had difficulty with a homework assignment, I looked to see what the purpose of the assignment seemed to be, and I compared that purpose to the aspect of the assignment that was causing my son difficulty. If the difficulty was due to something pretty much irrelevant to the task's purpose, I would bypass it. If it was the point of the task, I would work with my son on strategies to help him master it. For example, maybe the math worksheet is trying to teach the child to recognize the different forms that a type of problem might take, or to practice identifying which operation(s) he or she needs to perform for a particular problem. Having your child highlight or circle the critical words in the instruction or in the problem may be sufficient for directing attention to what the child should be doing. Also, your child's errors are often there for a reason. Sometimes you may be able to note a pattern to them, reflecting flaws in your child's understanding. If you can identify those flaws, you can work to correct your child's knowledge.

Are your child's spelling lists difficult to master? Often teachers and parents address such problems by requiring lots of practice of the words, for example, writing each word five times. But if you partner this repetitive learning strategy with a child whose attention span is limited, whose handwriting is awkward, or who is deluged with more work than he or she has the energy or motivation to manage—such a strategy almost ensures rebellion and failure. Instead of asking an already hard-working child to work *harder*, maybe the better approach is to ask him or her to work *smarter*. I'm a big believer in pre-tests (a test given before a unit of instruction, to identify what a child already knows) and error analysis. Which specific words is your child getting wrong? Those are the ones his or her energy should go into practicing. What was the error? Does your child tend to mispronounce the word or did they miss hearing a sound? What can you do to call attention to the erroneous part of the word and help them remember? Does an exaggerated pronunciation of the word or a little memory sentence help? (Michael came up with: "Don't fry your friend before the end!" to remind himself to include the letter "i" in the word "friend.") Yes, practicing the correct version of the word can help make it permanent, but if you and your child are hitting a wall with that approach, maybe there are ways around it that still accomplish the same goals. The night before a spelling test, I often offer Michael the opportunity to spell his words aloud to me. I offer pencil and paper nearby, in case he feels he needs to write and look at a potential spelling. It is only if he mis-spells a word orally, that I make him practice writing the word four or five times.

My solid understanding of my child leads me to expect certain types of assignments to cause difficulty for him. I know his lack of pragmatic communication skills means he doesn't always know how to seek help. So, I make an effort to be around when he does those more difficult homework assignments, and I provide more frequent homework accuracy checks. I find that when I get lax on these checks, I risk the unpleasant discovery that my child has been doing his homework wrong over the past few days. Because one lesson often builds onto the preceding one, he then begins to flounder in class. The resulting attempts to play catch-up are much more frustrating and difficult for him and for me, than staying on top of the work in the first place.

My point is that, in our family at least, making the effort to be nearby while my children work on their homework may be time-consuming and exhausting, but it is also extremely important. My children live closer to the edge than other children in terms of what taxes them, and my presence not only lends them motivational and emotional support, but my checks and timely interventions can provide the crucial scaffolding that makes all the difference in the world to their learning. If you are unable yourself to help your child with his or her homework difficulties, highlight the difficulty for other people to see, and ask them to help your child.

Modeling competent performance and making the implicit, explicit

Whenever I am trying to help my child develop more competent performance, I find that I must spend a lot of my time working to make the implicit, explicit. Just as watching the fluid motions of an accomplished athlete does not really help a *child* learn how to swing a bat effectively, I find that I often have to break tasks down into their individual parts and train my child on each of those parts separately. Modeling the behavior is not enough. You must also help guide the child's attention to the specific parts of the behavior that are of concern. Then, a very important part of teaching is to let the child try to do it him or herself, and give them feedback on their performance. It helps if your feedback can positively reinforce their attempts by being encouraging and specific. Instead of just listing everything they did wrong, comment on things they did right. That starts them off with success. Your child needs to be able to see that his or her work results in improvement, so take a careful look at their baseline performance and choose a reachable goal for him or her to work on next. You don't want to overwhelm your child by throwing all your criticisms or suggestions at them at once. Instead, you are going to want to get your child moving in a positive direction, by helping them achieve closer and closer approximations of what the final desired behavior is. Use frequent reinforcement—smiles, praise, encouraging remarks. Learning is hard work, and you want to show your child that you admire his or her efforts.

Grades, by themselves, are not very useful feedback to children for teaching better skills. Even when accompanied by summary comments, grades tend to show a final evaluation result. They don't help the child truly understand what better performance would look like. Making that understanding real involves looking at both what is *explicitly* stated, and what is *implicitly* meant by instructions. Our children often need help integrating the two. For example, I may see from a grading rubric that Michael's book report needed to identify its theme. The teacher's comments may even go further, by listing examples of some common themes like courage or loyalty. Sometimes these cues are enough. But if Michael is still unable to apply that cue to a particular assignment, we may need the teacher to actually tell him what the missed theme was. When either of my children seem to be struggling with teacher feedback, I will often ask if the teacher can show us an example of a few papers or answers that received full credit, so they can better understand what performance is expected and modify their future performance accordingly.

The appropriate use of practice

As one teaching adage goes, practice does not make *perfect*, practice makes *permanent*. If you want to ensure that what becomes permanent is correct, you need to monitor children closely until you are sure they are on the right track. Independent practice should only be used when a behavior is well established. You don't turn a child who is still struggling over to independent practice. If you do, then one of two things is likely to happen: either the child will give up, or the child will blithely practice (and so "learn") incorrect movements. Do not assume that just because the teacher gave a lesson, that your child is ready for independent practice on that assignment. Totally independent practice is more appropriate for review. Your child's practice at home may be his or her first practice away from the teacher, or away from his or her classmates. This home practice does not also have to be his first efforts away from all support or feedback about his work.

Marcus, for example, was getting very frustrated in seventh grade when he began learning how to simplify and solve more complex algebraic equations. Copying the problems incorrectly, forgetting a parenthesis, or multiplying by two instead of squaring a quantity obviously resulted in a wrong answer. Wrestling with these low-level difficulties made it even more difficult for him to learn the overall solution process the teacher was trying to have him follow. He was obviously trying so hard, but his answers would still be wrong. So I stepped in. For several weeks, he and I sat together while he completed his algebra assignments. I worked the problems alongside him, so we could compare answers at each step of the solution process. This close support by-passed his frustration because it stopped him from spending time and effort developing wrong answers. It also helped him recognize why going slowly and carefully was so important and would actually save him work in the long run. As our answers began to match more consistently, I was gradually able to pull back my supports. At first, I would still check his work, one problem at a time, before allowing him to move on to the next. When Marcus seemed to be meeting with consistent success, I pulled back further and started only looking over his completed assignment, to spot-check for difficulties. Again, when this seemed to be unnecessary, I backed even further away and now just monitor his regular assignment grades and teacher feedback for signs of difficulty needing my support.

You may be thinking by now that I'm sounding like a hovering mom. I admit that at times I am. Could I become a crutch? Worse, could the support actually undermine my children's independence and confidence in their own abilities? Of course it could, and so I also have the significant responsibility of monitoring for such negative effects. On the other hand, especially when people don't understand my children's disabilities, I've found that they are quick to question my parental concern or intervention. Those "societal checkpoints" on my supports are common. Although I sometimes bristle and get defensive about such challenges, I am also grateful for them. The questions posed are good ones, and ones I want to always be asking. Again, I have two goals. One of these is for my children to be able to participate and enjoy whatever activity they are attempting. My second goal is that they will be able to move towards competent independence in the activity. The intervention is intense when we first begin. But if I am providing scaffolding constructively, then I am helping them build their own knowledge, so that my supportive presence is needed less and less.

Because of his personality, my older son in particular provides great checks for over-protectiveness. In their desire to be competent in their own worlds, children often drive themselves to be independent. The worlds of an 11-year-old or a 13-year-old are very different than the world of a 50-year-old. Their concerns are different from mine. The timing of when they must deal with problems is different from the timing of the support I can provide. As they get older, a greater percentage of their day is spent out of my supervision, and they are left to the guidance of others or to fall back on their own abilities. I don't always need to motivate my children towards taking on more responsibility for themselves. Their world does it for me.

As you have seen, analysis and problem-solving is a mainstay of my life with my children. Of course, I also appreciate, accept, and love my kids unconditionally. I enjoy them and have fun with them. I'm not always trying to improve them! But I have learned how to "look" at them and at what is going on with them. By learning how to be a more careful observer of my children, I deepen my understanding of them. The better I understand my children, the better equipped I will be to meet their needs, and to stand up for them to see that others understand and address their needs as well. Creating a welcoming and supportive home life for my boys is only half my job. I also have to help extend that accommodating environment into the world beyond. My children spend a large portion of their day in school, and so the school becomes a special area of concern. In the next two chapters, I discuss using the special education mechanisms the law provides to help ensure that my children's needs are met.

9

The Special Education Process

Formulating an Individualized Education or Family Services Plan

This chapter discusses how to work with others to create a formal plan detailing what interventions and supports will be provided for your family and child to meet your child's needs and foster his or her growth and development. In the United States, this formal plan is called an *IEP (Individualized Education Plan)* for children aged three to 21 years old, or an *IFSP (Individualized Family Services Plan)*, for children from birth to three years old. The IFSP helps facilitate your infant or toddler's healthy development, and helps you and your family deal better with your child's special needs and foster his or her development. The IEP, on the other hand, protects your school-aged child from unfair expectations, while detailing how your child's right to an equal education will be protected. The IEP spells out the school's commitment as to what it feels an appropriate education that takes into account your child's differences should look like for the coming year. The IEP and the IFSP are actually legally enforceable contracts. They describe the supports, modifications, and interventions that will be provided to your child, the goals that will be addressed, and the performance measures that will indicate whether or not those goals have been met. It is vitally important that you pay close attention to the details of the IEP or IFSP to be sure you agree that it will sufficiently address your child's needs. In this book, I am primarily going to discuss the IEP process, although parent participation and advocacy will look very similar for both.

How is the IEP or the IFSP created?

There is tremendous variation in how individual states handle Early Intervention (EI) and the IFSP. As long as it follows general federal guidelines, each state is allowed to determine eligibility guidelines and to set up its own lead agency and procedures for providing and supervising Early Intervention services. The IFSP is created by family members and service providers together. Its goal is to identify those interventions and supports that will facilitate the particular child's development, and/or that will enhance the family's capacity to facilitate the child's development. The EI services an eligible child could receive in New York State, for example, are presented in Box 9.1. My personal experience is that EI services are much more family-centered and easier to access and use than the preschool and school-aged services. The National Dissemination Center for Children with Disabilities' website (www.nichcy.org) provides useful Early Intervention links specific to your state, including your state's lead agency for Early Intervention programs, and your state's Parent Training and Information Center (PTI). NICHCY also provides links to a wealth of other materials for families and professionals related to Early Intervention services, with each link clearly marked as to the types of resources available at that site. The Answers4Families website (www.answers4families.org/ifspweb) provides an online, self-paced tutorial designed to help professionals and families create better IFSPs. Although this tutorial was designed specifically for families in Nebraska, NICHCY highlights it as a useful basic guide for all. Just keep in mind that some of the particulars may vary in your state.

Box 9.1 Early Intervention and the IFSP, New York State's version

(The following information is from the guide to Early Intervention services in New York State, published by the Department of Health.)

In New York State, infants and toddlers from birth to age three are eligible for Early Intervention services if they have a disability or a developmental delay. A disability is defined as a diagnosed physical or mental condition that often leads to developmental problems (such as

Down Syndrome, autism, cerebral palsy, vision impairment, or hearing impairment). Developmental delay is defined by NY State to mean a significant delay in one or more of the following areas: physical, cognitive, communication, social-emotional, or adaptive (self-help) development. NY State, for example, defines a significant delay as a 12-month delay or a 33 percent delay in one area of development, or a 25 percent delay in each of two areas. Guidelines are also provided if standardized test scores are used to demonstrate delay.

Early Intervention services for eligible families in NY State may include the following:

- assistive technology services and devices
- audiology
- family training, counseling, home visits, and parent support groups
- medical services (only for diagnostic or evaluation purposes)
- nursing services
- nutrition services
- occupational therapy (OT)
- physical therapy (PT)
- psychological services
- service coordination services
- social work services
- special instruction
- speech-language pathology
- vision services
- health services (needed for your child to benefit from other EI services)
- transportation to and from Early Intervention services.

Your family may also be eligible for respite services, which is temporary care of your child, provided to give your family relief.

In NY State, all of these services are available at no cost or financial disadvantage to you, although the State may bill Medicaid or your private health insurance for some of the services. Early Intervention services also include assistance transitioning to CPSE (Committee on Preschool Special Education) services, as your child approaches three years of age.

The IEP for the preschool or the school-aged child is created by parents and service providers working together in a committee, called the Committee on Preschool Special Education (CPSE), or the Committee on Special Education (CSE), depending on the age of the child. Your child's IEP will be formally approved by the entire committee. Sometimes, as in this book, you will find the particular subgroup of the committee that works together to formulate the IEP referred to as the IEP team. The terms are pretty much interchangeable. The members of the committee are spelled out in IDEA 2004 to include parents, school representatives, evaluators, and service providers.

Each specialist on your IEP or IFSP team will make recommendations based on his or her area of expertise. The actual IEP or IFSP is a collaborative document, and the suggested program, services, and goals may be modified based on input from any and all members of the team—*including you*! Contributions to the IEP or the IFSP are based on each individual's knowledge of your child's usual functioning, anticipation of the upcoming curriculum and the expectations that will be made of your child, and awareness of possible supportive and remedial resources. You *may* choose simply to sit back, review, and approve or reject whatever intervention plan these professionals offer. That's the good news about the IEP process —you don't *have* to do anything further to get help for your child. However, if you want the Individualized Education Plan to be truly individualized to fit the needs of your child, you are going to have to get your hands dirty and actually help to formulate the IEP. The law recognizes the importance of the parent in the special education process. You may not have training in special education, but you are an expert on your child. Your presence on the special education committee is more than a courtesy. *It is your legal right.* The law also specifies a due process route for dealing with parental concerns and grievances that are not adequately addressed as part of the committee process. The more you do your homework, and the more you carry your weight to ensure that your child is well-represented in the individualized education process, the more likely your child will benefit from a truly customized IEP or IFSP.

When I went to my first IEP meeting, I expected it to be obvious what goals and interventions would be appropriate for my child. It was not! I have come to believe that formulating an appropriate IEP is as much art as it is science. Two children identified with the same disability may actually present in entirely different ways. Indeed, because you are writing the IEP for the *child* and not for the disability, your child's unique characteristics and situation will inevitably impact your child's IEP. Different team members may have different preferences and values as to what issues are important to address, what outcomes they feel are desirable or obtainable, and how they wish to work towards those outcomes. The law states that the intervention plan must be built around the child's needs, not around the options that your school district has readily available. You may need to remind your team of that obligation, offer positive examples of what meeting your child's needs would look like, bring in outside consultants, or otherwise encourage the committee members to be creative, if needed, to formulate something appropriate for your child. Your input into these decisions is crucial.

What is in the IEP?

When you complete these CSE or CPSE meetings, you will have a document that is a legally enforceable contract. It is an official recognition of your child's special educational needs, and the resources that will be brought to bear to address those needs. The basic parts of an IEP as specified by IDEA are presented in Box 9.2. I will briefly describe each of these parts below. There is not a single format that is required across school districts, and so the form used by your school district may vary somewhat. Your state education website may offer guidance documents. The specific *contents* of your child's IEP, however, will be created by you and your team. I recommend Siegel (2001) *The Complete IEP Guide* and Wright and Wright (2006) *From Emotions to Advocacy* (as well as the Wrightslaw website at www.wrightslaw.com).

The IEP begins with basic information identifying the student and guardian, and then states the recommended classification and placement information. If the CSE or CPSE officially decides your child warrants "classification," it means that you have successfully had your child evaluated and identified as eligible to receive special education services. The CSE or CPSE will then label his or her disability according to one of the 13 classification types specified in federal/state law (listed earlier in Box 3.1). Although your child's diagnosis influences your child's classification, the two are not synonymous. Diagnoses are medical terms. Classifications

Box 9.2 The main parts of the IEP

Federal regulations governing IEPs and model forms have been published by the US Department of Education. IDEA 2004 specifies that although the format of IEPs may vary from state to state, all IEPs must contain the following information (adapted from U.S. Department of Education 2007):

- A statement of the child's present levels of academic achievement and functional performance including:

    how the disability affects the child's involvement and progress in the general education curriculum (i.e., the same curriculum as for non-disabled children)

    for preschool children, as appropriate, how the disability affects the child's participation in appropriate activities.

- A statement of measurable annual goals, including academic and functional goals designed to:

    meet the child's needs that result from the child's disability to enable the child to be involved in and make progress in the general education curriculum

    meet each of the child's other educational needs that result from the child's disability.

- For children with disabilities who take alternate assessments aligned to alternate achievement standards (in addition to the annual goals), a description of benchmarks or short-term objectives.

- A description of:

    how the child's progress toward meeting the annual goals will be measured

    when periodic reports on the progress the child is making toward meeting the annual goals will be provided, such as through the use of quarterly or other periodic reports, concurrent with the issuance of report cards.

- A statement of the *special education and related services* and *supplementary aids* and *services*, based on peer-reviewed research to the extent practicable, to be provided to the child, or on behalf of the child, and *a statement of the program modifications or supports for school personnel* that will be provided to enable the child:

    to advance appropriately toward attaining the annual goals

    to be involved in and make progress in the general academic curriculum and to participate in extracurricular and other non-academic activities

> to be educated and participate with other children with disabilities and non-disabled children in extracurricular and other non-academic activities
>
> an explanation of the extent, if any, to which the child will not participate with non-disabled children in the regular classroom and in extracurricular and other non-academic activities.
>
> - A statement of any individual appropriate accommodations necessary to measure the academic achievement and functional performance of the child on state and district-wide assessments.
> - If the IEP team determines that the child must take an alternate assessment instead of a particular regular state or district-wide assessment of student achievement, a statement of why:
>
>> the child cannot participate in the regular assessment
>>
>> the particular alternate assessment selected is appropriate for the child.
>
> - The projected date for the beginning of the services and modifications, and the anticipated frequency, location, and duration of special education and related services and *supplementary aids and services* and *modifications and supports*.
>
> Each of these requirements references a particular section of IDEA 2004. Your state's regulations will also define the application of these requirements for your state, in accordance with federal law. The Wrightslaw website, or the book *Special Education Law* (Wright and Wright 2007) can assist with interpreting the application of each section to your child's particular IEP, and provide legal precedent and case law.

are legally defined categories used to justify services. Michael's ADD and low muscle tone, for instance, are medical diagnoses that have led the CSE to classify him as "Other Health Impaired." Marcus shared this classification until last year's IEP meeting, when I requested the change to "Autism" and submitted the supporting documentation for this change in classification. I prefer to use this classification because it makes the nature of his social and pragmatic communicative impairments more understandable to teachers. The autism classification also carries tighter measures of service under the law. With the change in classification label, his special education teacher and I will need to take special care to educate Marcus's teachers, to help them see what the impairment means in Marcus's case. Frankly, I believe these discussions with teachers are important when applying any summary label to a particular child.

For the next section of the IEP, the team must decide on suitable educational interventions to address your child's disability. These recommendations should be decided only after thoroughly discussing your child and his or her educational needs. Here the nature of the IEP as a contract becomes more obvious. The committee will set forth recommendations that, once approved, the school district will be required by law to provide for your child. It is very important that you understand what is being specified here, and the implications of what is agreed upon for your child. For many families, the biggest issues will revolve around the notions of inclusiveness and least restrictive environment. For other families, the issues may revolve around whether or not specific services should be provided for their child. Note that these programs and services are decided upon by the CSE or the CPSE based on the child's *needs*, not the child's diagnosis. Marcus's services, for example, did not change simply because I changed his classification from "Other Health Impaired" to "Autism." His services did change, however, as his educational needs changed.

Special education programs include a range of options, such as self-contained special educational classroom, resource room, and consultant teacher. They also include related services, such as aide support, counseling, speech therapy, OT, and PT. In considering what placement to make for your child, it is important to remember the "least restrictive environment" restriction on IEP development. The law specifies that the appropriate process for considering options is to first start with the educational placement most like your child's peers, and then to consider what modifications and supports could be made to that environment to allow your child to benefit from the placement. The committee should consider a more restrictive level of intervention only if the less restrictive one cannot be modified to accommodate your child's needs. Each school district is required to have a continuum of services available. You should discuss this continuum and where your child's needs fall with the other members of your child's IEP team. For example, the law requires that the first option to be considered is a regular educational classroom with no additional support. Next might be a regular educational classroom with "related service" support. Additional tiers include regular education with consultant services, regular education with resource room support, and only then does one begin to move into special education classroom options. You should discuss this continuum and how it would apply to your child with the other members of your child's IEP team. Begin and end these discussions, however, with *what your child needs, not what programs are available!* Special education is a set of educational *services* that your child receives. It is not a placement into a particular school or classroom.

I always feel at a disadvantage when it is time to design educational programs and services. The usual procedure is for the school personnel to present only their recommendations, and their list of options tends to be limited to what they have done in the past. My lack of awareness of other possible models limits my ability to contribute to this part of the discussion, unless I have done my own research into what is usually considered "best practices" for children with the same concerns as my sons.

For example, one year I was requesting more assistance helping Michael develop self-monitoring skills. The other members of the CSE recommended the use of direct instruction by the special education teacher in the resource room, which would have involved two hours a week out of the regular classroom. I told them that my concerns were especially regarding overcoming distractions and cuing applicability of these skills in the context of classroom work. In discussion of the pros and cons of these two options, we decided that this pull-out model was not the most appropriate one for Michael's needs. Instead, we added skills instruction to occur within the context of other psychological counseling focusing on emotional regulation, social problem-solving, and executive functioning (planning and decision-making) that would be provided to Michael once a week. We also added the assistance of a shared classroom aide, who would be guided as to how to cue the application of those executive skills within the context of Michael's daily classroom work.

Schools tend to have standard models for how they use various services. It is important to look more closely at the details of those models, to determine whether or not they need modification, or whether something entirely new may need to be created for your child's unique needs. If you are not happy with the options offered, you may need to request the services of an independent, educational consultant to help you advocate for your child. I know one parent of a child with Asperger's who has even gone so far as to have her son's IEP specify the services of an outside autism spectrum disorders consultant for up to ten times during the school year for assistance with IEP development, teacher education, and help with school-related social, emotional, and cognitive issues that cannot be resolved by the IEP team. *Anything your child needs can be possible in an IEP, it just may take some strong advocacy to acquire it.*

Similarly, the concept of "related services" is a more open-ended one than I realized from my school's usual offerings. Related services are services that a child needs to benefit from special education. The particular form that they take can vary. Different types of related services could be used to provide the same benefit to the child. Box 9.3 presents a list of some of the more common examples I obtained from an article published on the web by NICHCY (also accessible through the Wrightslaw website). I include this list because my vision of what could be possible for my child has often been limited by more traditional educational delivery models. You will decide, together with the other IEP team members, which related

---

Box 9.3 Related services most commonly provided to students with disabilities

The following list of related services is not meant to be exhaustive. It is adapted from "Related Services," published by NICHCY (2001). More detail on each of these services is provided in this NICHCY article:

- Artistic/cultural programs (including art therapy, dance/movement therapy, music therapy)
- Assistive technology devices and services
- Audiology
- Counseling services
- Medical services (for diagnostic or evaluation purposes only)
- Occupational therapy
- Orientation and mobility services
- Parent counseling and training
- Physical therapy
- Psychological services
- Recreation services
- Rehabilitation counseling services
- School health services
- Social work services in schools
- Speech-language pathology services
- Transportation

---

services are most appropriate for your child's unique educational needs. In true contract form, not only will the IEP include what services will be provided your child, but it will also specify details such as when the services will start and end, their frequency and duration, where they will occur, and at what provider:pupil ratio.

Your child's IEP will also list any accommodations and modifications to the regular educational program that you, along with the other CSE or CPSE members, decide are warranted by your child's needs. *Accommodations* are those things the school agrees to do to remove barriers to your child's learning and performance. Examples might include frequent breaks, preferential seating, the ability to type instead of write assignments, and frequent parent–school communication. *Modifications*, on the other hand, are the changes in standards or expectations of performance that you and the school agree are appropriate. An example might be lessened homework load, or use of a different textbook, or different curricular goals. Whatever assistive technology equipment and supports are needed will also be documented. Currently in the United States, schools are being held accountable for ensuring that teachers have appropriate training for the subject matter and types of students they teach. You should be sure that the staff working with your child have had training relevant to your child's specific disability. If not, then you should request such training be provided as part of your child's IEP.

Even when a child has special educational needs, the child's teachers are still required to help that student meet high educational standards. IDEA reinforces the notion of not "watering down" instruction for our children, bur rather differentiating the curriculum to meet the needs of each student. In other words, our children are not only offered access to the same educational *environments* as their peers. They are also offered access to the same educational *curriculum*, but modified appropriately for their needs. This, understandably, is a challenge for educators. However, cutting-edge instructional research and practice has been moving in this direction for 15 to 20 years now, to the point that these are the new standards to which schools should be held accountable. Federal and state efforts have focused on rewriting national educational standards, curricula, and assessments, and the emphasis now is on bringing classroom instruction into line with these. Educational conferences and teacher workshops will help teachers and administrators stay current in best educational practices. But also, a number of recent federal educational initiatives have been created to help improve school outcomes for all students. The Access Center (www.k8accesscenter.org), in particular, is one such initiative, which includes outreach to schools in each of the 50 states as part of its mission. If you want a sense of what more accessible curricula and lesson plans would look like, searching the Internet for "differentiated instruction" should begin to link you with useful sites. Professional organizations, such as the National Council of Teachers of Mathematics, and the National Science Teachers Association, have links to materials designed to help teachers and schools present high-quality subject matter instruction to *all* children, including students with disabilities. Some additional places to start your search, if your IEP team needs assistance, are listed at the end of this chapter. You do not have to become an educational expert yourself, but again, knowledge of what is possible will help you be a better advocate for the educational needs of your child.

Especially with the passage of the federal No Child Left Behind Act (NCLB), state and local student assessments have become especially important for schools. Both in regard to these standardized assessments, and in regard to regular classroom quizzes and tests, the IEP will discuss any testing accommodations to be provided for your child because of his or her disability. Examples of these testing accommodations might include extra time, separate location, or having items read to the student. This section of the IEP also details any times of day when the child will be removed from the general education environment or exempted from specific general education requirements. Or, program modifications may call for alternate assessments, so that your child is given different tests from those provided for classmates. If the latter is the case, be sure to check that the end result of these decisions are what you expect in terms of high school degree at graduation and post-secondary expectations.

The beginning of the IEP classified your child as needing special education services. The next part of the IEP begins to describe more thoroughly your specific child. To me, this is the heart and soul driving the IEP. It presents a thorough description of your child's present levels of functioning. This will include your child's academic achievement, descriptions of your child's functional performance within his or her usual environment, and characteristics of your child as a learner. This part of the IEP is also where you and the other members of the committee will translate this description of your child into a set of educational needs that must be addressed for your child. Let's look more closely at how to go about putting this section together, for neither the description nor the translation process is as straightforward as it sounds. As the person who knows your child the best, your contribution to these descriptions is especially important. You may be deluged with a number of abbreviations, technical terms, and acronyms here. Take the time to be sure you understand what they are, or ask for help deciphering the jargon.

One place for you to look for a description of your child's strengths and challenges is the set of formal evaluations that have been performed on your child. The school district's specialists may have performed some of these evaluations. Others may be ones you contracted to have performed. (See Chapter 3 on obtaining an evaluation.) The evaluations were probably multi-paged, detailed descriptions, separate from the IEP itself. The IEP uses shorter, summary descriptions from these evaluations, including achievement and intelligence test scores and other standardized measures. Although formal assessments contribute to these IEP summaries, informal reports are another, excellent source of information about the child. These may include classroom observations by the teacher or psychologist, as well as parent reports. These observations may then be summarized and presented in a way that highlights what a teacher can expect from your child's current functioning. The description of your child's present level of performance leads to certain expectations about the goals that might be set in the IEP or IFSP. You may be surprised by how the educational picture changes, depending on what is included and what is omitted from these descriptions of your child's present level of performance. I like to make sure that it contains the basic information needed to understand and appropriately react to my child. (You also should make sure that your child's teachers actually receive this information!) For example, Box 9.4 presents my son Michael's present levels of academic achievement, functional performance, and individual needs from his latest IEP. Please note that IEPs are confidential documents, and great care is taken to respect the child's right to privacy. I share this very personal information with you now (with Michael's permission) because I feel it will help your understanding.

Box 9.4 Present levels of performance and educational needs from Michael's fifth grade IEP

Academic achievement

Levels/abilities: Michael has above average cognitive and language skills and attends LEP (enrichment) classes. He is gifted in reading and has an extensive vocabulary. All reading, math, and writing skills are in the superior range relative to other children his age.

Needs: Michael has difficulty organizing his materials, taking notes, and checking his work. He also has problems following oral directions without visual cues. Processing of verbal directions is difficult for Michael, especially at times of transition, so checks for understanding of directions would benefit Michael.

Social development

Levels/abilities: Michael is friendly and interested in interacting with other children.

Needs: Michael has problems interpreting social situations and has some difficulty with social problem-solving. He tends to be very sensitive and can get emotionally "stuck" when he is overwhelmed. He needs adult support to process the situation and regain control of his emotions. Michael is overly sensitive to correction from adults, which he misperceives as criticism.

Physical development

Levels/abilities: Michael has low muscle tone, poor endurance, and inattention that often result in poor posture and can impact on handwriting as well.

Needs: Michael needs frequent breaks or opportunities to move around the room and change position. Michael uses a wedge seat to assist in sitting upright.

Management needs

Michael requires a clear statement of expectations in order for him to produce his best work, as he will have a tendency to produce the minimal requirement at times. He also responds well to verbal praise.

Organization is a problem and will require monitoring to ensure he has the appropriate materials to and from home, as well as a checklist for the classroom aide for writing support. Michael would benefit from opportunities for movement within or outside the classroom. He needs visual cues in order to follow directions independently, and needs assistance with transitions between activities. He would also benefit from assistance when he transitions from a pull-out activity (i.e., alternate math/LEP) and being given a brief summary of activities that were completed in the classroom during his pull-out time. Checklists have been helpful to him in the past. He should be encouraged to engage in positive "self-talk" to keep himself focused and organized.

The IEP will be written to show what adaptations, modifications, supportive services, and educational goals will be set in order to address the child's educational needs. Although your child's formal evaluations probably ended with a set of recommendations for meeting your child's needs, the special education committee does not have to accept those recommendations. Furthermore, unless the deficits noted by the evaluation translate into *educational* needs, they do not have to be addressed by the IEP at all. This is a very important distinction. The IEP is not a comprehensive plan meant to address all aspects of your child's disability or diagnosis. This distinction between diagnosed difficulty and acknowledged educational impact has caused me incredible frustration with my son, Michael. Michael has Attention Deficit Disorder, a Central Auditory Processing Dysfunction, low muscle tone, and numerous autism spectrum characteristics, including executive processing deficits and social and pragmatic language difficulties. But, because he is also extremely bright, has high grades, and is usually not disruptive in class, the school district has had difficulty recognizing that he still has extensive educational needs resulting from his diagnoses. It wasn't until his difficulties escalated to the point of emotional outbursts and clinical depression, that I was finally able to convince the CSE that it was educationally appropriate to work with me in a more intensive manner.

You may have to be creative to draw the connections between the difficulties you note, and the school's domain of concern. It helps if you can give specific examples. For example, you may present items from your child's schoolwork or homework, or you may describe behaviors you see at home that will likely extend into the school environment. Examples might also include your child's reaction to frustration, disappointment, or fatigue. I even asked Michael's teacher to describe what he found that he needed to do to help Michael. Although I appreciated this particular teacher's support, I pointed out to the team that it may be unrealistic to expect a classroom teacher with a full class to regularly be available for such responses, without additional help. Yet the consequences for Michael if such support was not available when he needed it, were high. Additional classroom support or intervention was clearly needed.

If you anticipate resistance from the committee, you may want to video-tape your child's struggles. This is an especially useful strategy if your child's difficulties are not well-represented by test scores. The intelligibility of your child's speech, for example, might be better demonstrated by a video of your child's attempts to converse, rather than by formal articulation or language measures. Similarly, videos of playground activities may more convincingly demonstrate gross motor limitations than would measures of motor development. I will often keep a sort of diary, in which I record brief anecdotes that illustrate difficulties or successes, and I keep a portfolio of concrete work examples to validate my concerns. Once I brought in an essay my third grader happily composed on the computer and compared it with the short, simple compositions he tended to write laboriously by hand. The obvious contrast quickly resulted in the committee agreeing that here was a case that adaptive technology—in this case, an AlphaSmart™ keyboard—would certainly be appropriate. Your child's self-esteem and attitudes towards learning are important and you may need to argue for a cumulative effect of mounting difficulties. Or you may have to demonstrate how your child's difficulties are creating a learned helplessness situation in which your child labels himself as a failure and so is reluctant to even try. Your child's *ability to communicate with others*, his or her *ability to participate physically in classroom or playground activities*, and your child's *emotional and social well-being*—these are all relevant educational dimensions. Your arguments can be further supported in the current educational climate in which our educational leaders acknowledge the schools' responsibility for developing the "whole child." The more reading you do, and the more you talk to other parents who have successfully navigated the process, the more likely you are to learn effective approaches towards enlisting the school's assistance. I find that it often helps if I can also suggest some examples of possible solutions to the problems raised. Getting the school to take action to help with various aspects of my child's disability is not always easy. It sometimes requires persistence, creativity, and negotiation skills. I'm not always successful, but I also know how to bide my time, do more research, collect more evidence, and raise my questions again at a later date.

So far, in our discussion of the IEP, we've described how you work with the other members of the CSE to design an appropriate educational program that meets the unique strengths and challenges of your child. The next step in creating the IEP is to decide what the goals of your child's education for the upcoming year should be. The instructional goals for a particular year are set by your school district's regular educational curriculum. Your child's IEP will set additional educational goals designed to address your child's unique needs. These goals describe what your child's IEP plans to accomplish, and what specific measures will be used to indicate whether or not the program has been successful. This usually takes the form of a set of annual goals detailing what your child will be able to do at the year's end. Sometimes these goals also include benchmark objectives that indicate what appropriate progress towards those annual goals should look like by the end of each grading quarter. The school district is not legally bound to accomplish the goals set in the IEP. However, failure to make sufficient progress on the goals set by the IEP team is a strong indicator that the Individualized Education Plan was insufficient for meeting your child's educational needs.

As you work with the other members of your team to formulate these goals, keep in mind that this is your opportunity to decide what specific needs *you* would like to see addressed by the plan. What would you like your child to be able to do, that she or he is not doing right now? These goals, after all, are descriptions of what the IEP team will be working on over the upcoming educational year. This is your opportunity to enlist their help on specific problems you see challenging your child as a result of his or her disability. IDEA does not specify the format or content of IEP goals, and so these will vary from school district to school district. Siegel (2001), Twachtman-Cullen and Twachtman-Reilly (2002), and Wright and Wright (2006) have good discussions of IEP creation. I urge you to follow up with further reading on this important topic. Box 9.5 includes some examples of the wide range of areas for which IEP goals may be written (from Siegel 2001). Remember, IDEA 2004 specifies that functional goals are "fair game," and just as important as academic concerns.

Box 9.5 Sample areas that are "fair game" for IEP goal development

- Academic skills
- Cognitive skills
- Emotional and psychological issues
- Social-behavioral skills
- Linguistic and communication skills
- Self-help and independent living skills
- Physical and recreational skills
- Vocational skills
- Transition to work or higher education skills

(adapted from Siegel 2001)

Over time, my children's therapy team and I have developed a strong working relationship. It was not uncommon for me to come to a meeting with a list of my concerns. We would all immediately start working together to translate these concerns into actual instructional or behavioral goals. Even though I have an education background, I am not expert in the actual technical wording of these goals. However, I can tell whether or not a proposed goal addresses my basic concern. I am always scouting around for other statements that better formulate what I would like to see happen in my children's IEPs. Your school district personnel will have goal banks at their disposal, or they may use a computerized program of options that can be tweaked to reflect your child's needs. At one planning meeting, the consultant teacher and I searched the goal bank together for ideas for formulating our goals. At other planning meetings, the team I have worked together to break new ground and write new goals. Goals banks are *tools* for helping the team write IEPs. They are not meant to restrict the IEPs' content. You may have to be a strong advocate for your child while formulating these goals. "We can't do that," or "That is not one of the choices available to us" are not acceptable reasons for rejecting a goal request. Rather, the goals are individualized to your child and related to the educational needs resulting from your child's disability. There are no set limits to the number of goals that your child's IEP can contain, so be sure that it includes those goals that you feel are most important. Do not give up on goal development until you are satisfied with the result as an appropriate focus for the team's intervention and support efforts for the upcoming year.

Although creating an IEP is a highly interpretive and individualized process, I thought it would still be helpful for you to see some specific examples. Box 9.6 presents the goals the team and I created together for Michael's current IEP. A different IEP team may have written a different set of goals for my child. As you can see, these were a very logical extension of the needs expressed earlier in his IEP, and these needs were tied closely into the struggles we noted in his home and school life.

Box 9.6 Goals from Michael's fifth grade IEP

Study skills

1. Michael will follow the classroom morning routine of unpacking his own backpack and putting away personal belongings and school materials while using a self-monitoring checklist.

2. Michael will use a planner to keep track of short- and long-term assignments and due dates.

3. Using the assignment list recorded in his planner, Michael will identify and select the necessary items required to take home in order to complete homework assignments.

4. Michael will maintain a portfolio with divisions for various subjects and will ensure that each section contains only information that belongs in that subject area.

5. Michael will independently seek out appropriate assistance from teachers and other support staff.

Social/emotional/behavioral goals

1. With the assistance of the school psychologist, Michael will assess his academic and emotional functioning on a weekly basis and choose one goal to work on for the following week.

2. Michael will communicate and interact in a socially acceptable manner with peers (e.g., appropriate eye contact, appropriate turn-taking, reciprocal conversation, and listening without speaking) as measured by teacher observation.

3. Michael will display appropriate coping skills to deal with changes or disappointments (e.g., student will redirect or self-soothe) as measured by teacher observation, psychologist observation, and self-report.

4. Michael will identify and display appropriate reactions and appropriate alternative solutions to challenging social situations that occur in the school (e.g., student accidentally bumps into him) as measured by teacher observation and self-report.

Motor goals

1. Michael will follow classroom routines, bring appropriate materials to class, and implement organizational strategies daily, with 80 percent success as measured by teacher recorded evaluation.

2. Michael will produce organized and legible written assignments as measured by teacher and parent observation.

3. OT will consult regularly with classroom staff to provide recommendations for techniques and/or modifications to enhance Michael's educational program.

Remember that the school's perspective and yours on appropriate goals may differ. The schools are looking for reasonable progress over the course of the year, but the definition of "reasonable progress" is sometimes fuzzy. That is why a detailed description of the child's current level of performance is so important. One year, I had intense disagreements with a particular therapist. This particular therapist did not usually work with my child, but, rather, supervised another individual who did. I felt strongly that Marcus had already mastered the OT goals these therapists were proposing for the next year, and I wanted new goals to be written. If necessary, I was prepared to bring Marcus to the meeting and actually ask him to perform the behavior described. However, my anecdotal description of my child's current level of functioning, coupled with the other team members' experiences with my child, was eventually sufficient to produce more appropriate goals that I felt would represent a true advance in my child's skills. Interestingly enough, this same therapist wanted to phrase all of her goals in terms of what the school or the therapist would provide my son, not in terms of what my child would be able to do as a result of this intervention. Other parts of the IEP are designed to describe how the services are going to be delivered. This part of the IEP really is meant to describe the target performance your IEP team is trying to develop in your child during the next academic year.

Pulling it all together to create an appropriate intervention plan

Now we've considered the basic parts of the IEP, Box 9.7 reviews the steps for creating this plan. Although the intent of the law clearly is to build an educational plan around the needs of the individual child, rather than to fit children into educational programs, the pragmatic reality of schools is that they are not going to want to re-invent the wheel for your child, if they already have a program in place that works for other children. There is nothing wrong with this, if the proposed program is appropriate for your child. The problem occurs when it is *not* appropriate, and sometimes schools imply that their already existing programs are your only option. This is not true.

Box 9.7 The steps to formulating an IEP

- Summarize your child's strengths and weaknesses relevant to the school's perspective.
- Translate those strengths and weaknesses into educational needs.
- Describe your child's current level of performance in those areas to be addressed.

- Select educational objectives to be addressed in the Individualized Education Plan, taking care that the objectives are appropriate, stated in terms of what the child will be able to do when they are achieved (also known as behavioral outcomes), with measurable indicators of progress towards those goals clearly stated.
- Consider which, if any, of the following are appropriate:
    accommodations to help your child meet educational expectations;

    modifications in what the child is expected to do;

    supportive services and personnel training.
- Clarify who is responsible for monitoring and accomplishing each part of your child's IEP—this will be your contact person for problems in that specific area.
- Evaluate the resulting, proposed IEP and request additional meetings and revisions as necessary.

The school's budgetary and staffing concerns are very real. However, the school's concerns are not the only legitimate ones. The law specifically states that your child's educational needs trump any budgetary objections that the school may have. That's where the disagreements sometimes arise—over what those educational needs are and what educational program is appropriate for your child. Both academic and non-academic benefits to your child may be relevant factors in the placement decision. School districts are not allowed to make placements solely on factors such as category or severity of disability, availability of educational or related services, availability of space, or the particular way a school usually delivers services. You and the schools will need to work together to formulate a plan that is "do-able" by the school, and that will still adequately address your child's educational rights and needs. Sometimes the school may need help in envisioning what form an alternative intervention could take. If you feel stymied in your efforts, dig deeper into the literature, consult with advocacy groups about successful strategies, or consider hiring an educational consultant or an advocate to help.

It will help you if you look at the meetings as a work in progress. Even when you formulate a tentative plan, think of this as reaching a consensus as to what you are going to try first. You are not locked irrevocably into that plan. If you find the plan isn't working well, call another meeting to discuss changing it. Sometimes, getting an effective IEP in place for your child will take several cycles back and forth between you and the other members of the committee. Sometimes, you may end up compromising, trying a less than desirable option first, to rule out whether or not it can be effective. When you are in a compromise situation, the catch is to get everyone to agree what a reasonable trial period would be, and to arrange a formal follow-up meeting to discuss how the plan is progressing.

Although IEPs do not have to follow a single, particular format, there are certain things you should look for in a well-designed IEP. In Box 9.8, I present the questions you should consider when evaluating the Individual-ized Education Plan resulting from your meetings with your special educa-tion committee. It is important for you not only to evaluate what you *see* in the document, but that you also keep an eye out for what *could be* in it, to

---

Box 9.8 Questions to consider in evaluating your child's proposed IEP

1. Do you agree with the description of your child's current level of functioning?

2. Do you agree with the school's assessment of how that level of functioning is or is not impacting your child's ability to benefit from his or her education?

3. Do you think the IEP targets the most important items for intervention at this time?

4. Do you agree that the IEP is setting reasonable and appropriate goals for your child, with a reasonable timeline for reaching those goals?

5. Do you agree with the way progress towards these goals will be assessed?

6. Do you approve of the accommodations, modifications, and supports described in the plan?

7. Finally, from your perspective, do you think the plan being offered adequately addresses your child's needs? Does it foster your child's growth, independence, and well-being?

---

make it an even better fit for your child. The school tends to offer what they readily know how to do. I spend a lot of time thinking about what might be missing from my children's educational programs. I watch my child to identify difficulties that might not be addressed. I keep up to date on the current literature on my children's area of disability, for reports of what seems to work for other children facing similar challenges, and I share that information with my child's IEP team.

How can you best contribute to the IEP or IFSP team?

How can you help ensure that this special education process best serves the needs of your child? First and foremost, be sure that you take your place as a team member. For your child's sake, *it is imperative that you attend both the building-level planning meetings and the formal approval meetings.* Furthermore, you are allowed to bring others to the meetings with you. If you are worried about your ability to stand up for your child, consider bringing in additional support—your spouse, an outside consultant, or a professional parent advocate, for example. These meetings are meant to be a dynamic process, instead of a mechanism by which everyone gives their rubberstamp approval to pre-formulated, canned programs. This means that you cannot predict exactly how the meetings will go, or what the outcome will be. You can, however, go into these meetings prepared. Although I know what I feel most strongly about, I go into the meetings willing to consider a range of options. I know what I most would like to see happen, and I have one or more fallback positions. I also have my arguments ready if I feel that my bottom-line, non-negotiable position is being breached. Although I may be emotionally braced, I try to go to these meetings with a constructive attitude. I assume that we are all there to work together towards a common goal, which is to design an appropriate education for my child. However, I recognize that we may disagree about what form this should take. I go to these meetings both prepared with information I have already collected, and yet ready to learn more. Your knowledge and preparedness will help you to be a strong advocate for your child at these meetings.

Know your rights

You don't have to be a legal expert, but it is important that you understand the basics of the laws governing special education. Otherwise, you may build your child's educational plan on inaccurate assumptions as to what the school district is and is not required to do. This does not mean that you automatically need to consult an attorney. There is often no need to make the meetings adversarial, but you don't want to be ignorant of your child's basic educational rights either. Your school district should give you a copy of a parent's guide to special education, explaining timelines, the complaints process, and your rights to appeal or request mediation in the case of a disagreement. Your state education office (and website) should have additional parent materials available. For many matters of disability law, I consult sources intended for the layperson. At the end of this chapter I list some of the more parent-friendly sources that I have encountered. These can at least get you started thinking about legal issues and how they might affect your special education advocacy for your child. You should definitely obtain a copy of the actual special education laws, and your state regulations. A helpful website, www.wrightslaw.com, periodically addresses common issues faced by parents and school districts. Wrightslaw is probably *the* single biggest lay source for legal information. Wrightslaw publishes a variety of guidebooks, a monthly Internet newsletter, and a website for exploring further information. Additionally, Wrightslaw offers parent training in many issues of disability law. I recommend that you include some legal resources in your general, ongoing education. The Wrightslaw newsletters are good monthly reminders for me, in terms of letting me dip regularly into the legal arena without becoming too overwhelmed and intimidated. In addition, the parent conferences I attend often have sessions dealing with the rights of families and individuals with disabilities. These also help me build a strong knowledge foundation.

Know your child

Take the time before the planning meetings begin to take a good, analytic look at your child's daily functioning at home and at school. Come prepared with concrete examples of difficulties you want to discuss. It often takes weeks for me to pull together those issues that I think are important for these annual discussions. Careful record-keeping along the way can help you have readily available a good picture of what you have noticed. Children change over time, and so do environments. As I described in Chapter 6, my son's needs and abilities certainly have changed over the years. It is important that I keep in mind a solid picture of who he is now and his current skills in relation to where we'd like him to be next year, as well as our longer-term plans for him. Also, my awareness should include more than his challenges. A strong IEP also requires an awareness of his strengths and those things that help him perform at his best.

Stay abreast of best practices in the area of your child's disability

The professionals on your child's IEP team have their own sources of continuing education in their respective fields. But they also have an invaluable educational resource in you! Parents are often a wonderful source of up-to-date information in the area of their child's disability. Be ready to share with them relevant information you have learned. The easier you make it for your committee to stay cutting edge, the more likely they are to apply that best practices information to designing a good educational program that meets the needs of your child. Also, stay abreast of what the various committee members are themselves thinking about your child and his or her educational program. Frequent, mutual sharing of information increases the odds that the team can work constructively together to build a good program for your child. Solid ongoing communication also helps troubleshoot potential problems, and makes it less likely that anyone will feel blindsided by information or arguments presented at the committee meetings.

Set your priorities

The IEP will not necessarily address each and every one of your child's documented needs. Not every deficit detailed in an evaluation will be considered educationally relevant, or of equal priority in establishing an Individualized Education Plan for your child. It is important that the IEP sets priorities that you feel are most important for your child for the upcoming year. In *How Well Does Your IEP Measure Up?*, Diane Twachtman-Cullen and Jennifer Twachtman-Reilly (2002) discuss how to go about setting your priorities, and even include rating scales that may be useful in this process. I especially recommend the book for parents of children on the autism spectrum, but I believe a look at some of their detailed examples will raise many a parent's expectations as to what effective service delivery could look like for their children. Lockshin, Gillis, and Romanczyk's (2005) *Helping Your Child with Autism Spectrum Disorder*, is another book that looks at IEPs or IFSPs, although this one is more explicitly within a family context, instead of a school setting.

Ask to be provided copies of evaluations and reports before the meeting

These documents can be dense. They often contain technical language. They also can evoke a lot of emotions in you, especially when you see your child's difficulties reduced to black-and-white words and numbers. Yes, you can expect the committee to help walk you through them. However, you do not want to be seeing these documents for the first time in a rushed setting. You are going to want to have time to think about what you are reading, and to make notes of any questions and concerns the documents raise for you. School districts are often pressed for time, preparing for these meetings. On the other hand, it is not fair for the school to expect you to help make decisions on documents you have not had a chance to review beforehand. A simple enough solution is to request (in writing, if necessary) to have all papers at least a few days before your scheduled meeting. If you are told that this is impossible, you should feel free to reschedule or table the rest of the meeting until you have had a chance to go over all the documents and proposals thoroughly.

Keep your focus in meetings

A concrete, written list is essential to keep you focused and to ensure that none of your concerns are omitted from the discussion. A lot can happen in these meetings, and you have a much greater chance of having your concerns addressed if you make a list and stay focused on it. You may even want to provide others on the committee with a list of your concerns ahead of time as well. Sometimes a person's first reaction to something different is to get defensive, or to dismiss a request as impossible. Given time to digest a position, however, people may reconsider their initial reactions and begin to see ways of reaching a position more satisfactory to all.

On a related point, I find it useful to go to these meetings focused on *problems* that I want to see addressed—and not necessarily on the form that *specific solutions* to those problems need to take. Sometimes if you go to the meetings demanding a particular solution, you may not be aware of the whole picture. The solution you *think* you want, may not actually be the best option for your child. On the other hand, if you can focus your team on collaborative brainstorming and problem-solving from a variety of perspectives, you may find a superior plan emerging. Of course you should stand your ground if your position is one that is critically important and non-negotiable. To be effective at the meetings, however, it is important that you listen to the other participants, assure them that you hear their points, and then communicate what concerns you about their position so that you can work through to a solution together.

Work to foster a team relationship

Attitude is very important to developing a successful IEP. Both schools and parents sometimes make the mistake of assuming they are adversaries of one another. Fanning the flames of such an us-against-them attitude is clearly not in your child's best interests. Although I go into the meetings determined to have my concerns addressed, at the same time I keep in mind that "they" are not "the enemy." "They" are not necessarily against my child. I am willing to grant that "they" also want to serve the best interests of my child—it is just that their perspective may be different. You must realize that you actually have two goals at these meetings. One goal of course, is to develop an effective IEP for your child. But your second goal is equally important, and that is to help build a quality IEP team. You and your child are going to have to continue working with these individuals for many years. Think of it as a sort of arranged marriage, if you will. Building a positive quality relationship with the other members of your team is well worth the effort. This does not mean that you cannot disagree! It does mean, however, that there are respectful versus disrespectful ways of expressing that disagreement. The ways in which you communicate with the other members of your committee establishes that sense of respect and helps build a quality relationship. These meetings are at their best when we look for areas of consensus, and work towards a plan that will address, or at least acknowledge, the concerns of each committee member.

Don't let emotions get in the way of problem-solving

I recognize that these meetings can be very emotionally draining. I'm aware of my strong feelings, and I try to keep them under control. My emotions might be quite valid, but to be an effective advocate for my child, I must go into these meetings very purposefully and keep my emotions from getting in the way. I watch out for anger and defensiveness, because these are likely to undercut my own position. I am aware of what I most fear. I rehearse several different dialogues, including possible constructive responses to imaginary conversations that would embody my greatest fears. If I am especially nervous or concerned about an issue, I ask someone to go to the meeting with me—my husband or a friend. As a parent, you are entitled to bring anyone you wish to the meeting, although it is a courtesy to let the school district know when you are bringing someone else. You also have the right to contest the presence of anyone at the meeting who you feel is not necessary or who does not seem to belong.

Plan ahead and avoid time pressure

Before I close this chapter on creating your child's IEP, I have to add a warning about how important it is that you prepare and organize yourself ahead of time for these meetings. The time pressure is very real. Don't take it personally, but the IEP process involves a timeline, and your child is not the only case that the team will need to consider. Because their time is limited, it will help if you try to be efficient, but at the same time make sure your child does not get lost in the process. To avoid letting myself get pressured into making these important decisions by tight time schedules, I started thinking about the next academic year's IEPs in January. In my school district, the meetings within my school (the building meetings) tend to take place in May, the school district usually meets in July to approve the IEP team's recommendations, and the school board vote that makes it official takes place in August. Different school districts will vary as to when in the process they invite you to become involved.

My own preference is to get involved *very* early. I initiate discussions with teachers and CSE staff in January, to start gathering their views on my sons' progress. I request to attend building-level IEP planning meetings. I request a rough draft of an initial proposed IEP a few days before the building-level meeting so I have enough time to seriously think about it and make recommendations. I ask for these initial meetings to take place early enough in the spring, that we have time for one or more follow-up meetings, as needed before the formal school district CSE meetings. I know that schools operate on a tight schedule, especially during the last two months. I do not want my child's educational program to be affected due to these understandable time pressures. Also, I feel that by the time the proposed IEP has reached the school district level, it has taken on a life of its own. Change is more difficult if I wait until then. Finally, practically speaking, I find these school-district-level meetings to be tightly scheduled, with other parents lined up in the hallway waiting their turn. I find that I can be a more effective advocate for my child if I have been included earlier in the process. Speak up and request to be included in those initial IEP planning meetings. If you have not heard from your committee, take the initiative and contact them first. Then, follow through at every level.

Keep your perspective

These meetings will not always go smoothly. That's ok. The point is not whether conflict occurs, but how it is negotiated. I have not always gotten what I requested from these meetings. I measure a meeting's success by whether the proposed approach seems reasonable to try, and whether it is one I can live with. Sometimes, to paraphrase the Rolling Stones, you may not always get what you want, but you can and should keep at it until you get what you need. If you are not satisfied with the school's offering, there are always other options available to you. Keep in mind that this IEP sets out a contract of what the school district is willing to offer at this point in time. You do not have to accept what is offered. You are always free to ask for another meeting, to seek further evaluation or opinions, to ask for mediation by an outside source, or to pursue a due process hearing in the case of a truly irreconcilable difference of opinion.

The IEP is not actually a complete, comprehensive intervention plan. It only covers what the school district is willing to consider as its role in supporting your child's growth and development. It may also be important for you also to pursue other avenues of support. These were described earlier, in Chapter 3. For example, the special education and legal advocates at Wrightslaw speak about the importance of developing a longer-range comprehensive plan for your child as a total person, including his or her interests, strengths, and long-term goals. Education is only a part of the picture. This might include giving significant thought to sports, extracurricular, and leisure activities for your child. What future do you and your child envision, and what are you doing to make that future more likely? It also includes giving thought to your child's developing self-awareness: what will your tell your child about his or her own disability, and how will you develop your child's self-advocacy skills? What medical interventions will you seek? Will you pursue pharmaceutical treatments for your child? The decision as to whether or not to use medications is an especially emotional and difficult one for parents. Our culture oscillates between wanting to throw a pill at everything, to going totally naturalistic and eschewing any biochemical meddling. It seems as though everyone has an opinion—and they are quick to voice it, solicited or not. At both extremes, arguments are often made without actually looking at the particular situation and the particular child. This is one reason I stress an analytical approach in this book. The more you learn how to truly look at your child and describe what you are trying to address, the more likely you will be to come up with a reasonable plan of action that will advance your child's developing competence and independence. A careful look at your child's actions following the plan's implementation will be enough to tell you whether or not you got your intervention right!

By now you are probably feeling the weight of all this responsibility. Remember, however, that you are putting together a team of people who can advise you and support you as you make these decisions. Seek out parent advocacy groups. Not only can they give advice and share resources, but also their emotional support can be invaluable. Work on keeping a sense of perspective. You can't "fix" everything, nor should you even try. Imperfections and uniqueness are a part of the human condition. I believe that observation of your child will help you know whether you are doing enough, doing too much, or doing the right things. Children change. Needs change. You will constantly need to reassess and reformulate your own plans in response.

Useful resources
Resources for increasing the accessibility of the general education curriculum for all children, but especially children with disabilities

There are a number of excellent, well-developed educational models and approaches focusing on making the general educational curriculum more approachable for all students. These methods stress the importance of meaningful learning and standards-based curricula and assessment. Current search terms that will help you locate such material, include "differentiated instruction," "understanding by design," and "universal design for learning." Any of these approaches will provide a wealth of useful curricular information for specific subject matter instruction, including position papers and explanatory briefs, sample lesson plans, curriculum guides, and teacher workshops. "We don't know how to do that" just means that someone needs to do some homework and find out how.

Valuable websites for resources for parents and teachers alike

The Access Center

www.k8accesscenter.org

NICHCY Connections for Curriculum Research

National Dissemination Center for Children with Disabilities

www.nichcy.org

The Center for Applied Special Technology (CAST)

www.cast.org

The Council for Exceptional Children

www.ideapractices.org

The Association for Supervision and Curriculum Development (ASCD)

www.ascd.org

The US Department of Education, Office of Special Education Programs' (OSEP's) IDEA website

http://idea.ed.gov

Useful books for teachers

Tomlinson, Carol Ann (2003) *Fulfilling the Promise of the Differentiated Classroom: Strategies and Tools for Responsive Teaching.* Alexandria, VA: ASCD.

Tomlinson, Carol Ann and McTighe, Jay (2006) *Integrating Differentiated Instruction and Understanding by Design.* Alexandria, VA: ASCD.

Wiggins, Grant P. and McTighe, Jay (2005) *Understanding by Design* (2nd edn). Alexandria, VA: ASCD.

Parent-friendly resources on the legal process and special education advocacy

Anderson, Winifred, Chitwood, Stephen and Hayden, Deidre (1997) *Negotiating the Special Education Maze: A Guide for Parents and Teachers* (3rd edn). Bethesda, MA: Woodbine House.

Siegel, Lawrence M. (2001) *The Complete IEP Guide: How to Advocate for Your Special Ed Child* (2nd edn). Berkeley, CA: Nolo.

Wright, Peter W.D. and Wright, Pamela Darr (2006) *From Emotions to Advocacy: The Special Education Survival Guide* (2nd edn). Hartfield, VA: Harbor House Law Press.

10

Monitoring the Progress of Your Child

Once your child's IEP has been created and everyone has signed off on it, you can finally relax and turn it over to the professionals, right? Wrong! Even if you are fortunate enough to be working with the best of professionals, you still have much to do. A good IEP on paper is one accomplishment. A good, actual working IEP, manifested in your child's day-to-day school life, is another. Your participation is crucial for both. *Never assume that everything is going smoothly.* Glitches in successfully implementing your child's IEP not only *may* happen, I can guarantee you that they *will*. It is the nature of the beast. The school environment is so multi-faceted, involving communication and cooperation between so many people, in so many different contexts, that problems inevitably are going to arise. When you, as your child's parent, take a vigilant, problem-spotting and problem-solving attitude, you put everyone involved with your child's education in a better position to address those problems quickly and productively, to help your child function better and develop throughout the school year.

Why am I such a pessimist, expecting glitches and problems? Planning is important, but it will not be perfect. Not only might your child have changed since your spring IEP planning meeting, but I believe it is impossible to anticipate completely how your child's special needs will play out in a particular classroom environment, with a new teacher, a new curriculum, new classmates, and new social dynamics. The individuals formulating the IEP in the spring may not even be the same individuals responsible for carrying it out in the fall. Successful IEPs involve staff cooperation at many levels, and the information needed to help your child succeed may not have reached all of the appropriate people, or may be inadequately understood or interpreted in a way that is not truly in your child's best interests. Monitoring the adequacy of your child's IEP emerges as a job custom-made for you, your child's parent and best advocate.

Are the terms of your child's IEP being implemented?

One of the guiding principles to being an effective advocate for your child is to be proactive and to try to anticipate problems/issues even before they arise. Your diligence can be vital for recognizing instances of oversight, neglect, interference, or misinterpretation. *Never assume that therapies have begun or that knowledge of IEP-directed accommodations and modifications has filtered to all of the appropriate individuals, or that they are being appropriately followed.* You do not have to do these checks in a suspicious, challenging, demeaning manner. Remember, even with the best of intentions on everyone's part, details can slip between the cracks. Drawing attention to potential problems may be necessary to introduce an element of accountability and responsibility for addressing the problems. Squeaky wheels attract attention, often followed by remedial action, so get used to squeaking, but also be prepared to jump in to help with the solution.

I often start my inquiries about the implementation of my sons' IEPs before the school year actually begins. In some years, my boys have needed adaptive equipment, such as an AlphaSmart™ for text processing, a seat wedge, or a special chair, and it is a good idea to confirm that the equipment has arrived and reached the classroom before the first day of school. A good time to do this is during the few days when teachers have reported to the school, but before school has been called back into session for the students. I also like to meet any aides and to touch base with the appropriate service providers in the first week or two of classes. Therapy usually doesn't begin until several weeks into the school year (the time by which services must begin is specified by law), but I like to confirm that the therapist is aware of my children and scheduling their therapies appropriately. Also, physical and occupational therapy require a physician's prescription, which it is your responsibility to obtain. I try to take care of that prerequisite when the IEP is written in the spring, but it is a good idea to confirm that the therapists have received copies so that services will not be delayed.

It is easy for paperwork to be misplaced, so photocopy any OT or PT prescriptions you have obtained, keep one copy for your records, send one to the CSE or CPSE, and send one directly to the therapist who will be providing the services.

Once school has been underway for two or three weeks, experience has taught me that it is vitally important to check to ensure that your child's scheduled services have actually begun, and then monitor their regular continuation periodically throughout the year. Overall, I would describe my experiences with therapists as very positive, but even so, we have experienced numerous difficulties over the years. Some problems have been due to minor oversights, but others have been due to more significant issues requiring extensive follow-up to resolve. One year the school was very late to begin Marcus's OT services because the district had not yet replaced an occupational therapist who left at the end of the previous school year. My complaint that the school was not in compliance with the terms of my son's IEP helped underscore the importance of expediting the hiring process. I called the CSE chair to tell her this concerned me a great deal and I asked her help: was there anything she could do to move things along from her end, to keep me from having to resort to my next step of filing a complaint? Another year, I discovered that several of Marcus's therapists were frustrated because school space was especially tight that year, and they had not been allocated an appropriate therapy room for their use. Following up on the therapy scheduling allowed me to add my voice to that of the therapists, and advocate for a better resolution to the space crunch. Yet another year, I became suspicious when Marcus's therapy communication book became noticeably void of entries from one of his therapists. In this case, I was able to call the school's attention to a chronic absentee problem with this particular therapist, and we ended up instituting a check-in policy for the therapist, to call her to be more accountable for her absences from my son. I find it interesting that although classroom teachers are expected to have substitute coverage if they are absent, school districts are not required to provide substitute coverage or make-up sessions in the event of a therapist's or student's absence. Missed sessions are not usually made up, yet frequent missed sessions risk undermining the attainment of your child's educational goals. You will have to use your judgment as to when to speak up, but the bottom line is that if services are included in your child's IEP, then your child is entitled to receive them. By speaking up, you raise the therapist's aware-ness and accountability. It also may be useful in alerting your school district to problems with inadequate space, equipment, or staffing. Your squeaky wheel may also help your district justify additional hires or restructuring of assignments.

Problems with implementing your child's IEP can come from many sources. By monitoring the implementation of your child's IEP, you can sometimes help identify and address the underlying source of the problem. In preschool, my son Michael had to use a special chair, called a Rifton chair, to help stabilize his trunk and provide better posture and positioning for fine motor tasks. We obtained the chair on loan from the school district, but whenever I dropped by the preschool classroom, I found Michael sitting in a regular chair. When I asked why, I was told that another child kept taking the chair apart. Of course, I protested the teacher's passive acceptance of the other child's behavior, and insisted the issue be addressed. I think there was an additional, unspoken issue at work as well. The chair really did look medieval. Although Michael did not mind using his special chair, it frequently drew gasps of surprise from other parents—and I admit I was not immune to that discomfort, the first time I had to seatbelt him into the chair to help his posture stay erect. I do not think the teacher was comfortable using the chair, and I also think that her personal classroom management style was seldom to use or enforce absolute mandates, such as "No taking apart Michael's chair." Too many years have passed for me to remember how we introduced the notion of the chair to Michael's classmates or to his teacher. I do know that *the degree to which the teachers are included in creating and discussing the IEP and its provi-sions will directly impact the consistency and quality of the service provided for your child.* Furthermore, some IEP provisions will be open to interpretation, and it is a good idea for you as a parent to keep an eye on what is happening to make sure it is following the intent, instead of merely the wording of the IEP. "Preferential seating," for example, could mean one thing for visual issues, and yet another for hearing or behavioral issues. Unless these differ-ences are discussed with each of your child's teachers, such classroom accommodations may be misinterpreted or ineffectively applied.

The use of aide support is another accommodation open to differential interpretations, both as to when and what kinds of support are appropriate. In fifth grade, for example, Marcus's class experienced a three-day, overnight camping trip as part of the science curriculum. The school's expectations about this activity and my own were drastically different, much to Marcus's detriment! The school interpreted the outing as "non-academic," and therefore not calling for aide support. Yet, it never crossed my mind that his shared aide might not accompany the class, providing Marcus with much-needed support during the uncertainties and stressors instigated by this foray into the unknown. Marcus's teachers returned very pleased with his successes over the camping trip—and totally oblivious to the embarrassing difficulties Marcus faced because he did not know how to ask what to do when he needed to go to the bathroom during a group activity in the woods.

Thorough training of the aide for the needs of the child is also important to ensure that the aide support is appropriate and does not undermine the development of independent behaviors. Michael, for example, seems to be especially prone to cue dependency—in which he over-relies on others to cue him with routines and transitions. Plus, Michael moves very slowly, which means that it is very tempting to step in and do tasks for him, in order to keep him somewhat on the same time schedule as the rest of the class. Discussions of these tendencies need to include teachers, therapists, parents, and paraprofessionals, to ensure that all those working with a given child are on the same page as to appropriate expectations and support efforts. The use of natural supports, such as peers, may sometimes be a more appropriate means of delivering assistance. Whatever your choice, it is important that the support should *enable*, and not further disable your child.

I'm incredibly supportive of the work paraprofessionals do, and I am also one of the strongest advocates for bringing them more into the communication loop with therapists and parents. Aides are an invaluable, pragmatic source of information about the day-to-day functioning of your child. Aides also are the daily, first responders who support your child through many of his or her difficulties, and so aides obviously need appropriate information to guide them in their choice of responses. It doesn't matter how much relevant information is in the head of the specialists—unless it is used to inform the people who work with your child, your child will not benefit. This is why appropriate training opportunities are now stressed in the latest reauthorization of IDEA 2004. It is also why I try to look for appropriate, easily digestible materials to help support my children's aides in their learning about my sons' disabilities. Diane Twachtman-Cullen's (2000) book, *How To Be a Para Pro*, is an informative, user-friendly book on autism spectrum disorders, and a useful model in this regard. I often purchase copies for aides and others working with my sons. National educational organizations, or centers for children and specific disabilities may provide other informative materials, such as the book, *The Puzzle of Autism*, recently released by the National Education Association (2006). Such introductory booklets are often available free or at a minimal charge, but I urge you to look carefully at them to be sure they are actually helpful to building understanding of your child. An alternative approach would be to put together a brief list of the informative sources you have found to be particularly useful, or targeted conferences you would especially like to ask your school district to attend. Everyone's time is tight. Your recommendations can assist school personnel in making more effective use of what time and resources they have available. Understanding our children's disabilities is key to appropriate implementation of their IEPs. Necessity has forced us, as parents, into the disabilities literature to learn how to support our children more effectively. As self-educated experts, we are in an excellent position to sift through and share this knowledge, to help teachers and paraprofessionals learn more easily what they need to know.

As you have seen, one of the first guiding principles for monitoring the effectiveness of your child's IEP is never to assume that your child's IEP is being appropriately implemented. Never assume that therapies are being provided, or that knowledge of IEP-directed accommodations and modifications has filtered to all of the appropriate individuals, or that the IEP is being followed. Never assume; always check. The second rule for monitoring the efficacy of your child's IEP is equally important. *Never assume that the plan is working, or think of that its implementation is adequate to support your child's education.* Again, never assume; always check. Your child's IEP is not set in stone—it can be modified, either formally or informally, as the year progresses, and you may often find that such adjustments are necessary. Your special job as parent will be to look not only for signs of what is or is not working in your child's Individualized Education Plan, but also to look to see what is missing and to advocate for action to address those missing pieces. You do not have to wait until the next academic year to address perceived insufficiencies, nor do you even have to necessarily call a formal IEP meeting to effect change in your child's school supports. I will discuss this process more extensively in the section that follows.

Is your child's IEP working?

Even when your child's IEP is being well implemented, you are often going to need to take lead responsibility for checking to see if it is working. Is it doing the job it was designed to do? Is it enough? As a legally empowered member of your child's special education team, you have the right and the responsibility to help monitor how well your child's IEP is working. Plus, it is your child, and so you probably have the most at stake. Feedback from all sides can be useful to determine how well the current implementation of your child's IEP is doing its job. The school's approach will be to look towards the formal benchmark and progress measures officially set in your child's IEP, but nowhere in special education law does it say that those are the only relevant measures. In fact, the wording of IDEA 2004 suggests that the evidence gathered about your child's day-to-day functioning is even more relevant and therefore important data for assessing the sufficiency of your child's IEP.

An IEP is working if your child is being a successful learner, making progress appropriate to his or her ability, and growing in competence and independence. The most common measurement of your child's growth used by the schools is the degree to which she or he is meeting the benchmarks set in his or her IEP. This is why the selection of benchmark objectives is so important. They should clearly and explicitly state what level of independence will be expected of your child on each instructional objective by the end of each quarter. I urge you, do not take "Steady Progress" as an adequate description of your child's progress on an objective, without accompanying sentences detailing what that steady progress looks like, and how the child's current level of performance compares with the established IEP benchmark! If the child is not reaching the benchmarks, then this is a clear indicator that further discussions need to take place. In fact, it may help you to think of these progress reports as not really indicative of your *child's* performance, but rather of his or her *IEP's* performance! These are the standards that the committee agreed would indicate whether your child is making sufficient progress. Failure to meet those standards is not the same thing as a less than desirable subject matter grade for your child. Failure to show acceptable progress on these IEP goals means that either the goals were inappropriate in the first place, or that your child needs more support and instruction to meet those goals than was anticipated when designing his or her IEP.

An additional problem with IEP progress reports is that they tend to report your child's progress primarily as measured by his or her IEP objectives. There are several problems with this. For each objective formulated in your child's IEP, many more *could* have been chosen. These instructional objectives were selected as the priorities to be addressed during the educational year, but that does not mean that they were meant to be the only needs addressed. Furthermore, there is nothing sacred about the particular benchmarks stated to measure progress on those instructional objectives. They are simply indicator behaviors that you and your IEP committee agreed upon as likely (but not exclusive!) sources of information about progress towards meeting selected objectives. Your child's vulnerabilities are actually likely to emerge in other forms as well, and it is often useful to step back and look elsewhere for evidence of your child's struggles. New manifestations can emerge, supports can be inadequate to develop greater competence and independence on the identified needs, and previously identified issues can transform and manifest in new ways.

Your child's report cards and progress reports appear, at least on the surface, to be a relatively objective measure of the success of your child's IEP. Especially when they include effort, achievement, and conduct dimensions, report cards seem to provide some objective measure of school performance. However, I urge you: *do not confuse educational performance with learning, or academic grades as the only school dimension that matters.* I offer two examples from my own children to illustrate the inadequacy of a child's grades alone as a primary criterion for determining whether or not a child's educational needs are being met.

Marcus, to give one example, is receiving very good grades in school, despite now taking advanced classes. I have no doubt that he is constantly learning new material in seventh grade, but I also see his exhaustion at the end of each day. I see the amount of organization I have to help him with at home, and the amount of monitoring I have to do to help him keep track of his assignments, or the coaching I have to do to prep him for how to talk to a teacher when he has missed a class or performed poorly on a particular assignment. I monitor his anxiety levels; I see him hyperventilate at night worrying over social issues in the lunchroom. I see his fingers peeled, not only of fingernails, but also of deep layers of skin. I heard him, at 12 years old, tell me that he does not want to sign up for Little League because he thinks that the amount of homework he is assigned will not leave him time and energy for the two nights during the week, and three hours on Saturday that baseball would entail! These difficulties are not reflected in Marcus's grades, which tend to be good—although paradoxically, his teachers sometimes feel that Marcus needs to try harder on his work. However, his school experience is being much more difficult than I believe we have the right to ask of *any* seventh grader. The difficulty of that school experience needs to be addressed in his IEP by helping him more effectively target his efforts.

Michael, to give you a second example, is so well read and bright, that I don't think he often really "learns" in the classroom; he is just given the opportunity to demonstrate things that he already knows. Therefore, Michael's "achievement" grades are unlikely to reflect his classroom difficulties, although his effort or conduct grades sometimes do. He has tremendous trouble with organization and transitioning between activities. He can see that he is usually last to get settled, that his desk is a mess, that he often can't find things he needs, and that he often has to admit to others that he forgot materials or assignments. Those behaviors disrupt the smooth flow of the school day and they are the source of many negative messages he receives. I am still struggling to get those difficulties adequately addressed in his IEP. As I frustratedly told the school one day, "If you are looking for my child to fail, to indicate the severity of his needs, that just isn't going to happen. He is too bright and I am too involved to let failure happen, or even to let his performance drop to what others would consider 'average.' He is not an average child!" *His* difficulties are shown in ways other than grades; a child can be gifted and still significantly struggling. Indeed, some of my self-esteem fears for him were realized last year when Michael struggled with a significant episode of clinical depression.

The biggest problem with report cards or grades is that, although they may measure products and describe my child's performance compared with the rest of the class, they do not capture what the experience was like for him as a learner. They reflect a *product*, not a *process*. I believe that the quality of my child's educational experience lies much more in the nature of the learning process—what engaged him, what frustrated him, what made him feel pride, and what gave him negative messages about himself. I also believe that the school experience is about so much more than just *academic* products. It is also about curiosity and creativity, emotions and self-esteem, character development, social interactions, and organizational and physical challenges. These aspects of the school experience shape my child every bit as much as the academic curriculum he is presented, and these aspects of the experience also need to be closely examined for our children with special needs. To get a picture of this more multi-faceted aspect of your child's school day is much more difficult than keeping track of returned papers or understanding a report card. Direct observations of your child's behavior, your child's self-reports, and the emotional tenor of your home after school and during homework time will help provide a more complete picture of how well the school's efforts are working. Talk to your child. More importantly, listen between the lines to what his or her words and actions are saying. Graded products may give one picture of your child's educational success, but observation of your child at work on those products may present quite another picture. This is why it is important for you to put yourself in the learning loop with your child, and then share what you see with others on your child's IEP team.

The importance of putting yourself in the learning loop with your child

It is easy for teachers to know what they have covered in class; it is much harder to discover what they have actually taught, what the students have learned, or what the students now can or cannot do. Because of the time pressures to cover curriculum, teachers often neglect to check for understanding, or such global checks may not reveal the confusions of individual students. If your child learns best at a slower pace or with a different presentation style than is the class norm, the shakiness of his or her comprehension might not be revealed until later. Homework time is when many otherwise masked difficulties emerge. As I discussed in Chapter 6, you can use homework time to help your child develop needed competencies. You can also use your child's homework time as a way to keep an eye on your child's educational progress, and to note patterns that you may wish to bring up later with his or her educational team. Your explicit feedback on patterns, recurrent difficulties, and even things that you discover to help your child, may end up resulting in IEP changes to further support your child in his or her learning. Teachers often cannot tell what goes on with your child's performance behind your home doors unless you tell them. Do not underestimate the importance or the usefulness of your own observations of your child's work at home.

An excellent example of the importance of my feedback to the school, came when Marcus was in third grade. It was late January, and over the past month Marcus and I had begun spending more and more time on homework. It was taking one-and-a-half to two hours nightly, and my poor eight-year-old was wilting. At first, we thought the increase was due to missed time at school due to having a tooth extracted. Then we assumed the reason was that transitions back after the holidays are always difficult. Then we attributed the increase to make-up work because of a mid-year class requirement that all assignments be in cursive. There always seemed to be a reason for a given night's homework to be so difficult. It took a while for me to realize that a consistent overload pattern was emerging, and that this pattern was something I needed to bring up with the school. The teachers only saw Marcus's completed work products: they had no idea of the amount of time and effort he was expending, or the amount of adult support needed to get him through that work at home. Although the specifics have changed from grade to grade, I've seen similar problems arise at various times with each of my boys. Your perspective and experiences with your child are different from the school's. *Do not assume that the school knows the same things about your child that you know,* or that the school just doesn't care. One of the most important things you can do when you note your child struggling is to pass on that information to the school. Don't be an Information Scrooge! You must actively work to help the school see what you are seeing. The school personnel cannot help you or your child if you don't tell them what you are concerned about, or help them to understand why. The attitude you take in these dialogues is central to the response you are likely to receive: remember, you are a team member, and you are giving strategically important feedback to the other members of your team.

At certain times of the year, I have learned I can predict that my children will "crash." Around February each year, the elementary school's curriculum seems to pick up pace. New concepts seem to be introduced more frequently around this time of year, and the sheer amount of the workload increases as teachers try to maximize their use of the long, relatively uninterrupted stretch of time before spring vacation. This is when underlying weaknesses in my elementary school children's IEPs are most likely to emerge. Secondary school is still too new to us for timing patterns to emerge with my older son. I do know that the first six to eight weeks of each school year have been rough, and that the sheer pace and volume of work at exam times is overbearing. The drill and practice format of the work teachers assign for students to study the material often does not mesh well with my child's energy levels or his more conceptual learning style. However, in either case, my feedback is important to the teachers to let them know the patterns that I see emerging, and to discuss with them what we can try, to assist my boys with their difficulties. Sometimes this is a matter of interpretation, and it helps if different individuals share their perspective and discuss different possible solutions.

I guess as parent, I would say that your role is to address the details of individual experiences, while at the same time stepping back to see the big picture of your child's life. You have to get in the emotional trenches with your child, while keeping enough distance to give your child the freedom to experience and to learn. You must decide when your support and intervention is enough, and when you need to call in additional troops. Your job is not an easy one. Even children without IEPs encounter problems with their school experience. A good school year does not necessarily mean one in which there are no problems. The trick is in recognizing what degree of difficulty is acceptable and within normal range, what degree warrants formal or informal intervention, and what warrants letting the child work it through on his or her own. We *do not* want our children to live in an unrealistic, protective bubble. We *do* want them to develop self-confidence and effective problem-solving skills.

What should you do when you see your child having problems?

First and foremost, when problems emerge, remind yourself that your child's teacher or school is not "the enemy." Although your goals and the school's for your child may not be identical, they probably are not at odds with one another either. Mutual recognition that you share a common desire to help your child, can help foster a problem-solving attitude instead of a hostile one, pitting one side against the other amid accusations and defensiveness. Box 10.1 presents characteristics of a constructive, problem-solving approach to working with your child's educational team. As you read through it, you will see that taking such an approach does not mean that you have to ignore problems, or passively accept the school's solutions. On the contrary, working with a team, contributing your voice and your perspective to the mix, is more likely to benefit your child than solo efforts on either side.

Box 10.1 Characteristics of a problem-solving approach with the members of your child's educational team

- Information sharing:
  - helping people to see what you see
  - working to see and understand what others see
  - enrolling their perspective and help, and offering your own.
- Listening to each other's perspectives and reconciling positions:
  - on data
  - on interpretation
  - on solutions.
- Evaluating results of solution attempts by cycling through the process again, as needed.

As a parent, you have the right to call for a program review meeting at any time you start to have concerns. I tend to write a program review meeting into my son's IEP, to occur around six or eight weeks into the school year. When you do call a meeting to discuss a problem, come prepared. Arrive organized, having done your homework, gathered your facts, mentally rehearsed possible scenarios and reactions, and ready to present your case. A summary sheet or perhaps a letter presenting your concerns in advance can be useful for keeping your focus during the meeting. You may also want to provide your team members with a checklist of the things you would like to see addressed.

At the beginning of the meeting, be specific when laying the perceived problem on the table and walk through your most important points. Do not assume that the school personnel have noticed the same things that you are noticing, or that they attach the same significance to it. State your concern clearly, and then back it up with specific examples of what has led you to that generalization or conclusion. Describe what you have seen, cuing into specific assignments or specific examples. It is one thing to complain "My child has too much homework," and quite another to voice a concern while showing the exact number of minutes spent on each assignment over the past week or two weeks. Maybe it is not homework as a whole that is derailing your child, but a particular subject matter or type of assignment. The more explicit the data you can provide your team, the better position you will all be in to analyze that data for patterns, and to propose possible solutions. When faced with your accumulation of data, your committee may very well easily come to the same conclusions that you have drawn. If not, they may present additional contrasting evidence, or information that supplements or provides an additional context to help you interpret what you are seeing. Be sure to listen carefully and take note of the team's reactions and responses.

Once the data is on the table, the next move is to hypothesize causes. If you believe some aspect of your child's disability has come into play, you need to present and explain that as a possibility. Often the school will respond that many of the children in the class are having the same problem. The fact that my child is not alone helps me feel better sometimes, but that perspective does not affect the fact that he needs help. Maybe the solutions we come up with for my child will be ones that can help others in the class as well. For example, if everyone is having trouble with cursive writing, I stay focused on my child and the way that the trouble is exhibiting in him. I can't help whether the general curricular demands are appropriate for the class as a whole or not, but I can discuss what I see in my child.

Once you have made your points, and especially if you have submitted them in writing for the team to consider ahead of time, it is now your time to listen. You've already said what you think. Now is the time to hear their responses. Don't be too quick to rebut or object to their responses, especially if their response or your initial reaction is negative. You owe it to your team to listen to what they think and why. Integrating perspectives into a coherent whole through authentic dialogue will be much more likely to lead to a constructive solution rather than arguing as to which *single* perspective is right. Listening is hard work. I find it useful to take notes on what I hear school personnel to be saying. You may also find it helps to restate and summarize the main points you are hearing from them—not only the ones you are presenting.

Sometimes a consultation with an outside educational, psychological, or other expert can be useful. An outside individual can sometimes bring in another perspective, add weight to your concerns, or help as a resource for possible solutions. You may hear from your team that the expert may perhaps be correct about your child, but that they do not understand schools. This criticism may even be deserved! However, it is your job not to let any statement be a trump card, nixing further discussion. Instead, work to keep the dialogue open, so the various perspectives can be melded into a solution that will address your concerns and still be feasible from the school's perspective.

Help your team to be constructive. I am convinced that one of our jobs as parents of children with special needs, is to help the school recognize how they can help our children. We can do this by providing very concrete examples of what strategies and solutions can look like. You may consider photocopying references, resources, or possible solutions. You should not presume to dictate solutions, but the more you can help your team start to brainstorm, the more likely they will be to join in with suggestions and possibilities of their own. Ideally, these meetings are not about "winning" and "losing," but about how to reach a consensus that both sides can find satisfactory.

Stay focused on your goal. Your team personnel are busy, as are you, and you need to make the most of your meetings together. Remember, your purpose is to solve the problem, not to vent your feelings. Vent with your spouse or with your friends, not with your school team. Your emotions can totally derail the meeting. As upset as you may be by what is going on, if you make the meeting about calming you down, your child will suffer. Here is where your statement of the problem will really matter, and it is important that you voice it concisely and clearly because your statement will influence the team's focus. I once made the mistake of putting into my descriptive letter a statement of how the anxiety levels and amount of time spent in homework were warping our family life. You guessed it! A large part of the ensuing discussion was the team's efforts to try to convince me to pull back from homework involvement. They dealt with the issue as I had (mis)stated it, and not with the issue that I actually wanted to have addressed. So, a large part of your personal challenge will be to manage your emotions. I've shaken with anger. I've cried from frustration. I've also worked hard to allow those manifestations only in private, or with people I trust. The emotions are real, and you will need to acknowledge and deal with them. But you cannot let these emotions take the driver's seat as you advocate for your child—not if you want to be effective.

Be sure to consult with your child. Your child can be a valuable source of information, giving his or her perspective about what is causing a problem. Your child can often give useful feedback on possible solutions, as to whether or not they think the solutions seem like a good approach. Although your child's perceptions may be based on incomplete or misunderstood data, discussing the situation with him or her may help both of you get a fuller sense of what is going on. Plus, practically speaking, your child's cooperation is often needed to implement IEP strategies. Discussions with your child ahead of time can help you uncover sources of resistance. Perhaps the two of you can brainstorm together to devise mutually agreeable solutions that are more likely to be carried through. Finally, I advocate talking to your child about what you are doing because it gives your child the message that you are in this together. You recognize their struggles and their accomplishments. Their opinions matter. These discussions model a problem-solving approach for your child, and lay the foundations for self-advocacy strategies that will be vitally important as your child grows beyond your immediate supervision and protection.

A further note on conflict

We live in a very cooperative school district, but I have encountered a number of problems over the years. Different school districts, with different personnel, may have different reputations for their willingness to work with parents in the best interest of the child. In an ideal world, life would always go smoothly. But I've come to adopt a more realistic mindset, which is that problems are going to arise. The mark of a quality program is not the absence of problems, but rather it is how the school and the district respond when the inevitable problems do arise. Often, simply bringing a problem to the school's attention through individual or team meetings has been sufficient to gain resolution of the problem. Whenever possible, I try to go directly to the person most directly involved in the particular aspect of my child's school day, saving going further up the chain of command as a back-up position. My basic approach is to try to treat others the way that I would want to be treated. So, if I were the one providing the care/services to my child, I would rather be alerted to a problem directly by the parent, rather than have the parent bypass me and go first to my supervisor. Also, practically speaking, a good supervisor is likely to ask you right away whether you have tried to talk to the staff directly about the problem. Keep in mind, however, that if the problem is not resolved to your satisfaction, you always have the option to appeal to others higher up in the authority chain, and you should not hesitate to do so.

Seeking the perspectives of other individuals can be useful when you feel that you and the school district are approaching an impasse. Parent support groups are invaluable for learning what other parents have done when faced with similar difficult situations. Engaging the services of a professional consultant or a parent advocate can be useful as well, by either advising you or accompanying you to meetings with the school. Parent to Parent, Families Together, or other family support agencies can often help you connect with a parent advocate who can support you in your dealings with the school district. The outside consultant may be an authority in the area of your child's disability. Or she or he may be someone useful in recognizing and countering power plays, unfair manipulation by the school district, or blatant violations of one's educational rights.

Finally, if nothing else seems to be working to resolve your conflict, seek legal representation. At some point in time, you may find your issues with the school beyond your ability to resolve satisfactorily without legal advice or support. What do you do? Your child's rights as a person with a disability are explicitly defined and protected by a number of state and federal laws. So, one option always available to you is to take legal action against schools or institutions on behalf of your child. Seek professional, legal help if your situation comes to this. But keep in mind that the general consensus across authorities appears to be that, if the matter has to end up in the courts, everyone loses. If you call your lawyer into meetings, the other side has to call their lawyer. Communication between parties becomes less open, less about addressing the child's needs, and more guarded and focused on the law. Pursuing the legal route is expensive, in terms of time, energy, and money. It is much better for both sides if issues can be resolved without such dire steps. However, situations may evolve so that the legal route is the only viable road left for you. If such dire steps are needed, by all means take them. Sometimes they are the only means of getting what your child needs. At other times, developing your own ability to speak knowledgeably and accurately about the law may be enough to get the results you need, without going through official legal channels.

Chapter 9 discussed the importance of including in your own, more general disability education, a basic foundation in your child's educational rights and the law governing special education. Useful resources at the end of that chapter listed general legal sources for building your knowledge. Preparedness ahead of time, when heads are calmer and reason more likely to prevail, is your best defense against an escalating conflict. But there are other tools that you may want to consult as well, and not all of them involve quoting legal precedent. At the end of this chapter I list some additional parent resources for dealing with conflict.

Sometimes the best way around conflict, is not looking at law, but rather looking at negotiation strategies. After all, problem-solving is still your ultimate goal. Negotiation strategies can be a useful tool in this regard. When we hit an impassable wall, it is not uncommon to find that if either side is willing to move their position a few inches to either side, a doorway to agreement can be discovered. Reconceptualizing an issue away from a specific solution, and back to a common goal can be another useful tool for finding another way around a problem. The resources at the end of this chapter can be useful for helping you back away from the particular issue, and look instead at the dynamics surrounding that issue. On the other hand, if a greater understanding of legal precedent on specific issues is more crucial to your problem-solving strategies, the Wrightslaw website (www.wrightslaw.com) often presents specific discussions of common conflicts, and connections to relevant case law showing what the courts' positions have been to date. We are fortunate enough where I live, to have a quality law school in our area, which offers a free clinic for advising parents and disabled individuals in matters of disability law. Many regions offer advocacy centers, which can provide legal guidance to you. For example, The Advocacy Center, located in Rochester, New York, serves upstate New York. There are likely to be similar centers in your region. The www.nichcy.org website or www.yellowpagesforkids.com can help you locate legal advocates within the United States.

The law is a complex entity, and one that is constantly in flux. New laws and regulations are passed regularly by federal and state legislatures. Court decisions create new case law. Interpreting how and what law applies to your particular situation, in your particular state may require the advice or services of a good lawyer. If so, select one who specializes in disability or special educational issues. If you have consulted other therapists and professionals, they may have names of lawyers or legal firms they recommend, based on their experience. If you have connected with a good parent network, they almost always will be able to refer you to someone in your community. Just as in hiring therapists or other specialists for your child, be sure to interview anyone you are considering employing for their specific training or experience relevant to a situation such as yours. The school district will have aggressive, experienced legal professionals making their case. You must ensure that you are equally well represented.

I have been very fortunate and have never had to file for a due process hearing in order to advocate for my sons. Therefore, I cannot offer further advice from my experience. I do know that the Wrightslaw website offers a training DVD on due process hearings, as well as specific books citing and explaining the applicable laws, to help you understand the arguments and the process. If this is a route you decide to use, keep your goal in sight: to help your child. Remember, you can't afford just to turn things over to the "experts." You need to understand at each step, what your options are, what is being done on your behalf, and why. You may not know the law, but you know your child and your situation. You know how to ask questions and you know how to learn. You know how to advocate for your child. Do not turn off your brain or your involvement just because you've brought in legal professionals. Learn from your legal advisors, but also help them to understand your situation and your child so they can make their arguments more effectively. They may be your "hired guns," but you will be building your case together.

Useful resources
Standing up for your rights without shooting yourself in the foot: parent guides to navigating conflict situations

Fisher, Roger and Ury, William (1991) *Getting to Yes: Negotiating Agreement Without Giving In*. New York: Penguin.

Mayerson, Gary (2004) *How to Compromise With Your School District Without Compromising Your Child: A Field Guide for Getting Effective Services for Children With Special Needs*. New York: DRL Books Inc.

Ury, William (1993) *Getting Past No: Negotiating in Difficult Situations. Confrontation to Cooperation*. New York: Bantam Books.

Wright, Peter W.D. and Wright, Pamela Darr (2006) *From Emotions to Advocacy: The Special Educational Survival Guide* (2nd edn). Hartfield, VA: Harbor House Law Press.

Wright, Peter W.D. and Wright, Pamela Darr (2007) *Special Education Law* (2nd edn). Hartfield, VA: Harbor House Law Press.

11

Advocating for Your Child

It Never Ends, or Does It?

One of my goals in this book has been to help you, as your child's parent, get a better picture of what successful advocacy for your child can look, sound, and feel like. I wanted to make advocacy real for you. I wanted to help you learn from some very concrete examples and then move beyond those examples to create your own way of advocating that is a custom fit for you and for your child. You see, for me, advocacy is not a particular set of things to do. Rather, advocacy is a way of life in which no detail of my child's experience is too small to be worth my examination, and no expert is so lofty that I unquestionably accept his or her advice. Advocacy, to me, is about really looking at and listening to my children, and making sure their perspectives and their needs are considered. Advocacy is about problem-solving, envisioning new choices, and taking action to make life better for my children and for others. Advocacy as a way of life does have some downsides, however.

At times, wearing the double hat of parent and advocate for your child will seem the most natural combination in the world. After all, that's what all parents do: we look out for our children to make sure they are protected, helped, and valued. Sometimes, that combination of advocate and parent will involve a difficult double vision. It can be painful to look closely at the parts of our children's development that are causing them problems, and it is hard work to develop plans to address those problems. My husband sometimes says I go looking for trouble, and in a way he is right. Yes, I do look for trouble spots—I believe that someone has to do so! On the other hand, because I want life to be so good for my children (as does any parent), looking for trouble hurts. What loving parent willingly and regularly schedules evaluations of their child meant to spotlight their child's deficiencies? Yet we regularly must do just that! Even though IEP paperwork includes spaces to list your child's strengths and abilities, the emphasis tends to be on examining the challenges and deficiencies to a degree that parents of typically developing children never have to consider. No wonder in the advocacy community, some people get upset about all of the focus on the *dys*functions and on the *dis*abilities! Yet the paradox is that those dysfunctions and disabilities are a part of the person who is my son. They are also the part on which we, as parents and as advocates for our children, must concentrate an inordinate amount of our attention. Sometimes we do so with focused efforts to help our children change. At other times we react by pushing for greater support and acceptance by others. Yes, we recognize and celebrate the many wonderful things about our children. But to enlist the help of others in supporting our children, we find we have to keep dragging up the negatives.

It is sometimes difficult to take on this analytical approach without slipping into the clinical mindset of our children as a set of "problems to be fixed." The entire medical model of disability, which looks to therapies and treatments, feeds this notion. So does the quite practical observation that, often, some aspects of our children's problems *can* be fixed or their impact lessened. As a parent, I have pushed to receive a great deal of intervention, designed to help build skills that were not developing naturally in my children. Many of these therapies have been highly effective, and my children's functioning has greatly improved as a result. I do not regret those efforts. The question that should always underlie these discussions, however, is this: how much therapy is enough, and when should one move into acceptance and support of difference instead of trying to change it?

Years ago, before I married or had any inkling that I'd ever have a personal connection with developmental disabilities, one of my professors at Yale said that he remembered sitting around with a group of researchers one day. They were talking about children with a particular diagnosis (the specifics of which elude my memory). Someone remarked, "I'll bet if we watched these kids in the snack room, we'd find they even drink Coke differently." In recounting this story, my professor was sending out the warning that if you are always on the lookout for *differences*, you're almost always going to find them. That is the nature of the diversity of humanity. But not every difference is of clinical significance. Not every difference entails a problem. And finally, "not every problem needs to be fixed!" as one of my favorite physical therapists once said to me. Even typical children are far from "perfect," so why should we burden atypically developing children with tons of therapy to try to shape them towards that illusory ideal? That's why as parents and advocates for our children, we always have to add in a healthy dose of self-examination and reflection. Am I pushing too hard? Is this a battle I should forget about? Have I lost my perspective? Have I become too much focused on the disability, and not enough on parenting my child? I admit, I've had to answer "yes," to some of these questions at one time or another. But in contrast to the few times I've perhaps done "too much," is the fact that *most* of the time, I've done exactly what was needed, and my children have thrived in so many areas as a result.

Another risk posed by being such a strong advocate for my children, is that I get so involved in trouble-shooting and problem-solving for my children, that I inadvertently cut my children out of the advocacy loop. I try to anticipate problems before they occur, to avoid them or mitigate their effects by building subtle supports and structures into my children's worlds. However, I am not always with my children to do this. Marcus's experience in middle school is certainly showing me that his world is moving outside of my range far faster than I can keep up. Eventually, my children won't be children any more. I really need to think more carefully about how I am preparing them to take on these advocacy responsibilities for themselves. My oldest has only barely turned 13—I thought I had a lot of time before I started planning for that transition to adulthood. Marcus, however, is quickly taking care of that delusion! My child may not be neurotypical, but in other respects he is a typical teenager, exploring his identity, making his own choices, and moving inexorably towards greater psychological and physical independence. Fueling this process, the junior high school environment is one in which greater independence is expected of him. I realize that the best gift I can give him at this time, is to make a concerted effort to teach him how to be a strong self-advocate.

Helping our children become advocates for themselves

We know what we, as parents, do to advocate for our child. What would *self-advocacy* look like, especially in a child or teenager with a disability? Self-advocacy is a set of skills that can be developed (look at how *you* have developed your own advocacy skills!). It is not about education, or about high intelligence, or even high communicative ability. At its basic root, self-advocacy involves speaking up about what you want or need. It involves asking questions or giving other people enough information about your wants and needs, that they can help you obtain and understand the information you need to make informed choices and decisions. Self-advocacy does not have to be about going it alone (just as we, as our children's parents, have found others to help us advocate for our children). Self-advocacy is about speaking up to make sure that what matters to you personally for living your life, is heard and taken into account, so that others work with you to further your goals. Self-advocacy is about laying claim to the rights and responsibilities of having input into one's own life. Box 11.1 lists the basic characteristics of self-advocacy proposed by the organization, People First of Missouri. I included it here because I think it does a wonderful job refocusing our attention, as parents, on what the basic skills of self-advocacy would look like for our adult children to function effectively in the world.

Box 11.1 What is self-advocacy?

Self-advocacy is:
- learning to speak up for yourself
- letting other people know what you want or need
- learning how to get all the information you need in order to make a good decision
- finding out what and who will support you in meeting the goals you set
- knowing your rights and responsibilities
- feeling good about learning from your mistakes
- problem-solving when things go wrong and making a new plan.

(adapted from www.missouripeoplefirst.org)

One of the most important steps we, as parents, need to take to help our children become strong self-advocates, may well involve a major attitude adjustment on our own part. Be careful. My experience is that many of your old preconceptions of ability and disability—those ghosts that you thought you'd exorcised when you first faced your children's developmental differences—may put in a repeat appearance. It is important that you do your homework, to move beyond those emotional reactions, as you work to evolve your relationship with your teen into its adult form.

But he/she is only a child... It's too complicated for him/her to understand... She/he cannot do as good a job as I can... She/he will have no one to provide good guidance... She/he will miss out on getting what she/he really needs... The stakes are too high... You may have other fears to add to this list—and they are real fears. The point is not to let our children's lives be governed by them. Instead, we need to acknowledge them, confront them, and find answers to them that enable our adult children to live rich full lives, as independently as possible.

"A parent's mentoring relationship must be based on an underlying trust and respect for one's child as someone capable of learning how to manage his or her own life," the National Center on Secondary Education and Transition (NCSET) and the Parent Advocacy Coalition for Educational Rights Center (PACER) advise (2002). We need to replace our focus on those fears, with a new focus, a focus on *what would it take*? What would it take to support our children as adults in living the lives they want for themselves, pursuing their goals and dreams? Helping our children develop the ability to speak up for themselves is a major step in preparing them for the adult world.

At the heart of self-advocacy is self-awareness. This includes your child's knowledge of him or herself, his or her strengths, weaknesses, preferences, and interests. Self-awareness develops and deepens over years, even for typically developing individuals. The self-awareness of a young child looks very different from the self-awareness of an adult. Young children describe themselves based on concrete, physical dimensions. It is only over time, that the self-descriptions develop to include comparisons to others, and abstract qualities. Although we are far from our children's only source of knowledge about themselves, one of our responsibilities as parents is to help shape our children's emerging self-concept.

Self-awareness is a particularly difficult skill, I think, for those individuals on the autism spectrum, but then again, even neurotypical adults have problems "knowing themselves." When my children were preschoolers, I gave them opportunities to make choices, helped them recognize and then name their apparent preferences, helped them try new things, and yes, allowed them to reject other things. This helped my children develop a sense of themselves. Rooted in our early physical attempts to seek pleasurable outcomes and avoid discomfort, self-awareness gradually becomes more abstract. It is built through continued experiences and shaped by the commentary of others: "Oh, you like to run a lot." "Loud noises frighten you, don't they?" "You really love books about dragons and knights!" Eventually, self-awareness develops into the ability to recognize and express preferences, and to make choices that take into account one's preferences and needs.

At some point, our children's self-awareness will need to include an understanding of their own disabilities. My children have *a right to know* about their disability—what it means, and perhaps equally important, what it does not mean! My children also *need to know* this information as a part of the puzzle they must consider when they are going about their daily activities, or when they are making plans for their futures. Helping our children learn about their own disabilities is an important task, which I discussed in Chapter 4. Because so much of our parenting life has been spent sheltering our children, and filtering their perceptions of ability and disability, the issue of what to tell your child and when, is a particularly difficult one for parents. But this self-knowledge is crucial for a person to make good choices for him or herself—both those big "life decisions," and those day-to-day choices we make as we go about our lives. An effective self-advocate must be self-confident and comfortable with their disability, and able to defend him or herself against others who might try to limit their life options because of their disability. Dinah Murray (2006) has a multi-faceted collection of essays exploring some of these self-awareness and self-advocacy issues for individuals, in *Coming Out Asperger*. As your child gets older, consider seeking out support groups and self-advocacy groups that would allow him or her to explore these aspects of his or her life.

A self-advocate also needs to learn how to develop and voice their own goals. Here I am not talking about IEP goals, or goals in the form of "I (the student) will be able to…" Rather, I am speaking of "real-life" goals. "What do I want for the near or far future? What is my plan going to be to accomplish or achieve that goal?" Setting goals, making plans to accomplish them, and then carrying through those plans, making adjustments as needed, is often at the heart of my advocacy life with my children. As I think now about developing self-advocacy skills in my children, I realize that I need to adjust my style, to start weaving more of a strand of self-advocacy into my parenting. My children alternate between shutting down and going passive when their needs are not met, and more dramatically melting down when they are overwhelmed. They often don't know how to ask for help. They often don't know how to decipher others' advice to understand what they should actually do to fix their current problem. Planning and organizational skills are a challenge for both my boys, whether it is motor planning, project planning, or organizing their rooms or even just their desks. I've targeted pragmatic language skills as important for both my boys. Along with that, however, I need to help demystify the planning process for them. I need to do more thinking aloud, and more modeling for them of how to speak up or ask for assistance. I also need to start to lower my scaffolding net, pulling back supports while I can still be around to help my boys recover if they fall. This means letting my boys try more things their own way, letting them make mistakes, and letting them learn from their own experiences of success and failure. Instead of doing it for them, I can help them learn from what they have tried themselves. I can also help them autopsy what happened and why, and brainstorm with them about what they may wish to try next.

Transitioning into the adult world: ready or not, it will come!

Initially, when I decided to explore the issue of transition to adulthood, I did so thinking it would be good to end my book with a glimpse at the future that eventually I would need to face with my sons. Marcus was only 12 at the time, and the issue seemed far off in our future. I expected to begin addressing these issues around the same time I started considering driving, dating, part-time jobs after school, or explorations into post-secondary education. I have already begun sharing with Marcus some of the discussions his consultant teacher and I have about his upcoming IEPs, and I have thought about inviting him to sit in on some of our meetings, but I have not taken any further action. I thought I was probably right on track, or perhaps even ahead of the game. When I researched this section of my book, however, I found that *federal law mandates a particular transition process*, and that it begins much earlier than I would have imagined. IDEA mandates that a transition plan should begin to be formulated at age 14, including provisions that children (yes, your child!) will be included in the IEP planning meetings, not just as observers, but as active participants. By age 16, specific goals addressing your child's transition into the adult world need to be in place. Teens are encouraged eventually to learn to run their own IEP meetings, and to educate others about their abilities and disabilities so they can represent themselves to others without your buffering presence. As one teenager challenged with mental retardation told me quite firmly, "No discussion about us, without us." At age 18, your parenting rights to participate as an equal member on your child's IEP team and to make educational decisions on his or her behalf, automatically revert to your child, unless the courts have declared your child to be legally incompetent. By this time, my parent advocacy role reverts to one of an advisory nature only, and therefore is only as good as my relationship with my child affords it to be!

Furthermore, by the time Marcus leaves high school, not only am I out of a job as his chief advocate, but the supports and accommodations my son will be afforded as an adult, are very different from those he is offered as a child. Adults with developmental disabilities deal with different agencies and funding sources, operating under different laws and regulations from those governing special education. Instead of educational entitlements, young adult needs are things to be argued under anti-discrimination or civil rights provisions, or to be applied for as social security, Medicaid, or health insurance benefits. Even when the schools and I have had differences of opinion regarding specifics, I have been able to rely on the fact that the school is required by law to address my children's needs. Now I find that the abrupt and unexpected (to me!) reality of special education laws is that their protections and responsibilities end with the completion of my boys' high school education. Absolute time to prepare Marcus and Michael for adulthood is much shorter than my intense, year-by-year focus on their unique developmental paths has let me see.

Instead of waiting for a distant future, I'm realizing that I need to start collecting new information and adjusting my sights. What does preparing my child to be an adult mean? I was so cognitively and emotionally floored at first, that I didn't even know what questions to ask or where to start to look for answers. I think that ignorance scared me as much as the sudden recognition of the time bomb itself. For the past ten years, I have been busy working with the school IEP teams to prepare my children for their school world, and their school world for them. I hadn't given thought to the fact that although this may be the life of a school-aged child, it is not "life." In school, it is very easy to become lulled into a rhythm in which, each year, we set IEP goals for the next year based on the challenges we expect our children to face in the coming year, coupled with what we've learned from the difficulties they experienced in the preceding year. The school is especially interested in classroom performance; I have occasionally pushed to have self-help or social goals included. But to be honest, we've never stepped back and systematically surveyed where this step-at-a-time preparation stands in terms of where my children will need to be when they are adults.

That is the purpose of transition services: to help provide this wake-up call for life after school, and for families and schools to work together with the child to help ensure a smooth start into adulthood. "Everyone needs supports to be successful in life… " Jed Baker reminds us in his book, *Preparing for Life* (2005).

> The important thing to know is the amount and type of supports your son or daughter wants and needs. This is determined by your knowledge of their abilities, skills, interests and preferences. There are three basic types of support that individuals use: people, materials, and services. (Baker 2005, p.29)

The purpose of transition services is for the student, parents, and professionals to work together, to best determine which are most appropriate to help ease your child from the school world and into the adult one. There is not a single way of deciding what might be appropriate. Navigating the various agencies and opportunities is not easy. Various resources tend to be kept separate from one another, and the full range of possibilities is never laid out in one place. One way to approach transition is for you and your teen to survey what resources are out there, and then to consider which of these might be worth pursuing for your teen's particular situation. From this view, if you don't know something exists, you don't even know that it is a possibility. Discovering the resources helps you begin to dream the dreams. This piecemeal approach has its disadvantages, however, because it can be so focused on obtaining services that it ignores the bigger picture: that of creating the life your adult child wants. What would that life be, and what would it take to help my child live such a life?

In facing this question, I came across a very helpful website, with a practical, downloadable curriculum to help parent and child work with their transition team to plan for the future. The curriculum, developed by Kathy Roberson, Rick Blumberg, and Dan Baker (2005), is called *Keeping it Real*. The curriculum offers one way to include one's young adult in developing short- and long-term goals for their future. These goals encompass all the major aspects of adult life, from further education, to jobs, to relationships, to pursuit of hobbies and interests, to housing and community involvement. Although the secondary transition team has the responsibility to help guide you and your teen through the transition process, I am a firm believer in doing some scouting on one's own. Just as you often encountered resistance or differences in views when you worked with your child's IEP committees, your child as a self-advocate will have to navigate differing opinions and obstacles when approaching questions of adult life. Not everyone will be open to new visions of what can be possible, preferring instead to steer your young adult towards ready-made programs that may or may not be suited to the life your teen wants. Not everyone is equally versed in what resources are available. At the end of this chapter I list some places to start your search. Odds are that you and/or your teen will come across at least most of the important options if you pursue these various avenues. It will be important for you, and for your young adult to stay connected in some fashion to the information grapevine. When I look at the options available now that were not even possible ten years ago, I'm actually optimistic about what other possibilities the future may offer my child. As self-advocates continue to work together to speak up for their needs, and to help others live their own visions of what they want in life, and as government and community agencies respond to those needs, I am confident that new resources will continue to be created.

Kathie Snow's website, www.disabilityisnatural.com, offers the following exercise that I find encapsulates what should be at the heart of long-term planning for your child. The exercise, "Best Hopes, Worst Fears," is described in Snow's essay of that same name. In it, Snow challenges parents (and teens) to make two lists. In one list are those things that one would most hope to see happen when envisaging the future. In the other list are the worst possible outcomes you could imagine when envisaging that same future. These two lists can open useful discussions. Snow writes that, as parents, we often find that hopes and fears are actually opposite sides of the same coin. In planning for the one, we are often taking very real steps to avoid the other. An open discussion of these fears and hopes often frees people to see beyond their general anxiety about change. It helps people take a more realistic, constructive attitude towards risk—and towards living their dreams.

The things I have learned about transitioning to adulthood are already shaping my year-to-year planning for both my boys. I plan on adding more self-advocacy and independence threads to their IEPs. I certainly have changed my vision of what the ultimate end-result of my children's education needs to be. Preparation for college is still very much in the picture for my children, but so also is working steadily on preparation for life. The two do not have to be mutually exclusive. Vocational, social relationships, recreational, and other life skills are important for anyone to develop in order to have full, satisfying adult lives. This means that I need to be more careful what I sacrifice when we are tempted to narrow our school focus to only academics.

On the other hand, I realize that most of my life advocating for my children has been right on track. My heart and vision still has a lot of the important themes needed for developing competencies and removing barriers—my revelation after this peek at the adult future, is a bigger focus on doing more *with* my child, instead of *for* him. Just as with other developing competencies, it's time to start considering how to scaffold his performance, and then to phase back my directions and even some of my supports. I need to let him to get more of the feel for taking over these responsibilities on his own, while I can mentor him and help him digest and learn from his experiences. Learning to let go then becomes my biggest parenting task. Along with it goes the task of learning how to respect and be supportive of our "children's" choices as the adults they have become.

When words matter: understanding the politics of "special needs" and how it affects your child

When you first found out that your child was not developing typically, you may have been so overwhelmed with the enormity of the task of coming to grips with your emotions, and your anxiety about what to do and how to help your child, that your world collapsed into a small, hard-shelled capsule, labeled "special needs." That is understandable. You'd spent your life up until then holding a certain set of assumptions about the way the world worked, and more specifically, about the way the world would work for you and for your child. You had probably never seriously considered any other perspective, or any other possibilities. And then you found that your assumptions were wrong. You found yourself having to spend inordinate amounts of time, energy, and money unpacking this dense, forbidding, "special needs" capsule, and trying to make sense of what its contents mean for you and for your family. As you learn more and more about the capsule, I hope you learn to use it as a set of possible tools to help build a good life for your child—and not as a set of confining boundaries your child has to live within.

Eventually, and I hope it will be sooner rather than later, you will discover that helping your child involves much more than learning how to work the special needs network. Yes, it is part that, and the more successfully you learn to work the network, the easier it will be to get help for your child. The more time you spend dealing with the special needs network, the more likely you are to come across the political and philosophical discussions concerning special needs. Some disability rights advocates question the language we use. They object to the way labels are used as a shorthand reference for people, and how those labels always stress dis-ability instead of ability. Some advocates question the critical eye always put on individuals with special needs. Why do we always focus on what is "wrong" with them, as though they were individuals who need to be "fixed?" Why are we so slow to consider that *maybe it is our schools or communities that are defective*, putting up barriers that make it difficult, if not impossible for people who don't meet certain arbitrary standards to be included or to function? Advocates turn a critical eye to the treatments and options offered to individuals with disabilities, especially in regard to the issue of whether they provide full inclusion of people with disability in our communities. Advocates work to ensure that individuals with special needs

243

are not treated as a "special" kind of people, but rather that they are offered the supports needed to give them the same chances as everyone else to pursue their dreams and reach their full potential. You might think that these are primarily political or terminology issues, and be tempted to dismiss these vocal advocates, along with bra burners, tree huggers, war protestors, or whatever other types of "extremists" you may have encountered in the past. Don't be quick to ignore them or to dismiss their points as only yet another quarrel about "political correctness." If you listen closely and take the time to understand, you'll often find that their arguments are at the very heart of how people with disabilities (like your child!) are treated and what kinds of futures they (like your child!) have opened to them. With the new perspective given to you because it is now your child that is involved, maybe you'll have a different sense of how important these political, philosophical, and linguistic issues are.

At every stage of your life, you will have to prioritize, peek and put up blinders, ration your energy and resources, and struggle to manage the items already on your "plate." But be careful. Do not let yourself become so busy doing for your child, that you don't ever step back and reflect on *what* it is that you are doing, where it is leading, and what its implications are for your child's future life. These broader philosophical and political stances actually underlie most of what we do with our children. If you don't at least occasionally take the time to reflect, you are implicitly supporting and being guided by the status quo. Then, the disability underlying your child's diagnosis is not the greatest limitation that your child faces—it is the way our society treats your child. By unquestioningly accepting that treatment, you become an unwitting accomplice to limiting your child's world.

Advocacy often involves searching out off-the-track solutions for your child's needs. Equally important, however, is learning to turn a critical, questioning eye towards any answers that you find or are offered. Theoreticians have the luxury of focusing on a single perspective, and trying to show the applicability of their own theory or approach (or book!) to a wide range of situations. You, on the other hand, need to consider the individual circumstances of your child and how the proposed approach fits within your values, your lifestyle, and your dreams—and those of your child.

Always, always, always—no matter how progressive or persuasive the message—you have to consider your particular child. Do not allow assumptions about your child's lack of ability limit your child. Nor should you let others' enthusiasms about their recommendations for you, trump your instincts about what is right. Almost every disability will require you to make complicated decisions: what standard or alternate treatment approaches are you willing to consider? How invasive are you willing for the therapies to be? How much emphasis are you placing on building up weaknesses, and how much on building up strengths? Is more support always better? How much is enough? These are often value-laden decisions. I'm not saying that all choices are equal—but often, legitimate arguments can be made on many sides. It will be up to you to weigh the evidence, to decide which choices to try for your child, and to decide whether the outcome warrants continuing to stick with those choices or trying something different.

Sometimes, advocating for your child will entail taking risks. As parents, we are always making choices based inevitably on incomplete knowledge. We don't always know all the options truly available to us, and we are certainly limited in our ability to envisage and create new options. We don't know all the ramifications of the choices we make for our children, or how they are going to play out in our child's lives. We are very hard on ourselves, and vulnerable to guilt about things we should have, could have, or would have done differently. Working with and for our children can be socially isolating. As a result, it is very important that we seek out others who can help us hold our lives in perspective, who can share their knowledge, who can support us in our anger, or frustration, or exhaustion, or worry, or guilt. As you work to help prepare your child for adulthood, also prepare yourself for the fact that your role will change, and be ready to change with the flow. You cannot and should not shelter your child so much that you protect him or her from realities and mistakes—that is how we all learn and grow. Keep a close eye on yourself so that your work with your child is towards greater inclusion into the mainstream of life, rather than isolating your child within the sheltered confines of a special needs bubble.

I wish you and your children joy in your lives—laughter and smiles in the present, not just gritted teeth and hopes for what relief may eventually come. I wish for you the wisdom and courage to see your child's life as one of possibilities and abilities, and not one of limitations and disabilities. I wish you the courage, the perseverance, and the insight not to let just the fact that something is unknown or difficult stop you and your child from soaring somewhere new.

And no, at some level, it never ends

One day while listening to my latest round of issues, a friend sympathetically said to me, "It just never ends for you, does it?" She was right, in a way. It doesn't. My legal rights and responsibilities towards my sons may end when they reach the age of majority, but my parenting concerns will never end (just ask my 78-year-old parents, who still worry about me!). As for now, no sooner do I get one set of issues resolved, than others arise. On those rare occasions when I feel like life is stabilized, I take a breather and then start out looking for more trouble, seeking to identify the next set of priorities and the next set of goals. I'm not a natural crusader, but I am a fierce advocate for my children. At heart, advocacy is about learning to see the world differently, from the underdog's perspective, and then trying to bring about change to make life better.

Almost inevitably, we find that our advocacy for those we love affects more than just our children. There's nothing special about us. But there is something special about the effects that our actions can have on those around us. For some of you, just helping your children navigate life from day to day will seem almost more than you can manage. That certainly has been the case with our family at times, so I know! Your plate is so absolutely filled to overflowing with just emotionally and physically surviving, you can't even begin to consider taking on anything more. Your world revolves around trying to get from one day to the next, while trying desperately to meet your family's needs—juggling bowling balls while trying to stay a least one step ahead of that speeding bus. That is a form of "advocacy." You are working to make the world a better place for your child. I can promise you that what you may see as efforts concentrated on just your child, will have a ripple effect touching many more people. Your advocacy is important work for us all. It is difficult work. It is slow and steady change by example.

Others of you will find yourselves moving more and more into the world of "causes." As you try to meet your child's needs, you'll discover that the best way to do that is to create different formal structures, to take bigger actions for societal change. It's not that you have more time on your hands than others, but it is that the actions you find yourself taking to solve problems for your child somehow involve more formally changing your corner of the world to make it a better place for your children to be. You find yourself not only challenging school policies, but also helping to write new ones. You run for school board—or create new schools. You form support groups, or not-for-profit consulting agencies. You lobby for insurance reform, or housing reform, or more accessible transportation, or greater self-determinacy. You take on new careers.

Advocacy has many faces, many styles, and many goals—some of them not even dreamed yet. I've recently had the privilege of becoming a part of an international organization called Partners in Policy-Making. Throughout our meetings, I've met a lot of parents and self-advocates. Many of these individuals ended up there because they didn't like the menu of choices they were offered for dealing with their disabilities, and they found themselves bootstrapping their way into something better. From the members of this group, I've learned that social reform change doesn't require a particular type of education or position. It only requires a vision of something new to try, and a persistent determination not to take "no" for an answer.

As we work to advocate for our children, we find that their lives are not the only ones changed. Our lives are offered that chance as well, not by coming out on the other side of hardship, but by being offered the opportunity to see people in all their complex wholes. Our children help us see beyond traditional labels of ability and disability, to extending a helping hand whenever it is needed, and to innovative thinking and problem-solving. Our vision, once stretched to accommodate our own children, quickly grows to encompass the differences of others. *My world* actually doesn't have any children with *special* needs in it. It only has children, and all children have needs. My world is richer because of my experiences with my sons. I see things I never would have noticed and I appreciate more of the significance of what I see. My actions may help my children, but I feel I have actually been the one healed—of a narrow, unrealistic vision of the world. I hope that by sharing those experiences, I've helped enrich your world as well. And if you don't like what you see around you…well by now you're developing your own vision for how you can bring about change. Go for it! I wish you well.

Useful resources
Your child's transition to adulthood

The National Dissemination Center for Children with Disabilities (NICHCY) has created an easy to navigate, and highly informative suite of web-based resources on transition to adulthood. Interest- and need-specific paths are separately targeted for parents, students, and professionals. NICHCY also publishes state-specific resource guides applicable to individuals with disabilities of all ages.

www.nichcy.org/resources

The National Center on Secondary Education and Transition (NCSET) provides some helpful parent briefs promoting effective parent involvement in secondary education and transition.

www.ncset.org/publications

Resources on person-centered planning

www.ilr.cornell.edu

www.allenshea.com

www.capacityworks.com

Department of Vocational and Educational Services for Individuals with Disabilities

www.vesid.com

Regional non-profit agencies for independent living

www.ilusa.com/links/ilcenters.htm

State Developmental Disabilities Agencies

www.disabilityresources.org/DD.html

Social security income supports

www.socialsecurity.gov

A review of self-determination training curricula

www.uncc.edu/sdsp/sd_curricula.asp

**Information on special needs trusts, letters of intent, and other options
to help provide guidance/care in the event of your death**

www.kidsource.com/kidsource/content4/estate.dis.all.3.3.html

or www.nichcy.org

References

American Psychiatric Association (1994) *Diagnostic and Statistical Manual of Mental Disorders* (DSM-IV) (4th edn). Washington, DC: APA.

Anderson, Winifred, Chitwood, Stephen and Hayden, Deidre (1997) *Negotiating the Special Education Maze: A Guide for Parents and Teachers* (3rd edn). Bethesda, MD: Woodbine House.

Attwood, Tony (1998) *Asperger's Syndrome: A Guide for Parents and Professionals.* London: Jessica Kingsley Publishers.

Attwood, Tony (2006) *The Complete Guide to Asperger Syndrome.* London: Jessica Kingsley Publishers.

Baker, Jed (2005) *Preparing for Life: The Complete Guide for Transitioning to Adulthood for Those with Autism and Asperger's Syndrome.* Arlington, TX: Future Horizons, Inc.

Bates, Ames, Louise and Chase Haber, Carol (1985) *Your Seven-Year-Old: Life in a Minor Key.* New York: Dell Publishing.

Bates, Ames, Louise and Chase Haber, Carol (1989) *Your Eight-Year-Old: Lively and Outgoing.* New York: Dell Publishing.

Bates, Ames, Louise and Chase Haber, Carol (1990) *Your Nine-Year-Old: Thoughtful and Mysterious.* New York: Dell Publishing.

Bates, Ames, Louise, Ilg, Frances L. and Baker, Sidney M. (1988) *Your Ten-to-Fourteen-Year-Old.* New York: Dell Publishing.

Boehme, Regi (1990) *The Hypotonic Child: Treatment for Postural Control, Endurance, Strength, and Sensory Organization* (Revised). Tucson, AZ: Therapy Skill Builders.

Brazelton, T. Berry revised with Sparrow, Joshua (2006) *Touchpoint Birth to Three* (2nd edn). Cambridge, MA: DaCapo Press.

Fisher, Roger and Ury, William (1991) *Getting to Yes: Negotiating Agreement Without Giving In.* New York: Penguin Books.

Ginott, Haim G. with Ginott, Alice and Wallace, H. Goddard (eds) (2003) *Between Parent and Child: The Bestselling Classic that Revolutionized Parent-Child Communication* (2nd edn rev.). New York: Three Rivers Press.

Goddard, Sally (2002) *Reflexes, Learning and Behavior: A Window into the Child's Mind.* Eugene, OR: Fern Ridge Press.

Greene, Ross (2005) *The Explosive Child: A New Approach for Understanding and Parenting Easily Frustrated, Chronically Inflexible Children.* London: Harper.

Hieneman, Meme, Childs, Karen and Sergay, Jane (2006) *Parenting with Positive Behavior Support: A Practical Guide to Resolving your Child's Difficult Behavior.* Baltimore, MD: Brookes Publishing Co.

Hodgdon, Linda A. (1995) *Visual Strategies for Improving Communication: Practical Supports for School and Home.* Troy, MI: QuirkRoberts Publishing.

Jackson, Luke (2002) *Freaks, Geeks and Asperger Syndrome: A User Guide to Adolescence.* London: Jessica Kingsley Publishers.

Kaplan, Melvin (2006) *Seeing Through New Eyes: Changing the Lives of Children with Autism, Asperger Syndrome, and Other Developmental Disabilities Through Vision Therapy.* London: Jessica Kingsley Publishers.

Klein, Stanley D. and Kemp, John D. (eds) (2004) *Reflections From a Different Journey: What Adults with Disabilities Wish All Parents Knew.* New York: McGraw Hill.

Klein, Stanley D. and Schive, Kim (eds) (2001) *You Will Dream New Dreams: Inspiring Personal Stories by Parents of Children with Disabilities.* New York: Kensington Books.

Kranowitz, C. (1998) *The Out-of-Sync Child: Recognizing and Coping with Sensory Integration Dysfunction.* New York: Skylight Press.

Kutscher, Martin L. (2005) *Kids in the Syndrome Mix of ADHD, LD, Asperger's, Tourette's, Bipolar, and More! The One Stop Guide for Parents, Teachers, and Other Professionals.* Philadelphia: Jessica Kingsley Publishers.

Lockshin, Stephanie B., Gillis, Jennifer M. and Romanczyk, Raymond G. (2005) *Helping your Child with Autism Spectrum Disorder: A Step-by-Step Workbook for Families.* Oakland, CA: New Harbinger Publications, Inc.

Mayerson, Gary (2004) *How to Compromise With Your School District Without Compromising Your Child: A Field Guide for Getting Effective Services for Children with Special Needs.* New York: DRL Book, Inc.

Mercado, Denise (2006) *They Created Us: Special Education, Medicaid Waivers, EPSDT, Independent Case Management: A Family's Journey Through a Bureaucratic Maze!* Milton Keynes, UK: AuthorHouse.

Murkoff, Heidi, Eisenberg, Arlene and Hathaway, Sandee (2002) *What to Expect When Your're Expecting.* New York. Workman Publishing.

Murkoff, Heidi, Eisenberg, Arlene and Hathaway, Sandee (2003) *What to Expect the First Year.* New York. Workman Publishing.

Murray, Dinah (ed.) (2006) *Coming Out Asperger: Diagnosis, Disclosure and Self-confidence.* London: Jessica Kingsley Publishers.

Nadeau, Kathleen G. and Dixon, Ellen B. (2005) *Learning to Slow Down and Pay Attention* (3rd edn). Washington, DC: Magination Press.

National Center on Secondary Education and Transition and the PACER Center (2002) "Parenting Post-secondary Students with Disabilities: Becoming the Mentor, Advocate, and Guide Your Young Adult Needs." Available at http://www. ncset.org/publications/viewdesc.asp?id=208.

National Education Association (2006) *The Puzzle of Autism.* Washington, DC: NEA.

NICHCY (2001) *Related Services.* Washington, DC: National Dissemination Center for Children with Disabilities. Available at http://www.nichcy.org/pubs/newsdig/nd16txt.htm

Powers, Michael D. with Poland, Janet (2002) *Asperger Syndrome and Your Child: A Parent's Guide.* New York: HarperResource.

Prince-Hughes, Dawn (ed.) (2002) *Aquamarine Blue 5: Personal Stories of College Students with Autism.* Athens, OH: Swallow Press/Ohio University Press.

Roberson, Kathy, Blumberg, Rick and Baker, Dan (2005) *Keeping it Real: How to Get the Support You Need for the Life You Want.* New Brunswick, NJ: The Elizabeth M. Boggs Center on Developmental Disabilities. Available at www.rwjms.umdnj.edu/boggscentre/products/keepingitreal/Keeping_It_Real.htm.

Schor, Edward L. (1999) *Caring for Your School-age Child: Ages 5 to 12.* New York: Bantam Books.

Shelov, Stephen P. and Hannemann, Robert E. (2004) *Caring for your Baby and Young Child: Birth to Age Five* (4th edn). New York: Bantam Books.

Shub, Jeanne and DeWeerd, Amy (2006) *Ready to Learn: How to Overcome Social and Behavioral Issues in the Primary Classroom.* Portsmouth, NH: Heinemann.

Siegel, Lawrence M. (2001) *The Complete IEP Guide: How to Advocate for Your Special Ed Child* (2nd edn). Berkeley, CA: Nolo.

Stehli, Annabel (ed.) (1995) *Dancing in the Rain: Stories of Exceptional Progress by Parents of Children with Special Needs.* New York: Beaufort Books.

Tomlinson, Carol Ann (2003) *Fulfilling the Promise of the Differentiated Classroom: Strategies and Tools for Responsive Teaching.* Alexandria, VA: ASCD.

Tomlinson, Carol Ann and McTighe, Jay (2006) *Integrating Differentiated Instruction and Understanding by Design.* Alexandria, VA: ASCD.

Twachtman-Cullen, Diane (2000) *How To Be a Para Pro: A Comprehensive Training Manual for Paraprofessionals.* Higganum, CT: Starfish Specialty Press.

Twachtman-Cullen, Diane and Twachtman-Reilly, Jennifer (2002) *How Well Does Your IEP Measure Up? Quality Indicators for Effective Service Delivery.* Higganum, CT: Starfish Specialty Press.

Ury, William (1993) *Getting Past No: Negotiating in Difficult Situations. Confrontation to Cooperation.* New York: Bantam Books.

US Department of Education (2007) *Building the Legacy: IDEA 2004.* Washington, DC: US Department of Education. Available at http://idea.ed.gov

Vygotsky, Lev (1978) *Mind in Society: The Development of Higher Psychological Processes.* Cambridge, MA: Harvard University Press.

Wiggins, Grant P. and McTighe, Jay (2005) *Understanding by Design.* Alexandria, VA: ASCD.

Willey, Liane Holliday (1999) *Pretending To Be Normal: Living With Asperger's Syndrome.* London: Jessica Kingsley Publishers.

Wright, Peter W.D. and Wright, Pamela Darr (2006) *From Emotions to Advocacy: The Special Education Survival Guide* (2nd edn). Hartfield, VA: Harbor House Law Press.

Wright, Peter W. D. and Wright, Pamela Darr (2007) *Special Education Law* (2nd edn). Hartfield, VA: Harbor House Law Press.